Mischief Reef

Senan Fox

Mischief Reef

China, the Philippines, and a Disputed Atoll in the South China Sea

palgrave
macmillan

Senan Fox
School of International Studies
Kanazawa University
Kanazawa, Japan

ISBN 978-981-16-3883-1 ISBN 978-981-16-3884-8 (eBook)
https://doi.org/10.1007/978-981-16-3884-8

This Palgrave Macmillan imprint is published by the registered company Springer Nature Singapore Pte Ltd.
The registered company address is: 152 Beach Road, #21-01/04 Gateway East, Singapore 189721, Singapore

Dedicated to my family

"A happy family is but an earlier heaven."

George Bernard Shaw

Preface

As one of the so-called "Big Three" present day and strategically well-placed Chinese outposts in the South China Sea, and whose occupation since 1994 has oft times disrupted bilateral, regional, and Sino-US ties, Mischief Reef has certainly lived up to its name. This book examines the atoll's take-over, the feature's significance, and important related developments since the mid-1990s. For reasons explained inside, it also places the dispute within the context of the wider South China Sea disagreements, a geo-political impasse which now stands front and center of the rising China's relationship with the Philippines, its neighbors, and the only power that can seriously challenge Chinese designs in the area, the United States. Frictions regarding the feature have been accompanied by wider regional developments related to China's ascent and its greater capability and willingness to physically display its control and "rights" in disputed areas.

Initially, the work was a product of research conducted at the University of Tokyo, as part of a post-doctoral research fellowship there. Funded by the Japan Society for the Promotion of Science (JSPS), that project followed on from my PhD thesis, which tackled the question of why bilateral approaches to the East China Sea disagreements between Japan and China have a tendency to fluctuate. It also complemented my November 2018 Palgrave book *China, South Korea, and the Socotra Rock Dispute* and other related published works. The central goal of this work was to identify the push factors that persuaded Beijing to occupy, and then consolidate their control of the atoll, to draw lessons from the take-over, evaluate the arguments made by all sides, position the dispute within the wider strategic environment today, and reflect on how the issue may develop in the coming years.

Addressing the origins and developments related to a twenty-five year plus occupation was not without its challenges. For example, tracking down and analyzing sources from the pre-digital area meant that a small number of journal sources are not easily accessible due to the lack of digital availability. Some journals had no records of the issues published during the gap period. Some universities, such as Oxford University, did not have complete collections of these journals. Nonetheless, these sources were retained and utilized in this book for the following reasons: some of these very much fell in line with other well established facts. Thus, it was decided to include them and let the reader decide on their reliability. With these cases, incomplete references were triangulated with two or more existing credible and fully detailed references, and when they complemented each other, they were included.

As the Biden era begins, and China's rise continues, despite the COVID-19 interruption, this book comes at an opportune time. For example, will the US fatigue from China's apparent gains in the South China Sea during the Obama and Trump years see an escalation around Mischief Reef? Or will Beijing head off Washington by marginalizing the Americans via less confrontational means? These timely questions are addressed in this work. As the book explains, the dispute is not merely a spat over a reef, but is entangled in much more significant and wider questions over maritime disputes, geo-strategic rivalries, freedom of navigation and over-flight, regional diplomacy, international law, domestic politics, and resource competition, and more. By presenting insights into such issues as well as East Asia, this work provides observers with much to reflect on. While numerous scholars and journalists have written on the issue, this is the first publication in monograph form that provides a comprehensive, direct, and chronological account of the Mischief Reef dispute. By reading the seven chapters contained herein, the reader should receive a solid grounding with regards to the political, economic, legal, historical, and present-day strategic implications, and of the challenges faced by the littoral states of East Asia. It is my sincere wish that readers will learn about the commonalities between these issues and will possess a greater appreciation of their utility for present and future policy prescription and analysis. I also hope that insights into the dispute's impact upon bilateral, regional, and Sino-American ties and why a resolution has proved elusive will be broadened.

I also acknowledge those without whom the work may not have seen the light of day. These include my family, whose unceasing love and support provided me with much needed emotional sustenance. Thanks also to my good friend Junichi Ooshima for his encouragement and support as I dealt with various deadlines and challenges in the writing process. Special thanks goes out also to the book's editor, Dr. Mary Jane Fox (no relation). She will never truly know how much her skill, patience, and refusal to give up in spite of looming deadlines was the determining factor in finalizing the book. I would also like to thank the Japan Society for the Promotion of Science (JSPS) who provided me with all the necessary funding to come to Japan and to complete the research as a post-doctoral fellow.

In particular, I wish to express my deepest gratitude to Professor Akio Takahara (Faculty of Law) at the University of Tokyo who kindly agreed to act as my research host, and who throughout my time there, acted with the utmost professionalism and kindness with regard to my various requests and enquiries. Thanks also to the administrators and staff at the said Faculty of Law for all their kind help. I would also like to express my gratitude to Ashwini Elango (Project Coordinator), Jacob Dreyer, and all the staff at Springer Nature and Palgrave Macmillan for their professionalism, patience, kindness, and assistance with my questions and requests. Last but not least, I would like to thank my colleagues and the administrative staff at the School of International Studies at Kanazawa University for their advice and help as I endeavored to complete the book.

Kanazawa, Japan Dr. Senan Fox

Contents

Abbreviations

ADIZ	Air Defense Identification Zone
AFP	Armed Forces of the Philippines
APEC	Asia-Pacific Economic Cooperation
ARF	ASEAN Regional Forum
ASEAN	Association of Southeast Asian Nations
BRP	Barko ng Republika ng Pilipinas (Ship of the Republic of the Philippines)
CBM	Confidence-Building Measures
CCCC	China Communications Construction Company
CCCPC	Central Committee of the Communist Party of China
CCMOA	Cabinet Committee on Maritime and Ocean Affairs
CCP	Chinese Communist Party
CITES	Convention on International Trade in Endangered Species of Wild Fauna and Flora
CJIL	Chinese Journal of International Law
CMC	Central Military Commission
CNOOC	Chinese National Offshore Oil Corporation
CNPC	China National Petroleum Corporation
CoC	Code of Conduct
CPPCC	Chinese People's Political Consultative Conference
CS	Continental Shelf
CSIS	Center for Strategic and International Studies
DoC	Declaration on the Conduct of Parties in the South China Sea
ECS	East China Sea
EEZ	Exclusive Economic Zone
EIA	Environmental Impact Assessment

FON	Freedom of Navigation
FONOP	Freedom of Navigation Operation
ICJ	International Court of Justice
ISI	ImageSat International
ITLOS	International Tribunal on the Law of the Sea
JMSU	Joint Marine Seismic Undertaking
KIG	Kalayaan Island Group
MIMA	Malaysian Institute of Maritime Affairs
MOFU	Memorandum of Understanding
NFFAA	National Federation of Filipino American Associations
NSC	National Security Council
PAF	Philippine Air Force
PBSC	Politburo Standing Committee
PCA	Permanent Court of Arbitration
PHL	Republic of the Philippines
PLA	People's Liberation Army
PLAAF	People's Liberation Army Air Force
PLAN	People's Liberation Army Navy
PRC	People's Republic of China
PRCFM	People's Republic of China Foreign Ministry
REE	Rare Earth Elements
ROC	Republic of China (Taiwan)
SCS	South China Sea
SLOC	Sea Lines of Communication
SOA	State Oceanic Administration
SONA	State of Nation Address
SRV	Socialist Republic of Vietnam
TAC	Treaty of Amity and Cooperation
UN	United Nations
UNCLOS	United Nations Convention on the Law of the Sea
UNSC	United Nations Security Council
VFA	Visiting Forces Agreement
WPS	West Philippine Sea

List of Maps

CHAPTER 1

The Circumstances of Mischief Reef

Abstract Here recent developments as well as preliminary background and contextual information to China's occupation of Mischief Reef since 1994–1995 are introduced. The chapter presents the positions of the claimant states, China, the Philippines, Vietnam, and Taiwan, and also explains why the furtive takeover of the feature, which today contains a runway and extensive military facilities, was disturbing for several reasons. These include the fact that it was the first major occupation of a South China Sea feature in the post-Cold War era, and the first militarized SCS dispute involving China and a state other than Vietnam. The move also appeared to be an opportunistic and unprovoked take-over of territory under the jurisdiction of an ASEAN member state. This occupation raised questions about the rising dragon's intentions in the region. It also seemed to confirm fears regarding the objectives of PLAN since its strategic shift further out to sea after the mid-1980s. These are discussed herein. The feature's important geographical location and potential economic value in terms of fisheries, oil, gas, and other natural resources are also described. The chapter then provides an historical overview of the important events and developments relevant to Mischief Reef before China's take-over of the atoll.

Keywords ASEAN · China · Exclusive Economic Zones (EEZs) · Historical background · Natural resources · The Philippines

S. Fox, *Mischief Reef*,
https://doi.org/10.1007/978-981-16-3884-8_1

Introduction and Current Developments

Mischief Reef is found in the South China Sea (SCS), within a large archipelago called the Spratly Islands which is located between the Philippines' elongated Palawan Island, southern Vietnam, and Malaysia.[1] Being the focus of a dispute mainly between the Republic of Philippines (PHL or PH)[2] and the People's Republic of China (PRC), it may appear to be just another one of many clashes over sovereignty and jurisdiction in the SCS. However, it stands out from the other disputes for several reasons, and not just because the PRC has occupied it since the mid-1990s. Among those reasons would be that as of December 2019, for example, it is currently one of China's biggest outposts in the disputed Spratlys with "an airfield capable of handling an Airbus A320" and is additionally monitored by "high powered aerostats".[3] Needless to say, there has been considerable concern over both China's overt militarization of their questionable occupation of Mischief Reef as well as interfering with freedom of navigation and over-flight in and over international waters.

The background to and consequences of the PRC occupation of the disputed Mischief Reef in the mid-1990s are both interesting and complicated. While this occupation was just one of several occupations carried out by virtually all claimants of Spratly Islands disputes, over the years Mischief Reef has been particularly significant. Most notably, its seizure by the PRC took place within the Exclusive Economic Zone (EEZ) of the PHL, also a member state of the Association of South East Asian Nations (ASEAN); this alone sent alarm bells ringing amongst all the other disputants throughout the region.[4] It was also the first militarized South China Sea dispute involving China and a state other than

[1] The term 'Mischief Reef' is applied herein as the most commonly used term in international English language publications. China refers to the Spratly Islands as the Nansha Islands.

[2] In October 2010, the government of the Philippines announced they would officially use the abbreviations PH and PHL to refer to their country, and that they would discontinue the use of the initials RP (Republic of the Philippines) (*Official Gazette of the Republic of the Philippines*, October 28, 2010).

[3] Zhen, "China Deploys Airship."

[4] The definition and details of EEZs are covered in Part V of UNCLOS from 10 December 1982. https://www.un.org/depts/los/convention_agreements/texts/unclos/unclos_e.pdf.

Vietnam. Prior to Mischief Reef, the Chinese had confined physical military activities over features in the area to the Vietnamese. Disagreements between Manila and Beijing over the eastern Spratlys had existed for many decades but were latent rather than active since the early 1970s.[5] The furtive takeover in 1994–1995 was widely perceived to be the first occasion in which an ASEAN member state had its own territory occupied by China.[6] In reality, the Chinese had already physically occupied Filipino claimed features (six in total) in the Spratly Islands in the late 1980s when American military forces were still stationed in the Philippines. These included two of the other "Big Three" PRC outposts, Fiery Cross Reef and Subi Reef, both claimed by China, Taiwan, the Philippines, and Vietnam. In November 1987, China's Central Military Commission and State Council sanctioned the deployment of the PLAN to occupy features in the Spratlys, and early 1988 saw violent clashes between China and Vietnam over control of features. In September 1988, the Chinese ambassador to the Philippines informed the PHL government that the PRC was open to and hopeful of putting the Spratly disputes aside via consultations.[7] This bloody and much-publicized 1988 confrontation between two long-standing South China Sea rivals who claim all the Spratly area as their own, perhaps overshadowed the losses suffered by the Philippines at that time and hid the impact of what had actually happened. China may also have been viewed regionally as reacting defensively, right or wrong, to Vietnamese activities in the island group. The quiet and clandestine take-over of Mischief Reef six years later left the Filipinos in no doubt as to the threat posed by China, no doubt a sign of a shifting power balance in the region.

It also underscored the limitations of ASEAN's ability to discourage the Chinese. The occupation of Mischief Reef also flew in the face of ASEAN's Declaration on the South China Sea in 1992, the first attempt by the regional body to persuade China to respect international norms of behavior.[8] Following the declaration, China agreed with the stated position "to resolve all sovereignty and jurisdictional issues pertaining to the South China Sea by peaceful means, without resort to force." The

[5] Swanstrom, "Conflict Management and Negotiations," 98.

[6] Vietnam did not join ASEAN until July 28, 1995.

[7] Raditio, *Understanding China's Behaviour*, 102.

[8] Meng, "Sea of Cooperation," 327; Oishi and Quang, 301.

same document also urged "all parties concerned to exercise restraint with the view to creating a positive climate for the eventual resolution of all disputes" and "to explore the possibility of co-operation" in various areas.[9] There was an irony to the fact that the take-over happened during a series of meetings initiated by Indonesia in 1990 which involved the various claimants.[10] The way in which the Chinese took possession of the reef, amidst efforts to peacefully address the disputes, meant that it, in comparison to earlier standoffs, did more to damage China's reputation in the region.

Virtually every prior military confrontation in the SCS was exclusively confined to China and Vietnam. China's claimed "indisputable" sovereignty is not based on, nor consistent with, globally accepted international law. The occupation also seemed to confirm fears regarding the objectives of PLAN since its strategic shift further out to sea after the mid-1980s. Despite the 1988 reverses, the PHL had been cautiously confident about its revised security arrangements with the United States, particularly in relation to Beijing's intentions. The reef's occupation, however, turned such sanguine views on their head, and represented a classic case of a weaker state being caught flat-footed by a stronger territorial rival who had seen a strategic window of opportunity in which to act. At the same time, the initial regional response to the takeover took the PRC by surprise, and amongst other reasons, compelled it to counter China Threat warnings, for example by ratifying UNCLOS in 1996, signing bilateral agreements with Malaysia and the Philippines over Spratly features, and most significantly, consenting to at least discuss the South China Sea disputes multilaterally.[11]

The PRC's occupation of Mischief Reef also opened a Pandora's box of an entire series of questions about the rising dragon's regional intentions. As stated, prior to the 1994–1995 takeover, Manila held the view that the tactile and military element of the SCS disputes was an overwhelmingly China-Vietnam affair. China differs from the other claimants, however, since it does not merely claim a portion of the SCS as other claimants do, but instead claims virtually all of it, and contends that its

[9] For the full declaration, see http://cil.nus.edu.sg/1992/1992-asean-declaration-on-the-south-china-sea-signed-on-22-july-1992-in-manila.

[10] Swanstrom, "Conflict Management and Negotiations," 119; Sheany, "South China Sea Workshop."

[11] Meng, "Sea of Cooperation," 327.

sovereignty over the area is "indisputable" and not open to compromise. These assertions are not based on nor consistent with the United Nations Law of the Sea (UNCLOS) or customary international law. The reef's takeover thus fed fears that Beijing was choosing "might" over "right" by sanctioning its People's Liberation Army Navy (PLAN) to surreptitiously occupy the feature and then later defend the act with force. The occupation also seemed to confirm fears regarding the objectives of PLAN, which had surfaced since its strategic shift further out to sea after the mid-1980s.

Prior to the incident, the PHL government had felt assured about its revised security arrangements with the United States and in relation to Beijing's intentions. The reef's occupation however, turned such sanguine views on their head, and represented the classic case of a weaker state being caught flat-footed by a stronger territorial rival who had seen a strategic window of opportunity in which to act. The once barely submerged feature is now controlled by the PRC but is claimed by the Republic of the Philippines (PHL), Vietnam (the Socialist Republic of Vietnam/SRV), and Taiwan (the Republic of China/ROC).[12] China has since consolidated its control over the atoll in various ways. Due to the fact that the on-going dispute centers largely around two protagonists, the PRC and the PHL, the latter being the closest among the claimants and within whose EEZ the reef rests, it is Manila and Beijing's competing claims which are primarily addressed here. Actual and potential economic, security, and political values are also discussed, as well as the question of why the Chinese decided to occupy the reef when they did, and the various factors leading up to when the Philippines first publicized the development in February 1995. These factors include the feature's important geographical location and the area's significance in terms of fisheries, oil, gas, and other natural resources. In addition, this book addresses the consequences of the occupation, the lessons learned from it, and how China and the Philippines have dealt with the issue ever since. The reasons why the two countries are still unable to definitively resolve the dispute, and the challenges they faced and continue to face in managing the Mischief Reef conundrum are also examined. This introduction provides

[12] The reef is referred to differently by its various claimants. Besides *Mischief Reef* there is the Filipino *Panganiban Reef*, and then Vietnamese *Đá Vành Khăn* and finally *Meiji Jiao*, used by the PRC and Taiwan; see Dzurek, 70.

some preliminary background and contextual information to the occupation in order to prepare the reader for more detailed discussions later in the book.

Background and Context

Looking at Mischief Reef in view of the larger context includes being aware of the stated positions of the competing claimant states other than China and the Philippines, specifically Vietnam, and Taiwan. Knowing that the feature today contains a runway and extensive military facilities following years of incremental and extensive construction work by China, is crucial. Another consideration is that with the Philippines as a member state of ASEAN, the takeover marked the first occasion in the new post-Cold War era in which an ASEAN state had territory occupied by the PRC. For these reasons, the occupation came as quite a shock to the region and none more so than to the Philippines. Although the Chinese had begun to place structures upon stilts on the reef in 1994, the poorly resourced PHL did not realize the gravity of the situation until early 1995. The takeover was a calculated gamble that ultimately paid off because the Philippines could only watch as China consolidated its control of and presence on Mischief Reef; it remains so to this day. Initially, China officially claimed that the small structures built on the reef were constructed for the benefit of fishermen and were not military in nature. Mischief Reef today, however, is a completely transformed feature, one of China's so-called "Big Three" outposts in the Spratlys, due to the construction of a military base and runway, land reclamation, and several other facilities.

Even though the feature is now controlled by the PRC, it is not only claimed by the Philippines but also Vietnam, and Taiwan. Due to the fact that the ongoing dispute centers largely around two protagonists—the PRC and the PHL—this research addresses Manila and Beijing's competing claims to the feature. It also discusses its economic, security, and political value, the question of why the Chinese decided to occupy the reef when they did, and the various factors which led up to February 1995 when the Filipinos first publicized the development. In addition, it addresses the consequences of the occupation, the lessons learned from it, and how China and the Philippines have dealt with the issue ever since. The reasons why the two countries are still unable to definitively resolve the dispute, and the challenges they faced and continue to face in managing the Mischief Reef conundrum, are also examined.

As stated earlier, prior to the occupation of Mischief Reef, military confrontations in the South China Sea were overwhelmingly confined to China and Vietnam, and to their disputes over territory in the Paracel Islands[13] to the north of the SCS, and far from the Spratly group in the south-east. The PHL claims rights to Mischief Reef primarily on the basis of UNCLOS regulations in that it rests within 200 nautical miles (nms) or 370.4 km (kms) of the country's territorial baselines. Palawan Island, the nearest undisputed Filipino territory, is located 129 nms (239 kms) east of the reef.

While the 1994–1995 occupation is distinctive for the reasons provided above, it is also regrettably just one of many disputes between rivals for territory within the Spratly Islands. China's occupation of what initially seemed to be a worthless reef needs to be understood in the context of growing speculation concerning potentially vast energy resources in the Spratly area from the 1970s onwards. The lead-up to the mid-1990s is particularly relevant to this case. This period saw a rush of activity by claimants who felt compelled to delineate their maritime territory, to assert their sovereignty, and submit their claims to the United Nations in advance of ratification in accordance with UNCLOS. It was also a time of dynamic change in a new security, economic, and strategic environment, and one in which the Chinese military presence in the form of PLAN had increased its presence in peripheral waters, giving added importance to the Spratly area and its adjacent shipping lanes. In reflecting upon the occupation of Mischief Reef, all of these factors are examined. Given that geography figures so fundamentally in this issue, it is important to review this aspect before proceeding to further discussions on the key topics, which influence how the dispute manifests itself. The relative economic value of the waters around the contested reef is also discussed in the following section.

Geographical Context

Mischief Reef is a barely submerged horseshoe-shaped reef situated at 9′55″ North and 115′ 32″ East on the eastern edge of the Spratly Islands group. Its status as a feature that rests below water at high tide means that

[13] To the PRC, these are the Xisha Islands.

it is not entitled to claim any maritime zone around it under UNCLOS provisions. The reef extends to about nine kilometers in length and six kilometers in width, covering an area of 51.5 square kms. It also has a lagoon, and some of the reef's rocks are visible, but only at low tide. Its location places it well within the Philippines' delineated 200 nm EEZ in accordance with the Filipino interpretation of UNCLOS. It is situated 239 kms (129 nms) west of the undisputed Philippine island of Palawan, which guards the strategically important Balabac Strait at its southern end, and 1110 kms (599 nms) south-east of the PRC's Hainan Island, located at China's underbelly. Manila, the Philippine capital, is located 796 kms to its east. The reef sits roughly 100 kms equidistant between Filipino and Vietnamese occupied features in the area such as Nanshan (Lawak) Island (PHL) and Sin Cowe East Island (SRV). The largest PHL-administered island of Pagasa (Thitu), within the disputed Spratly group and Philippine-controlled since 1973, is 135 kms north-west of the feature.[14] Thitu is also home to one of the largest naval bases outside the Philippines[15] (Map 1.1).

To offer an idea of scale, the Spratly Islands group consists of 38% of the South China Sea's area or approximately 414,400 square kms (160,000 square miles), and are scattered about 926 kms from North to South and about 740 kms from East and West.[16] They are made up of 12 main islands and 390 reefs, banks, islets, shoals, and cays. Out of all of these, a mere 33 are visible above the water at high tide and only seven have a land mass of more than 0.5 square kms. All of these features are claimed in whole or in part by six neighboring states: Brunei, China, Malaysia, the Philippines, Taiwan, and Vietnam[17] (Maps 1.2 and 1.3).

Economic Value

The Spratly Islands are located in close proximity to vital shipping lanes which connect the oil-producing regions of the Middle East with the rising economies of East Asia. Up to one quarter of global maritime traffic also pass through adjacent waters, making the southern South China Sea

[14] Klare, *Resource Wars*, 119–120.

[15] Swanstrom, "Conflict Management and Negotiations," 98.

[16] Himmelman, "A Game of Shark."

[17] Klare, *Resource Wars*, 119–120.

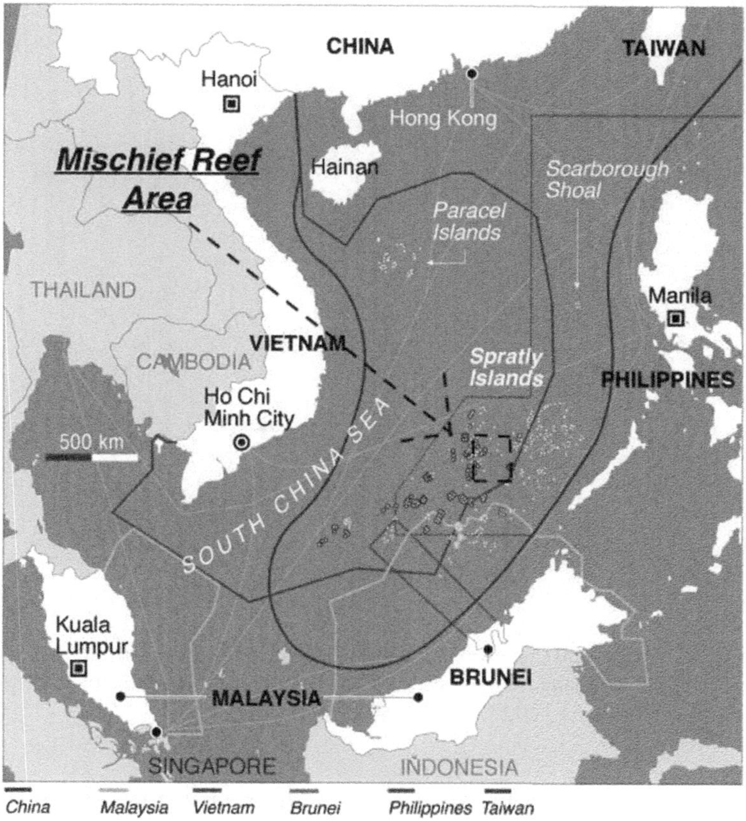

Map 1.1 Image (from July 2012) showing the area in which Mischief Reef is located. Note China (and Taiwan's) claim to virtually all of the South China Sea as well as the overlapping EEZ claims of Vietnam and the Philippines. Public Domain Image (*Source* "Challenging Beijing in the South China Sea", Voice of America, July 31, 2012: https://blogs.voanews.com/state-department-news/2012/07/31/challenging-beijing-in-the-south-china-sea/; https://en.wikipedia.org/wiki/Territorial_disputes_in_the_South_China_Sea#/media/File:South_China_Sea_claims_map.jpg)

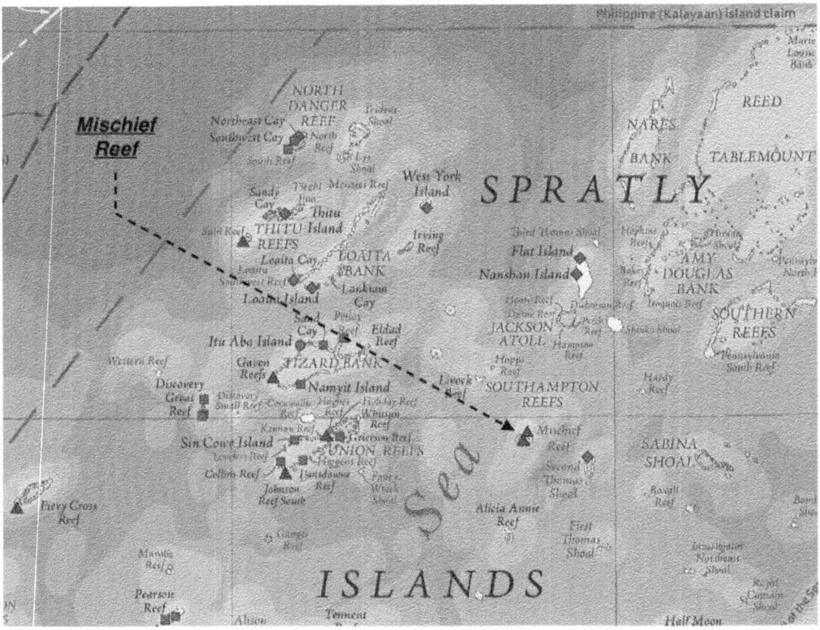

Map 1.2 Image (2015) showing Mischief Reef's location within the Spratly Islands. Public Domain Image (*Source* US Library of Congress, 2015: https://www.loc.gov/resource/g9237s.2016587286/)

area one of key importance to powerful states such as the US, which are committed to the freedom of navigation of vessels in international waters. While the islands are not in the direct path of major shipping lanes,[18] their juxtaposition between numerous states in East Asia draws attention to the Spratlys' potential for conflict and disruption if disputes are not managed properly.[19]

One scholar writing on energy and resource competition, Michael T. Klare, sees incidents such as the takeover of Mischief Reef as energy rather than defense related, where clashes in the area increased in frequency after the late 1980s. Klare argues, for example, that because ownership and control of features in the Spratly group could, under UNCLOS

[18] For further insight into shipping lanes and the Spratly Islands, see Dzurek, 65–71.

[19] Varner, "How China's Belt."

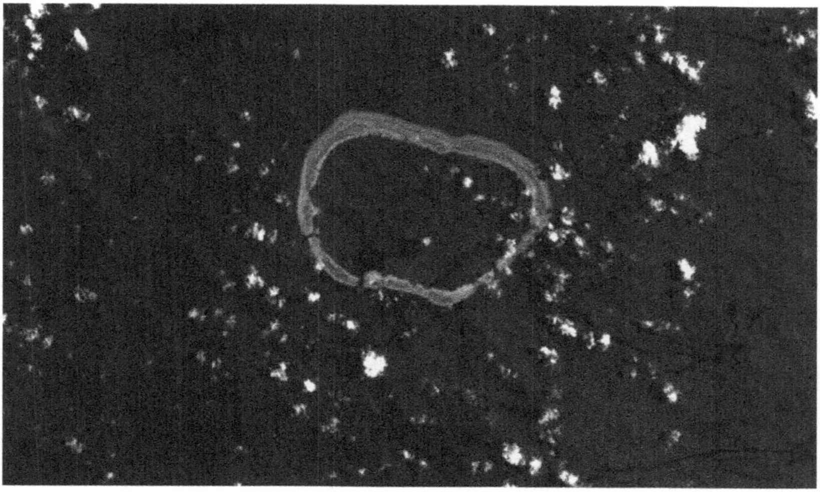

Map 1.3 NASA Landsat Satellite Image showing Mischief Reef in April 2001. Public Domain Image (*Source* Oceandots.com, April 21, 2001: https://web.archive.org/web/20120611094819/http://www.oceandots.com/pacific/spratly/mischief.php; https://en.wikipedia.org/wiki/Mischief_Reef#/media/File:Mischief_Reef_LANDSAT_2001.jpg)

guidelines, strengthen the hand of claimants eager to utilize maritime resources in these features' surrounding waters, the 1990s saw a rush for an island grab with rival claimants, and not just the PRC, seeking to control as many features as possible for themselves. For example, as many as five states (China, Malaysia, the Philippines, Taiwan, and Vietnam) have military and naval installations on features within the island group. The strengthening or defense of claims has also seen an increase in risky and potentially conflictual activities, such as the attempted undoing of occupations, the removal of "foreign" markers and installations, and the fending off of vessels of a rival state in sensitive waters. In addition, China's more pressing quest for essential oil and gas to feed its economic prosperity and secure the legitimacy of the communist regime began in earnest in 1993, when it became a net importer of hydrocarbons. A US Department of Energy report in 2000 stated that the PRC's oil consumption is expected to increase from some 3.8 million barrels a day in 1997 to some 9.5 million barrels a day by 2020, an almost three-fold increase.[20]

The issue of the actual quantity of energy reserves in waters near features such as Mischief Reef, however, is characterized by both conflict and consensus. On one hand, a 1969 United Nations seismology survey reported that the SCS was potentially rich in hydrocarbon deposits. In 1994, the PRC Ministry for Geology and Mineral Resources, without specifying whether they were referring to only the Spratly group, also estimated that there could be as much as 225 billion barrels of oil in the area. Other reports, however, have collectively proven to be inconclusive and inconsistent in terms of the scale of the resources. For example, the East–West Center in Hawaii stated in 1995 that in the Spratlys, the oil and gas resources are a mere "drop in the bucket".[21]

No matter what one's position on the exact quantity of energy resources in the Spratly Islands actually might be, it is also apparent that the rivalry for access to the area's seabed oil and gas deposits is increasingly being fed by the rise of the Asia–Pacific region as an economic power-house. This has consequently led to higher demands for sources of energy to sustain economic growth and prosperity. During the 1990s, for example, energy consumption in the region grew by a rate of 5.5% per year, or more than ten times the global average. This development had significant ramifications for the economic strategic value of the Spratly Islands because it compelled neighboring states to seek out alternative energy sources to feed their own growing economies' demands and to address the vulnerability of relying too much on resources from the distant Middle East.[22] This has placed pressure in particular on states such as China, where the Chinese Communist Party's (CCP) legitimacy in the post-Cold War era is increasingly dependent on securing economic prosperity for its citizens.[23] These economic shifts have also meant that non-claimant states such as Japan and South Korea now place a greater emphasis on the safety and stability of Sea Lines of Communication (SLOCs) in which oil and gas tankers pass in proximity to the more

[20] Klare, *Resource Wars,* 112–115. In fact by 2020 it exceeded this and 14.23 million barrels a day was reported: https://www.statista.com/265235/oil-consumption-in-china-in-thousands-barrels-per-day/.

[21] Meyer, 5; Valencia, Van Dyke and Ludwig, 9.

[22] Klare, *Resource Wars,* 110–111.

[23] For more on this issue of communist party legitimacy and economic prosperity in the PRC, see Esteban, 2006.

volatile Spratly group. Regarding Japan, for example, up to 70% of its oil transits through the SCS. In addition, improvements in deep water exploration techniques have also made once inaccessible resources available for extraction by oil and gas companies.[24] The potential of these resources in the area is discussed in more detail later.

Alongside the oft-discussed oil and gas potential of the Spratlys is the actual value of fish stocks in the eastern Spratly area, which accounts for almost 20% of the total fish catch for the Philippines. In 1993 PHL fishermen hauled in some 162,455 tons of commercial fish in waters off the island of Palawan.[25] Nine years later, in 2002, the country's Foreign Affairs Secretary Teofisto Guingona Jr. estimated that upwards of 50 billion US dollars worth of maritime resources was lost annually as a result of illegal poaching and fishing activities within the PHL's territorial waters. This, he argued, was largely attributable to the poorly funded Armed Forces of the Philippines' (AFP) inability to carry out adequate surveillance within the Philippine EEZ.[26]

Notwithstanding the arguably more important and complex security and legal interests involved in this dispute, the economic value of the immediate area must surely have been an influence in the Chinese decision to first act and then to later reinforce their position on the feature.

Structure and Content

Besides the first of this book's seven chapters providing some preliminary background and context to China's occupation of Mischief Reef, the remaining chapters provide discussions in and around the legal and security aspects, decision-making, time frame, historical implications and then more recent implications. To be more specific, Chapter 2 looks at the legal disagreements at the center of the dispute, and where the dispute is positioned from the perspective of maritime law as well as China and the Philippines' stated legal positions in relation to the reef. Chapter 3 provides the security issues to the occupation. It locates the occupation in a post-Cold War security environment when the USA was scaling down on defense spending and disengaging from Southeast Asia. Relatedly, it discusses why, from a Chinese military planning perspective, the operation was seen as possible due to the PHL appearing weak and incapable of a

[24] Klare, *Resource Wars*, 111; Meyer, 5; Emmers, 49.

[25] Storey, "Creeping Assertiveness," 104.

[26] Chung, "The Spratly Islands Dispute," 251.

concerted response. The following chapter further explores the dynamics behind the decision to occupy. After details of China's strategic motivations and the timeline of events are presented, evidence is examined in regard to why the Chinese acted when they did, and why that reef was selected. It also looks at the influence of domestic politics in the PRC on the decision to occupy. Chapter 5 discusses the occupation's various stages, detailing the immediate responses of the Philippines and other regional players as well as the USA, and the lessons learned in its immediate aftermath. The chapter provides the contrasting opinions regarding what happened, most notably the initial PRC claim that the activities were of "no military character at all". Chapter 6 discusses the implications of developments after the 1994–1995 occupation and also presents the significance and reasons for the so-called "Second Mischief Reef Incident" in late 1998, which took place when the PRC began to construct much more extensive structures on the reef. It then presents contrasting scholarly arguments regarding the PRC's strategic objectives vis-à-vis Mischief Reef, the incentives and restraints that influence its behavior, and related Spratly Island developments since the late 1990s. It shows how potentially dangerous incidents, "salami slicing" and "cabbage tactics" strategies by China in particular, and behavior designed at emphasizing claims continue to complicate this dispute. It also looks at the significance of the 2002 Declaration on the Conduct of Parties in the South China Sea (DoC), and why the Spratly disputes appeared to stabilize somewhat from the late 1990s to the late 2000s, before escalating again. Special attention is given to the groundbreaking Arbitral Tribunal proceedings (from January 2013) and findings, which were announced in July 2016, as well as their ramifications for approaches to the Mischief Reef issue.

The concluding Chapter 7 looks at Mischief Reef developments in recent years. The future outlook is then considered, factoring in variables such as domestic political circumstances, economic incentives, the policy goals and strategic objectives of the two protagonists as well as those of the US, the only power capable of seriously challenging Chinese aspirations in the South China Sea. The chapter shows there are compelling incentives to address the dispute peacefully. Included are the lessons learnt to date from the Mischief Reef issue, as well as proposals for resolving or at least managing the dispute. Because international maritime law has such a role to play here, however, understanding its strengths and weaknesses and how the law has been interpreted is crucial, and so the law discussion follows accordingly.

References

Dzurek, Daniel J. "China Occupies Mischief Reef in Latest Spratly Gambit." *International Boundaries Research Unit (IBRU) Boundary and Security Bulletin* (April 1995): 65–71.

Himmelman, Jeff. "A Game of Shark and Minnow." *The New York Times*, October 27, 2013. http://www.nytimes.com/newsgraphics/2013/10/27/south-china-sea/index.html.

Klare, Michael T. *Resource Wars—The New Landscape of Global Conflict*. New York: Owl Books, 2001.

Meng, Lai Yew. "'Sea of Cooperation or Sea of Conflict'?: The South China Sea in the Context of China-ASEAN Maritime Cooperation." *International Journal of China* 8, no.3 (December 2017): 321–345. https://icsum.org.my/wp-content/uploads/2020/02/IJCSV8N3-FULL-ISSUE.pdf.

Official Gazette of the Republic of the Philippines. "DFA shifts to ISO initials 'PH' and 'PHL'." October 28, 2010. https://www.officialgazette.gov.ph/2010/10/28/dfa-shifts-to-iso-initials-ph-to-phl/.

Oishi, Mikio, and Nguyen Minh Quang. "Brothers in Trouble: China-Vietnam Territorial Disputes and Their Bilateral Approach to Conflict Management." *International Journal of China* 8, no. 3 (December 2017): 287–320. https://icsum.org.my/wp-content/uploads/2020/02/IJCSV8N3-FULL-ISSUE.pdf.

Raditio, Klaus Henrich. *Understanding China's Behaviour in the South China Sea—A Defensive Realist Perspective*. London: Palgrave Macmillan, 2019.

Sheany. "South China Sea Workshop Aims to Manage Potential Conflicts in Disputed Waters." *Jakarta Globe*, November 16, 2017. https://jakartaglobe.id/news/south-china-sea-workshop-aims-to-manage-potential-conflicts-in-disputed-waters/.

Swanstrom, Niklas. "Conflict Management and Negotiations in the South China Sea: The ASEAN Way?" *Institute for Security and Development Policy*. Nacka, Sweden, January 1999, 93–125. https://isdp.eu/content/uploads/publications/2001_swanstrom_conflict-management-and-egotiations.pdf.

Varner, Joe. "How China's Belt and Road Policy Affects Global Security." *Diplomat and International Canada*, January 2, 2020. http://diplomatonline.com/mag/2020/01/how-chinas-belt-and-road-project-affects-global-security/?utm_source=rss&utm_medium=rss&utm_campaign=how-chinas-belt-and-road-project-affects-global-security.

Zhen, Liu. "China Deploys Airship on Outpost in Disputed South China Sea, Satellite Firm Says." *South China Morning Post*, December 2, 2019. https://www.scmp.com/news/china/military/article/3040019/china-deploys-airship-outpost-disputed-south-china-sea.

CHAPTER 2

The Perspective of Maritime Law

Abstract This chapter addresses China and the Philippines' legal positions in relation to Mischief Reef, particularly in regard to the United Nations Convention on the Law of the Sea, tasked with addressing maritime disputes. When the Philippines and Vietnam ratified UNCLOS in 1984 and 1994, and China followed suit in 1996, they laid out the extent of their respective maritime areas. Although China remains the primary concern, this chapter also describes how virtually all the disputants have selectively interpreted UNCLOS. The chapter then covers how disagreements over South China Sea features became more complicated from the 1970s onwards with the discovery of potentially substantial energy resources. It shows how activities related to EEZ delimitation and control over perceived maritime spheres significantly increased after the late 1980s, prompting a pre-emptive rush by claimants to control features. Analysis of China's arguments is provided. The chapter also points to a number of significant flaws in the Philippines' claims, and explains why both parties are at an impasse. The conclusion addresses the implications of legal developments in the SCS, most notably the landmark South China Sea Arbitration findings in July 2016, which found overwhelmingly in favor of the Philippines, prompting angry responses in word and deed from China.

S. Fox, *Mischief Reef*,
https://doi.org/10.1007/978-981-16-3884-8_2

Keyword Continental shelf · Historic rights · Maritime law · Nine-dash line · South China Sea Arbitration · United Nations Convention on the Law of the Sea (UNCLOS)

Legal Positioning

Understanding where China and the Philippines are legally positioned in relation to the reef is crucial, and particularly so with regards to the United Nations Convention on the Law of the Sea (UNCLOS III), adopted in 1982 and not only tasked with addressing maritime disputes, but providing avenues for dispute settlement.[1] In this regard, it is of course subject to specified limitations.

The Chinese defend their position by citing historical evidence of first discovery and the occupation, albeit sporadic, of the SCS' various features. The question of who has rightful sovereignty has been a contentious issue for many years, and long before the 1970s, when the discovery of potentially substantial energy resources in the area increased the strategic and economic value of the sea for the claimant states. This was particularly the case with China, Taiwan, and Vietnam. The Philippines, however, has also cited historical discovery and effective occupation to reinforce its UNCLOS-derived EEZ and continental shelf claims in the eastern Spratlys.

When the Philippines ratified UNCLOS with China following more than ten years afterwards, these states were anxious to lay out the extent of their respective Exclusive Economic Zones (EEZs) and continental shelf areas.[2] UNCLOS came into force in November 1994. Although China remains the primary concern in terms of international law regarding Mischief Reef, it is worth noting how virtually all the disputant states have interpreted UNCLOS in selective ways, and with the aim of maximizing their own claims. In the midst of the relevant states aiming to conform to UNCLOS ownership criteria before ratification, their actions related to EEZ delimitation and control over perceived maritime spheres

[1] For the complete document, see: https://www.un.org/depts/los/convention_agreements/texts/unclos/unclos_e.pdf.

[2] Batongbacal, "Arbitration 101: Philippines V. China."

significantly increased after the late 1980s. Vietnam was the most active in the occupation of features as well as the construction of military outposts in the late 1980s and early 1990s, prompting a pre-emptive rush by other claimants to take control of certain features.[3]

As will be discussed, international legal opinion considers that China's historically based assertions and nine-dash line claim are weak under international law. Specifically in relation to Mischief Reef, the Arbitral Tribunal in 2016 (discussed later) for example stated that "the 'nine-dash line'... cannot provide a basis for any entitlement by China to maritime zones in the area of Mischief Reef..." and that there exists no legal basis for any entitlement by China to maritime zones in the area of Mischief Reef...."[4]

The Philippines' position is that their own arguments are stronger than China's due to their decades-long administration, apparent adherence to UNCLOS, and more consistent display of sovereignty in the Spratly Islands. While international law supports most if not all of the arguments and submissions presented by the Filipinos, there are nonetheless flaws in both sides' claims.

There have been implications of some major legal developments on the SCS in recent years, as mentioned, most notably the historic, landmark South China Sea Arbitration case which published its findings in July 2016, of which the legal details make up a 500 page tome.[5] Following the PHL's January 2013 request for the UN to arbitrate on their competing claims with the PRC, a tribunal held its first meeting in The Hague on July 13 of that year. The Chinese repeated their rejection of the body in a Note to the Tribunal on August 1, and on August 27, the Tribunal issued its first Procedural Order. The Permanent Court of Arbitration (PCA) adopted the Tribunal's Rules of Procedure and initial timetable. It was formally designated to serve as registry of the proceedings. However, given that media and other sources tend to mistakenly state that it is a PCA Tribunal, it should be noted that the Tribunal is in fact a body separate and independent of both the PCA and the International Tribunal on

[3] Emmers, "Maritime Disputes," 50; Storey, "Creeping Assertiveness," 95.

[4] Permanent Court of Arbitration, PCA Case No. 2013–19, 256, 631, 633.

[5] Permanent Court of Arbitration. PCA Case No. 2013–19.

the Law of the Sea (ITLOS). In its role as registry, the PCA basically hosts the tribunal and offers it administrative assistance.[6]

The Tribunal's final decisions were deemed to be so momentous that in the months preceding the findings, China made determined efforts to lobby other nations.[7] Even though the Philippines lost on some minor points, its greater wins were largely seen as not unexpected. Understanding not only the legal complexities of such disputes, including the ambiguity of UNCLOS, but also the history of its beginnings provides meaningful insight into the behavior of the PRC and the PHL in recent decades.

Legal Disagreements

The rise in tensions surrounding features such as Mischief Reef can mainly be understood, at least in legal terms, in the context of UNCLOS III, the third major international UN convention tasked with addressing maritime disputes.[8] This convention, which was ironed out after lengthy negotiations in the 1970s, was adopted in April 1982 before finally coming into force in November 1994. In the years prior to this, states with rival claims in the Spratly Islands sought to stake their territory in advance by various means, and this included the laying down of markers and granting of exploration rights to companies, often in areas within or near two or more overlapping EEZs. It also witnessed a rush by countries to occupy uninhabited features, which were claimed by others. The Philippines and Vietnam ratified UNCLOS in 1984 and 1994 respectively, and Brunei, China, and Malaysia followed suit in 1996. Virtually all the disputant states in the Spratlys have interpreted UNCLOS in selective ways and with the aim of maximizing their sovereign jurisdiction over disproportionately large EEZ and continental shelf areas.[9]

[6] Batongbacal, "Arbitration 101: Philippines V. China"; "Kotani, "The South China Sea Arbitration, No."

[7] Liu and Wong, "China Intensifies Lobbying."

[8] The first UNCLOS conference (UNCLOS I) took place in 1956 and resulted in four separate treaties which entered into force in the 1960s. These were Conventions on: the Territorial Sea and Contiguous Zone; the Continental Shelf; the High Seas; and the Fishing and Conservation of Living Resources of the High Seas. UNCLOS II took place in 1960, but with no results for a range of reasons.

[9] Emmers, "Maritime Disputes," 50; Storey, "Creeping Assertiveness," 95.

In the case of Mischief Reef, there is a critical distinction between the claims made by the PHL and those made by the PRC. The Philippines, for example, used UNCLOS as a guideline for its claims and asserted sovereignty over only a portion of the Spratly group. Beijing and Taipei,[10] however, claim rights to all of the Spratly group as well as virtually all of the SCS, and base these assertions largely on historical and archaeological evidence. Procedurally, the PRC has declared certain co-ordinates for baselines through which it would measure its territorial sea areas (May 15, 1996), an EEZ (June 7, 1996), and adopted a Law on the EEZ and Continental Shelf (June 26, 1998).[11]

The PRC's historical assertions for example include that "the earliest discovery by the Chinese people of the Nansha Islands can be traced back to as early as the Han Dynasty" [206 BCE to 220 CE] and that "the Nansha Islands came under the jurisdiction of China from the Yuan Dynasty" [1271 to 1368].[12] A statement by the PRC's Foreign Ministry in 2000 also includes claims that numerous states, global opinions, and publications throughout the world have provided evidence of "international recognition" of China's sovereignty over the Spratly Islands over many decades and as far back as 1912.[13] Another PRCFM statement from the same day and year complained that despite such records:

> In recent years, countries like Viet Nam and the Philippines have sent troops to seize some uninhabited islands and reefs of the Nansha Islands, destroyed the marks of sovereignty erected by China there, and arrested, detained or driven away by force Chinese fishermen fishing in the South China Sea.[14]

Friction over Mischief Reef in the mid to late 1990s should not be seen in isolation, but rather as part of a wider pattern among the disputants of strengthening and more actively laying down their claims. The vague and often ambiguous guidelines set out by UNCLOS have not helped to

[10] For a concise account of Taiwan's position vis-à-vis the Spratly Islands, see "Sovereignty Over the Spratly Islands," 2009.

[11] Robles, "The South China Sea Arbitration," 126.

[12] Ministry of Foreign Affairs of the People's Republic of China, "Historical Evidence to Support China's."

[13] Ibid., "International Recognition."

[14] Ibid., "Basic Stance and Policy."

lower tensions, and indeed appear to be a decisive factor in understanding why rival states behave as they do in the area. As Ramos-Mrosovsky contends, the convention's regulations effectively promote the display of sovereignty by claimant states, and punish countries that seem to acquiesce in a rival state's claim to a disputed area. UNCLOS also encourages states to be extremely selective in choosing aspects of the law, which serve their own interests.[15]

Background to China's Presence

China's record of using force in the South China Sea to reinforce its position has been a cause for concern for neighbors since the 1970s, even though until the 1994–1995 Mischief Reef occupation, this was confined to clashes with Vietnam, for example over the Paracel Islands in the northern SCS in the 1970s. From one perspective, this use of force sometimes could be understood as reflecting the PRC's opportunism and well-timed exploitation of a rival's weaknesses at any given time. In January 1974, for example, the Chinese, as part of their attempts to check Soviet influence in the region, consolidated their control by force over the Paracel Islands. Known as the Battle of the Paracel Islands, it resulted in the deaths of 53 Vietnamese soldiers and 18 Chinese soldiers, as well as a significant number of injuries and vessel damage and losses on both sides. This was at a time when South Vietnam held sovereignty over features in that area but was distracted by the Vietnam War, which was coming to an end. The Saigon regime was also about to fall, and its ally, the United States, had effectively disengaged from the country. Despite being an ally to Saigon, Washington was unwilling to entangle itself in a maritime standoff with a PRC already hostile to the USSR, the patron of the Vietnamese communists, and with whom rapprochement had been reached in 1972 with President Nixon's famous visit to China. North Vietnam was also still dependent on vital material and financial aid from the Chinese at a critical end phase juncture of the Vietnam War, and was distracted by much more pressing issues. Under such circumstances, it was less likely to protest this challenge to Vietnamese sovereignty over the islands. Despite PLAN's inability to project significant naval power

[15] Ramos-Mrosovsky, "International Law's Unhelpful Role," 906–908.

beyond its coastal waters and the fact that it could not realistically countenance an ongoing military presence in the Spratly area, they nevertheless took control of all the Paracel Islands after this. It was not until the late 1980s when changes in capabilities and strategy would lead them to an increased presence in the southern South China Sea. The desire to establish a foothold in this area was also fed by the consolidating activities of Vietnam, which remained a major threat to the PRC's maritime interests throughout the 1970s and into the 1990s.[16]

From the mid to late 1980s onwards, PRC defense planners placed a greater emphasis on countering rival disputants by physically asserting Chinese claims in the Spratly Islands rather than simply declaring them. As observed by Emmers, most of the various parties involved in the SCS disputes had, at one time or another, constructed permanent foundations on tiny, uninhabitable and high-tide submerged features in order to assert their sovereignty over that particular reef or islet. In the late 1980s, the pattern of action and reaction had some very serious consequences. The result in the Spratly Islands was an unusually violent naval showdown between the PRC and Vietnam at Johnson South Reef (now occupied by China) and the deaths of over sixty Vietnamese soldiers on March 14, 1988. As the casualties suggest, the Chinese prevailed, and over time, reinforced their presence in the area as a result, occupying Fiery Cross Reef and at least five other features. The incident, however, garnered relatively little attention from an ASEAN distracted by peace efforts aimed at ending conflict in Cambodia (1978–1991).[17] Tiglao et al. also observe that at the time of the Johnson South Reef Skirmish in 1988 communist Vietnam was endeavoring to portray a "less warlike image" to the outside world.[18] Since then, China has been involved in a sovereignty dispute over the Spratly Islands with virtually all of the other claimants.

In February 1992, Beijing passed the "Law of the People's Republic of China on the Territorial Sea and the Contiguous Zone", reiterating the PRC's claims to a broad sweep of maritime territory in the East China Sea and the South China Sea. The law also emphasized the right to use force if Chinese sovereignty was threatened or undermined.[19] Notably,

[16] Emmers, "Maritime Disputes," 52; Tiglao et al., "Tis the Season," 18.

[17] Emmers, "Maritime Disputes," 52.

[18] Tiglao et al., "Tis the Season," 18.

[19] See article 14: http://www.asianlii.org/cn/legis/cen/laws/lotprocottsatcz739/.

this took place nearly two and a half years before UNCLOS III came into force in November 1994. This claim, alongside its later 1996 ratification of UNCLOS and formal declarations of sovereignty over practically all of the SCS, meant that the PRC now found itself in direct confrontation with those states who claimed portions of the Spratly Islands in accordance with their own interpretations of UNCLOS. There appeared to be a disconnect between China's domestic laws (and strategic behaviour) and its stated support for the previously mentioned July 1992 ASEAN Declaration's commitment to "peaceful means" and creating a "positive climate".

With countries aiming to conform to UNCLOS criteria for ownership prior to ratification, activities related to the delimitation of EEZs and of control over perceived maritime spheres of influence within the Spratly group significantly increased from the late 1980s onwards. The methods included, amongst other activities, the building and maintaining of military outposts on reefs, laying down flags and markers, and keeping a closer watch on "foreign" military and civilian vessels in sensitive areas. It is clear that the PRC is not the only state, which kept and still keeps and maintains military outposts in the area, nor does it hold the highest number of such outposts. In fact, Vietnam had been much more active in strengthening its claims.[20] In the aftermath of the Mischief Reef takeover in 1994–1995 for example, China held control over only seven features while Vietnam held twenty-seventy and the Philippines held eight. Taiwan and Malaysia held one and three respectively.[21] China is thus also hardly alone in terms of physically occupying territory claimed by another neighbor in the Spratly Islands. As shown, two prominent examples include the Philippines and Vietnam, who currently occupy Commodore Reef (SRV), Amboyna Cay (SRV), and Barque Canada Reef (PHL) respectively, features claimed by Malaysia. Malaysia, for its part, occupies Louisa Reef (Terembu Semarang), which is also claimed by Brunei.[22] Occupation of a feature does not automatically bestow maritime area benefits to the holder in terms of UNCLOS-derived rights to EEZ and continental shelf resources. Nonetheless, the prevailing attitude is that

[20] See, for example, https://amti.csis.org/vietnam-expands-another-outpost/; and the Council on Foreign Relations' Global Conflict Tracker: https://www.cfr.org/interactive/global-conflict-tracker/conflict/territorial-disputes-south-china-sea.

[21] Raditio, *Understanding China's Behaviour*, 102.

[22] Guan, "The South China Sea," 17–18.

to occupy has its benefits over not occupying, especially so when viewed through a defensive security lens. The occupation of a reef also allows the occupier to display its presence, to exert control over claimed areas, and to deny a rival the opportunity to use a contested feature for the same reasons.

PRC Claims

As briefly mentioned earlier, China has asserted that its people first discovered and gave a name to the Spratly archipelago during the Han Dynasty [206 BCE to 220 CE] and has displayed jurisdiction in the area since the Yuan Dynasty [1271 to 1368]. A statement in 2000 by the PRCFM entitled "Jurisprudential Evidence To Support China's Sovereignty over the Nansha Islands" provided a detailed historical account of China's presence in the island group as proof of its "indisputable sovereignty over the Nansha Islands." The evidence they claim is both Chinese and foreign, and can be seen in such books as the "Records of Rarities" by Yang Fu (of the eastern Han Dynasty), in the "Records of Rarities in Southern Boundary [sic]" by Wan Zhen (of the Three Kingdoms Period), and in "A History of Phnom" by General Kang Tai (of the East Wu State). Fishing and coral collecting were chronicled by Fei Yuan of the Jin Dynasty (265 to 420 CE) in his article "Chronicles of Guangzhou". "Fishing, planting, and other productive activities" by Chinese people on the islands and their adjacent waters have been taking place since at least the Tang (618 to 907 CE) and Song (960 to 1279) dynasties. These activities continued during and after the Ming (1368 to 1644 CE) and Qing (1644 to 1912 CE) dynasties, and the fishermen from the Chinese mainland involved in productive activities "never failed to pay their taxes and fees to the Chinese government."

"Continued effective government behavior" is also evident over the centuries. For example, Emperor Zhenyuan of the Tang Dynasty, included the Nansha Islands in an administrative map during his reign (785 to 805 CE). Since the beginning of the twentieth century, various Chinese governments have "undauntedly maintained" sovereignty over the area. Republican China (1912 to 1949 CE) commissioned a map and an agency was tasked with approving and deciding on new names for all the SCS' features and island clusters. When France invaded and occupied nine features in the Spratlys in the 1930s, the Chinese government made diplomatic protests and Chinese fishermen staged a demonstration. When the Nansha Islands were occupied by the Japanese during World War Two, China made "unremitting efforts" to win them back. The Cairo Declaration of 1943 promised that all territories taken from China by Japan should be "restored to China" including "Manchuria, Taiwan, and the Penghu Islands." The Spratlys during the occupation fell under the jurisdiction of Taiwan, according to Japanese law. The Potsdam Declaration of 1945 also promised the return of lost territories to China. According to the PRCFM statement, "China recovered the Nansha Island [sic] in 1946."

The era of Republican China also saw the government authorizing the sending of soldiers to the archipelago "on garrison duty", holding a "take-over ceremony," drawing up an official map with new names for the features,[23] and the publication of "the earliest book of the physical geography of the Nansha Islands."[24] Sources also show that at the diplomatic level, the Chinese Nationalist government of Chiang Kai-Shek first formally outlined its perceived SCS area in 1947, when it used a line characterized by nine interrupted lines which included nearly all of the SCS.[25] When the PRC was established in 1949, the country's Premier, Zhou Enlai, followed suit by formally making a similar claim in 1951.[26] In 1950, the nationalist Republic of China (ROC) government, having lost the Chinese Civil War (1927 to 1936 and 1945 to 1949) withdrew its garrisons from (Taiping) Itu Aba Island in the Nansha Islands and Yongxing (Woody) Island in the Paracel (Xisha) Islands. This did not mean that China had relinquished its claims. According to Wu, the Philippines only recognized the value of the Spratlys in the 1930s and even at that did not challenge China's claims until the late 1950s. In fact, they assert that the Filipinos had recognized China's rights in the area at the end of World War Two. On top of that, the San Francisco Peace Treaty of 1951 and the "Treaty of Peace between the Republic of China and Japan" (more commonly known as the Treaty of Taipei) in 1952, confirmed, in China's eyes, their sovereignty over the Nansha

[23] For details from earlier decades and a Chinese perspective, see Wu, "Competing Claims."

[24] Foreign Ministry of the People's Republic of China, "Jurisprudential Evidence."

[25] The "nine-dash line", was declared "contrary to the Convention" and "without lawful effect" in §1203: B (2) of the South China Sea Arbitration ruling from July 2016.

[26] Emmers, "Maritime Disputes," 51.

Islands and the promised transfer of the islands from defeated Japan. To emphasize China's treaty rights, Premier Zhou Enlai released an official statement prior to the San Francisco Conference in 1951 in which he said that the PRC's sovereignty over the Nansha Islands (and throughout the South China Sea) would not be altered regardless of what the final draft of the San Francisco Treaty looked like.[27] Under the PRC government, the islands were incorporated into the mainland's Guangdong and then Hainan Province where the communist government has "maintained China's sovereignty over the Nansha Islands" ever since.[28] These historical reasons, the PRCFM contended, illustrate why "no country in the world has the right to change China's legal status as the owner of the Nansha Islands in any way."[29]

More detailed explanations of the PRC's counter-arguments are covered later in the section on China's responses to the July 2016 South China Sea Arbitration findings. Suffice to say here that Beijing views the vast majority of the South China Sea as its own exclusive maritime territory and declares its right to possess virtually all the features in that area. The PRC authorities thus see it as their unquestionable sovereign right to exercise authority in the area and on all the features, including Mischief Reef.[30] In a pre-emptive June 2016 statement by the Chinese Society of International Law released by the PRC's Ministry of Foreign Affairs, it declared "China has always maintained and enjoyed territorial sovereignty over the Zhongsha Islands (including Huangyan Dao [Scarborough Shoal]) and the Nansha Islands (including the above-mentioned eight features such as Meiji Jiao [Mischief Reef]) in their entirety".[31] The 2016 Tribunal also wrote in its case details that the PRC considers Mischief Reef to be a high-tide feature entitled at least to a territorial sea. The PRC also views the Spratly Islands in general as being entitled to a territorial sea, an EEZ, and a continental shelf. The Tribunal likewise noted Beijing's diplomatic correspondence with Manila that "China possesses indisputable sovereignty over Nansha Islands and its adjacent waters, and the construction, usage and other activities at the relevant

[27] Wu, "Competing Claims," 13–22.

[28] Foreign Ministry of the People's Republic of China, "Jurisprudential Evidence."

[29] Ibid.

[30] Guan, "The South China Sea," 3.

[31] Foreign Ministry of the People's Republic of China, "The Tribunal's Award."

islands, reefs, shoals and sands are actions completely within the scope of China's sovereignty, sovereign rights and jurisdiction"[32] and on February 12, 2015, that "the development of any facility in the Nansha Islands falls within the scope of China's sovereignty."[33] The PRC's Foreign Ministry also declared on September 14, 2015 that "[c]onstruction activities taken by the Chinese side on some stationed islands and reefs in the Nansha Islands are completely lawful, reasonable and justified."[34] This reveals why China sees no issue with construction activities on the reef, surveilling "foreign" vessels and aircraft nearby, or obstructing "foreign" fishermen, a frequent source of tension. Manila has claimed that the Chinese obstructed their fishermen in the reef area since occupying it in 1995. In its case details, the Tribunal stated that, from the available evidence, it seems the PRC has never directly responded to the accusation that it has illegally prevented Filipino fishermen from fishing close to Mischief Reef, an area well within the PHL's EEZ. In addition, Beijing's numerous statements indicate its view that the Philippines does not have rights in the said area. China likewise has not appeared to do anything to prevent its own fishermen from fishing in the Mischief Reef area. In fact, the issuance of the "Nansha Certification of Fishing Permit" in 2008 for instance, which incorporated Mischief Reef, is a clear example of actively encouraging unlawful fishing activities let alone preventing them.[35]

Weaknesses of PRC Claims

Mainstream legal opinion considers China's assertion that the features of the South China Sea have always been Chinese territory is weak under accepted international law. At best, any record of authority over the area was sporadic and occasional throughout the centuries and certainly not consistent until recent decades. Indeed, it did not become effective and continuous in select locations from north to south until after the late 1980s. There are also inconsistencies in historical documentation vis-à-vis the Spratly Islands, within which Mischief Reef sits. Valencia et al., for example, cite an official Chinese government report in 1928 in which

[32] Permanent Court of Arbitration Case No. 2013–19, §730; 290.

[33] Ibid., §1006; 403.

[34] Ibid., §1009; 403–404.

[35] Ibid., §747; 294.

nothing is stated about the Spratly group, and where the southernmost boundary of China's territory is described to extend to only just beyond the Paracel Islands. Chinese scholars have defended their position by arguing their country was not observing Western-inspired international law principles and procedures until at least the nineteenth century.[36] China was also racked by foreign interference, occupation, and internal strife for the first half of the twentieth century. In this context, it was also unwilling and unable to physically assert its control over perceived Chinese territory in the SCS. Under international law, however, it is clear that in the Spratly Islands, the PRC did not "effectively" occupy any part of that area until 1987–1988, when the PRC constructed a marine observatory on Fiery Cross Reef, as well as weather stations, air control centers, and military facilities on other occupied features. Similarly, it was not until the 1990s that China, in displaying its sovereignty, attempted to regulate and restrict "foreign" commercial and fishing vessels in the southern SCS.[37] This was decades after the Philippines had begun to physically exercise their sovereignty in the islands and waters around such features as Mischief Reef in the eastern Spratlys. Alfredo C. Robles Jr., an authority on the South China Sea Arbitration Tribunal and its 2016 findings, has stated that the Chinese first formally claimed "historic rights" as late as May 2009 and prior to this, had not claimed SCS sea areas beyond the territorial sea.[38] The PRC's Declaration on the Territorial Sea in 1958 for example stated that the Spratly Islands are "separated from the mainland and its coastal islands by the high seas".[39] China's apparent treatment of Mischief Reef as a high-tide feature also does not stand up to scrutiny. Decades before man-made constructions, detailed British, Japanese and even Chinese surveys proved that Mischief Reef is a low-tide elevation in its natural state.[40] Thus it cannot be used to lawfully claim EEZ or continental shelf rights or even a territorial sea. Robles, dismissive of China's assertions, refers to internationally-agreed maritime laws and contends

[36] Some might consider this a moot point, since international maritime law was not widely codified, accepted and practiced in the West until the later nineteenth century. Prior to that it was primarily limited to national "admiralty" laws.

[37] Valencia, et al., "*Sharing the Resources*," 22–24.

[38] Robles, "The South China Sea Arbitration," 115.

[39] People's Republic China's Declaration on the Territorial Sea, Appendix 18, 21.

[40] Robles, "The South China Sea Arbitration," 144.

that the sea was "subject to only two principles, the freedom of the seas, which prohibited appropriation by any State, and control over a limited area by the immediately adjacent coastal State, which prohibited appropriation by any other State." On both counts he states, China's claims falls flat. On the issue of historic rights, he argued that "evidence that the Philippines or China had historically made use of the South China Sea islands would at most support the claim to historic rights to islands but would not establish historic rights to the waters beyond the territorial sea. The converse is true: historic usage of the SCS waters cannot lead to rights over islands."[41] Unfortunately for China, such views are congruent with UNCLOS, the last word on maritime law. When the Philippines sent a Note Verbale to the Chinese in February 2015 demanding that they "desist" and strongly protesting the PRC's island-building activities at "Panganiban [Mischief] Reef", they reminded China that the feature is a low-tide elevation situated inside the PHL's EEZ and on its continental shelf. They also cited the convention's Articles 60 and 80 to assert, "the Philippines has the *exclusive* right to authorize the construction of artificial islands, installations, and other structures in the vicinity of Panganiban [Mischief] Reef."[42] The Tribunal noted in their case details that China had created "an artificial island" now permanently above water at high tide, a clear contravention of Article 60's "unequivocal" regulations and that the Chinese had continued their island-building activities "without receiving, or even seeking the permission of the Philippines" ("the coastal State") and in despite of Filipino protests. In response, the case records declared: "In light of these provisions of the Convention, the Tribunal considers China's violation of its obligations to be manifest."[43] The next section will describe and examine the Philippines' claims regarding Mischief Reef.

Republic of Philippines' Claims

The Philippines lays claim to the eastern portion of the Spratly Islands. Since September 2012, in a counter move against Chinese activities, the Filipino government has officially referred to the broad area in which

[41] Ibid, 135.

[42] Permanent Court of Arbitration Case No. 2013–19, §1005; 402–403.

[43] Ibid., §1037; 414; §1038; 415.

Mischief Reef rests as the "West Philippine Sea". This followed the signing of Administrative Order 29, which refers to Presidential Decree No. 1599, a 1978 decree that established the country's EEZ. The "West Philippine Sea" move followed on the heels of the Filipino congress' Republic Act No. 9522 (the Baselines Law)[44] in 2009 defining and describing the country's baselines and emphasizing sovereignty claims over the Kalayaan Island Group (KIG) within which Mischief Reef sits (see below). Broadly speaking, the largely symbolic and not specifically demarcated "West Philippine Sea" designation refers to a wide area adjacent to the west of the Philippine archipelago located within the South China Sea and in which PHL sovereignty and jurisdictional rights apply in accordance with UNCLOS.[45]

Mischief Reef is also located in an area known in Tagalog as Kalayaan (meaning "Freedomland") as well as the Kalayaan Island Group (KIG). The group consists of 53 islands, reefs, and shoals and takes up an area of 64,976 square miles out of a total of 150,000 square miles for the entire Spratly Archipelago. Original PHL claims in this area (to around 33 features in total) had their roots in declarations made by a Filipino lawyer and businessman, Tomas Cloma, who claimed to have discovered several unoccupied features on behalf of the Philippines. This "discovery" was later reinforced by the businessman's 1956 proclamation of a new state named Kalayaan with Cloma himself as its first governor. Cloma defended his position by stating that the area's features were *res nullius* (no one's property) or *terra nullius* (no one's land) because their previous owner, Japan, had relinquished its various wartime possessions at the 1951 San Francisco Peace Conference.[46] Cloma's claim was met by shows of strength in the area by the navies of other claimants as well as through diplomatic protests. China, France, the Netherlands, South Vietnam, and Taiwan responded with claims of their own, with France and the Netherlands later dropping their claims. Banlaoi writes that in

[44] For more details, see *Official Gazette of the Republic of the Philippines*, "Republic Act No. 9522."

[45] Ubac, "It's Official: Aquino Signs Order"; Batongbacal, "Arbitration 101: Philippines V. China"; "Philippines Renames Coast," *South China Morning Post*; Heydarian, "The West Philippine Sea?"

[46] Emmers, "Maritime Disputes," 51; Dacanay, "China Builds on Five More"; Storey, "Creeping Assertiveness," 96; Banlaoi, *Security Aspects*, 87; Buszynski, "ASEAN's New Challenges," 10.

1947,[47] the PHL Foreign Affairs Secretary Carlos P. Garcia called on the victorious post-war Allied Forces to place these "New Southern Islands" under Filipino jurisdiction for security reasons and that the country had asserted its sovereignty over the KIG in the 1950s before the UN General Assembly. Since 1968, the PHL's military has occupied and administered eight islands in the KIG.[48] These take-overs of features claimed by China (in 1970, 1971, 1978, and 1980) have led Chinese experts such as Wu to point to the Philippines doing decades earlier what China is doing now.[49]

Manila's approach to Cloma's activities was generally "vague and non-committal" until the businessman legally transferred his claims to the Philippines in 1974.[50] Presidential Decree 1596 of June 11, 1978 declared that the KIG was "vital to the security and economic survival of the Philippines", and that "much of the above area is part of the continental margin of the Philippine archipelago". The following sections of the decree are also worth noting:

> WHEREAS, these areas do not legally belong to any state or nation but, by reason of history, indispensable need, and effective occupation and control established in accordance with international law, such areas must now be deemed to belong and subject to the sovereignty of the Philippines;
>
> WHEREAS, while other states have laid claims to some of these areas, their claims have lapsed by abandonment and can not prevail over that of the Philippines on legal, historical, and equitable grounds.[51]

On the same day as Presidential Decree No. 1596, President Ferdinand Marcos decreed a 200 nm EEZ for the PHL (the aforementioned Presidential Decree No. 1599) and declared that the features within Kalayaan, which include Mischief Reef, were sovereign territory on the basis of their proximity. The Philippines also regarded them as an appendage of the province of Palawan. Since then, PHL military personnel have occupied and maintained small outposts on numerous features out of over fifty in the KIG area.[52] On the basis of Manila's claims in that area, Mischief

[47] Banloi, Security Aspects, 87.

[48] Ibid.

[49] Wu, "Competing Claims," 13–22, esp.19.

[50] Ibid.

[51] *Official Gazette of the Republic of the Philippines*, "Presidential Decree No. 1596."

[52] Tordesillas, "Bring China's 9-Dash Line"; Emmers, "Maritime Disputes," 51.

Reef, even though it is not entitled to a sea area of its own, falls well inside the country's EEZ at 130 nms. According to Article 13, its low tide elevation exempts it from being an island and thus any state from insisting on sovereignty or possession, which had led to it being classified only as a maritime feature, but located well within the Philippine EEZ. It is on that basis that China's flurry of industrious building on Mischief Reef in the 2013 to 2016 period is understood to be violating Philippine sovereignty. UNCLOS Article 73 (1) outlines the rights and privileges of EEZ ownership as follows:

> the coastal State may, in the exercise of its sovereign rights to explore, exploit, conserve and manage the living resources in the EEZ, take such measures, including boarding, inspection, arrest and judicial proceedings, as may be necessary to ensure compliance with the laws and regulations adopted by it in conformity with this Convention.[53]

The PHL also cite Article 56(1) providing the coastal State with "the exclusive right to regulate the establishment and use of artificial islands, installations and structures" located within its EEZ. China's activities on and near Mischief Reef also represent a violation of Articles 60 and 80 which regulate the construction of the above in the coastal State's EEZ and on its continental shelf.[54]

When held up to UNCLOS, the PHL's confidence in their claims is not surprising. From the historical standpoint, China feels particularly aggrieved. From the Philippines' perspective, their country's decades-long unbroken administration of the area leads them to believe that there was no doubt about whose remit held sway over the reef prior to 1994–1995. The fact that Filipino fishermen had a long history of utilizing Mischief Reef during fishing expeditions only strengthened their convictions. Foreign oil companies had also been granted exploration and development contracts by Manila in the early 1990s to potentially rich offshore fields in the area straddling Palawan Island and the main Spratlys group.[55] These legal realities alongside cautious optimism regarding the security environment meant that, prior to the occupation, many Filipinos felt like they had little reason to fear the seemingly distant China.

[53] UNCLOS III (United Nations Convention of the Law of the Sea).

[54] Permanent Court of Arbitration Case No. 2013–19, *passim*.

[55] Klare, *Resource Wars*, 122.

Weaknesses of the PHL's Claims

Looking at its original claims to the area, one source asserts Manila's *res nullius*-influenced claims in the smaller Kalayaan area of the Spratlys are flawed for a number of key reasons.[56] For example, the argument that the features in question were ever abandoned by other claimants such as China and Vietnam does not stand up to scrutiny. This is evident in the aforementioned historical developments and arguments presented by Wu. In addition, when Thomas Cloma claimed a section of the archipelago for his own country, he only physically occupied features in the area for a number of months. For the best part of two decades, it was also apparent that he was acting in a private capacity rather than with any official backing or sanction from the government. This weakened the assertions made prior to the mid to late 1970s when Manila made formal declarations of ownership. Up to that point, the central government had publicly neither approved nor disapproved his actions.

As with the PRC, PHL historical documents point to inconsistencies in Manila's adoption of Cloma's claims. For example, a 1955 government declaration concerning straight baselines around the state's archipelago does not include the Kalayaan area. Manila's continental shelf claims in the area are also weak because the main archipelago is separated from the Spratly Islands by the deep Palawan Trough. This denies the Philippines a reasonable claim to the 'natural prolongation' of its continental shelf beyond the trough as stipulated in UNCLOS Article 76,[57] and also weakens any continental shelf claims to the area, which extend beyond 200 nms.[58] Dzurek also argues that the PHL's unilateral EEZ claims do not consider any other potential EEZs, which would extend around the above-water islands within the Spratly archipelago. In addition, as the Philippines is not sovereign over the Spratly Islands and its features, which are occupied by a number of states (including the PHL itself), Dzurek claims it is not accurate to say that Mischief Reef unquestionably falls with Manila's EEZ jurisdiction, despite it being only 130 nm west of the Philippines' Palawan Island.[59] Despite these flaws, it is clear that, from the perspective of international law and in the court of international opinion, the Philippines appears to stand on firmer ground than China.

[56] Hong, *UNCLOS and Ocean Dispute*, 19.

[57] Article 76 stipulates the extent of the continental shelf in detail; see UNCLOS III.

[58] Valencia, et al., "*Sharing the Resources*," 35.

[59] Dzurek, "China Occupies," 68.

The Philippines Initiates Proceedings Against China

On January 23, 2013, Manila declared that it had initiated an arbitration case against the PRC (on January 22) with reference to their competing claims in the South China Sea.[60] This involved the issuance of a "Notification and Statement of Claim" that fell under the dispute settlement provisions of UNCLOS. Specializing in maritime law, Batongbacal commented in 2015 that the case "currently stands as the most significant, and most closely watched, development for specialists and observers of the maritime disputes in the South China Sea (SCS)."[61] Robles likewise described it as a "landmark legal case" which represented the first that saw the PHL and the PRC becoming parties to a compulsory dispute settlement procedure, and which applied unprecedented interpretation and application of UNCLOS. These include the compatibility of historic rights with UNCLOS, determining whether features are above water or permanently submerged at high tide, and distinguishing features entitled to maritime zones around them and those that are not. The five member body was also tasked with judging on diverse but no less significant issues such as near-collisions, the destruction of coral reefs caused by island-building activities, and the illegal fishing of giant clams and sea turtles, the latter reported as far back as 1995.[62]

This was in response to the formal request by the PHL in January 2013 for a tribunal to be initiated, and which related to fifteen submissions by the Filipinos that addressed four central issues. These included historic rights (and China's nine dash line claim), the status of features, the lawfulness of China's actions, and the aggravation of the disputes. The Filipinos also emphasized the harm caused to the marine environment by China's reclamation and dredging activities. The tribunal was subsequently set up on June 21st of that year in accordance with the procedures outlined in Annex VII of UNCLOS. Acknowledging that the PRC had refused to recognize the proceedings, the tribunal noted that even if one party refuses to participate, the other side may ask a tribunal to proceed in making an award. Such a scenario should not bar proceedings. However,

[60] For a full account, see Permanent Court of Arbitration Case No. 2013–19.

[61] Batongbacal, "Arbitration 101: Philippines V. China."

[62] Valderama, "Speaker Urges Speedy Trial."

a tribunal "must satisfy itself not only that it has jurisdiction over the dispute but also that the claim is well founded in fact and law."[63]

As explained in detail here by Batongbacal, these questions mainly relate to Article 287 and Annex VII, which allow disputants to peacefully resolve maritime disagreements through non-binding means when involving the disputant themselves and binding means that include third parties that arbitrate and adjudicate on cases brought before them. Even though states can recourse to non-binding means whenever they wish, Article 287 (3) requires states to choose a preferred binding means that involves third parties. In a situation in which one disputant refuses to make a choice, then Annex VII is automatically selected as the default mode of arbitration and dispute settlement.

Whichever the selection, there are a number of express limitations as outlined in Article 297 (2) and Article 297 (3). There are also optional exceptions outlined in Article 298 (1). When they ratified UNCLOS, neither the PRC nor the PHL declared any preference in terms of a third-party dispute settlement mechanism. As such, both states were formally deemed to have decided that arbitration could be initiated in order to investigate and decide upon their contrasting interpretations of UNCLOS except when any of the aforementioned limitations and optional exceptions apply. On February 19, 2013, the Chinese formally rejected the "Notification and Statement of Claim" and returned it to the PHL. Despite this, Article 9 of UNCLOS Annex VII, stipulates that a state's failure or refusal to legally defend its position or to participate in procedures do not prevent proceedings from advancing. Annex VII's Article 3 allows for the setting up of an arbitral tribunal consisting of five judges. The PHL set the ball rolling by nominating Rudiger Wolfrum (from Germany) as one of the five. The rules allowed the PRC thirty days to respond in kind by nominating another judge, however, no response that granted recognition to the tribunal was given due to China's rejection of the body. In such circumstances, Annex VII permits the President of ITLOS, then Shunji Yanai (from Japan), following a request from the state that initiated proceedings, to appoint a judge to the body.[64] Yanai duly obliged on March 23, 2013 with the appointment of Stanislav Polack (from Poland), and the three remaining judges afterwards, again

[63] Permanent Court of Arbitration Case No. 2013–19, §117; 45.

[64] Batongbacal, "Arbitration 101: Philippines V. China."

following the required request from Manila. These were Jean-Pierre Cot (from France), Chris Pinto (from Sri Lanka), and Alfred Soons (the Netherlands). Chris Pinto quit his post on May 31, 2013, just one month after his appointment, due to the fact that his wife is Filipino.[65] His position was then filled by Thomas Mensah (from Ghana) on June 24, 2013.[66] As will be seen later in this chapter, China protested that the overall make-up of the tribunal was evidence of bias against the PRC and of an inability to grasp the cultural and historical complexities of the Spratly disputes. Regardless of Chinese complaints, there was no getting away from the harsh reality for the Filipinos of Chinese activities within the "West Philippines Sea", a situation that compelled them to act. As explained by PHL Secretary of Foreign Affairs, Albert del Rosario, on the day they commenced their legal case against China:

> Within the maritime area encompassed by the 9-dash line, China has also laid claim to, occupied and built structures on certain submerged banks, reefs and low tide elevations that do not qualify as islands under UNCLOS, but are parts of the Philippine continental shelf, or the international seabed. In addition, China has occupied certain small, uninhabitable coral projections that are barely above water at high tide, and which are "rocks" under Article 121 (3) of UNCLOS.[67]

The Philippine's Arbitration Claims

Briefly, the details of the PHL's "Notification and Statement of Claim" were as follows:

a. that the PRC is asserting invalid rights and entitlements that greatly exceeded what was permitted by the internationally agreed UNCLOS, most notably the nine-dash line map which assumed sovereign, jurisdictional, and historical rights and titles for China within that area. Nonetheless, Manila also acknowledged that the tribunal's jurisdiction did not extend to the question of sovereignty over features within that area such as Mischief Reef nor did they call

[65] China would cite this as evidence of the Tribunal's "biased" composition. See "South China Sea Arbitration Decided"; Callar, "For Having Pinay Wife, Sri Lankan Judge."

[66] Batongbacal, "Arbitration 101: Philippines V. China."

[67] *Official Gazette of the Republic of the Philippines*, "The Secretary of Foreign Affairs."

on the tribunal to make a ruling on same.[68] This is a moot point given the PRC's complaint that the tribunal was in reality a cleverly disguised attempt to undermine Chinese sovereignty in the eastern Spratlys.

b. that China illegally occupies and controls eight features within the South China Sea, including Mischief Reef. The PHL contended that title and sovereignty related claims by Beijing to permanently submerged features, to control of navigational rights in surrounding waters, and to historic rights to living and non-living natural resources were illegitimate. Maritime rights and entitlements in relation to features like Mischief Reef they argued should fall under the remit of UNCLOS' Article 121. They detailed how the PRC had obstructed the PHL and its vessels from exercising their right to explore and exploit marine resources within or close to such reefs. This was a flagrant breach of Article 121. The Filipinos also acknowledged that, at most, five features with rocky protrusions, not including Mischief Reef, might be entitled to a maximum 12 nm territorial sea zone around them. Chinese claims and activities beyond 12 nms thus stood no ground in the eyes of international law.[69] Regarding Mischief Reef, a low-tide elevation (LTE), China's position was even weaker because it is entitled to no maritime zone but is in fact part of the PHL's continental shelf. Manila therefore should enjoy exclusive rights and jurisdiction.[70]

c. that China illegally asserts rights and entitlements in other areas of the PHL's EEZ and CS including the exploitation of living and non-living natural resources in these areas. The Philippines claimed that the Chinese were likewise obstructing them from doing the same, and that UNCLOS-enshrined navigational rights were interfered with.[71]

According to Batongbacal, the PHL hoped that the Tribunal could buttress their position and weaken China's by publishing findings in the form of declarations and orders. Most notable of these, they hoped, would

[68] Batongbacal, "Arbitration 101: Philippines V. China."

[69] Ibid.

[70] Ibid.

[71] Ibid.

be a declaration invalidating the PRC's nine-dash line and emphasizing UNCLOS as the template through which rights and entitlements are determined. In addition, they sought a declaration stating that the occupation of, and construction of facilities on, features like Mischief Reef were illegal and that the occupation must end. The Filipinos also wanted the Tribunal to order the PRC to reform its domestic laws so that they were in line with UNCLOS as well as a command to end the obstruction of PHL vessels and any other activities that breached UNCLOS regulations. They also called on the Tribunal to declare that the PHL was wholly entitled to its twelve nm territorial sea and two hundred nm EEZ and CS from its archipelagic baselines as enacted in 2009.[72]

The Tribunal's first Procedural Order (one of four) asked the Philippines to submit its so-called Memorial, outlining its arguments in detail, by or on March 30, 2014. The PHL submitted their non-public Memorial on March 30, 2014, a paper consisting of some 4000 pages of arguments, documents, and maps. On May 14, the Tribunal met and called upon the Chinese to respond with a Counter-Memorial by December 15, however, on May 21, the PRC issued a note repeating that they did not and would not recognize the proceedings.[73] The body released another Procedural Order on December 17 of that year, in which the PRC's non-submission of a Counter-Memorial was noted, as well as China's refusal to participate in or accept the arbitration. It also stated that the body's members had received copies of China's "Position Paper". Manila was given until March 15, 2015 to submit a supplemental submission that outlined the tribunal's jurisdiction as well as the merits of the legal case. It especially called on the Filipinos to respond to China's "Position Paper". The Chinese were allowed ninety days in which to respond.[74] This position paper is described below.

[72] Ibid.

[73] Ibid.

[74] Batongbacal, "Arbitration 101: Philippines V. China."

PRC December 2014 Position Paper and Other Counter Arguments

China had stated publicly via an official "Position Paper"[75] on December 7, 2014 as well as in other formal and diplomatic statements that the tribunal has no jurisdiction over features such as Mischief Reef, and that it would not be partaking[76] in proceedings.[77] In brief, the Chinese government protested that the PHL's commencement of arbitration was in breach of bilateral agreements, contravened UNCLOS, and was contrary to general practice in terms of international arbitration.[78] The Position Paper did not address the merits of the Philippines' arguments and focused only on criticizing the Tribunal's rights and suitability to decide on the issues in question. These criticisms are discussed subsequently.[79]

It has also declared that its statements and declarations in response to the January 2013 initiated arbitration "shall by no means be interpreted as China's participation in the arbitral proceeding in any form."[80] China has refused to participate in or recognize the Tribunal and declared it had no jurisdiction over features such as Mischief Reef.

The 2014 Position Paper cited some key reasons for not accepting, and not participating in, the arbitration. These include (a) that the issue of territorial sovereignty over a number of SCS features "does not concern the interpretation or application of the Convention" (i.e. UNCLOS) and is "beyond the scope of the Convention"; (b) that the PHL has failed to honor its international law obligations by acting unilaterally because the two countries have previously agreed, through various declarations and bilateral agreements to bilaterally resolve the disagreements via negotiations, and (c) the matters put forward by the PHL, even if accepted, for argument's sake, fall "within the scope of the declaration[81] filed by China

[75] Foreign Ministry of the People's Republic of China, "Position Paper."

[76] China did try to indirectly influence the Tribunal. Robles noted that China had informally been taking part in arbitration and provides examples; Robles, *The South China Sea Arbitration*, 51–52, 120.

[77] Permanent Court of Arbitration, Press Release.

[78] Ministry of Foreign Affairs of the People's Republic of China, "Statement on the Award."

[79] Batongbacal, "Arbitration 101: Philippines V. China."

[80] Permanent Court of Arbitration, Press Release.

[81] Government of the People's Republic of China, "Position Paper."

in 2006 in accordance with the Convention, which excludes, *inter alia*, disputes concerning maritime delimitation from compulsory arbitration and other compulsory dispute settlement procedures."[82]

Similarly, the Chinese point to the 2002 Declaration of Conduct (DoC) which they viewed as a commitment and an obligation by the two neighbors to find a resolution via friendly consultations and negotiations, and through a mutually agreed means of dispute settlement. The Chinese reject Filipino assertions that the PRC had already frequently violated the DoC and that this had compelled the PHL to act. In addition, the Chinese called attention to a number of bilateral agreements[83] or "joint statements" in 1995, 1999, and 2000, and afterwards in 2004 and 2011 as evidence that both had given assurances over two decades to settle their disagreements through negotiations that both sides agreed to.[84] They charge also that the Philippines upped the ante by being the first to use force around Scarborough Shoal in 2012, as described later.[85] Batongbacal neatly summarized a number of key points in China's "Position Paper" criticisms. These were that the arbitration was in principle based on the question of sovereignty over SCS features and even if the body dismissed sovereign-related questions, they would first need to delimit maritime areas before deciding on PHL claims. This meant that whatever happened, "the case falls outside the Tribunal's jurisdiction since it is within the optional exceptions to the jurisdiction of binding dispute settlement mechanisms that China invoked in a 2006 declaration in accordance with the terms of UNCLOS Art. 298(1)."[86]

[82] Government of the People's Republic of China, "Summary of the Position Paper."

[83] The Tribunal found that the multilateral and legally binding 1976 Treaty of Amity and Co-operation (TAC, Chapter IV, Articles 13 to 17) of which China and the Philippines are parties, could not preclude submission of the dispute to arbitration or recourse by any party to compulsory dispute settlement; Robles, *The South China Sea Arbitration*, 27, 28. For China's statement on bilateral negotiations, see https://www.fmprc.gov.cn/nanhai/eng/snhwtlcwj_1/t1370476.htm.

[84] These joint statements are dated August 10, 1995, March 23, 1999, May 16, 2000, September 4, 2004, and September 1, 2011.

[85] Robles, *The South China Sea Arbitration*, 23, 26.

[86] Batongbacal, "Arbitration 101: Philippines V. China."

The Tribunal's Findings

The Arbitral Tribunal rendered two awards, an award on jurisdiction and admissibility,[87] on October 29, 2015 and the final award on July 12, 2016. This marked a watershed for the Mischief Reef dispute in terms of how the Tribunal publicized to the world the legal weaknesses inherent in China's claims and activities in the South China Sea. This was in spite of the historic arguments made by the Chinese to the area.[88] On the four key issues, the Tribunal declared that on the first issue, "Historic Rights and the 'Nine-Dash Line'," China's historic rights "were extinguished to the extent they were incompatible with the exclusive economic zones provided for in the Convention." On the "Status of Features", the tribunal sided with the PHL in their contention that reefs that "have been modified by land reclamation and construction" such as Mischief Reef (and three other features in the areas of dispute) "were submerged at high tide in their natural condition." It also stated that the Spratly Islands as a collective unit were not entitled to any maritime zone. As such, on both counts, certain maritime areas fell within the PHL's EEZ because there was no circumstance in which China could possibly argue for an entitlement. Regarding the "Lawfulness of Chinese Actions", the Tribunal found that because the legitimacy of the PHL's EEZ (within which Mischief Reef rests) in accordance with UNCLOS was confirmed, then it followed that the PRC was violating the PHL's internationally agreed rights in three ways. These are (a) interfering with Filipino fishing and petroleum exploration activities (and illegally creating "a serious risk of collision when they [PRC law enforcement vessels] physically obstructed Philippine vessels. The PRC has "physically obstructed Philippine vessels"); (b) constructing artificial islands through land reclamation[89]; and (c) failing to prevent fishermen from the PRC from fishing inside the PHL's EEZ. Specifically with regards to Mischief Reef, it noted

[87] This declared the Tribunal could decide on a number of jurisdictional issues and deferred other issues for further consideration. See Kotani, "The South China Sea Arbitration, No." See also Permanent Court of Arbitration Case No. 2013–19, "Award on Jurisdiction and Admissibility."

[88] See Permanent Court of Arbitration Case No. 2013–19.

[89] In the PHL's Submission No.12, a declaration was sought stating the PRC's island building activities had breached UNCLOS' Articles 60 ("Artificial Islands, Installations and Structures in the Exclusive Economic Zone") and 80 ("Artificial Islands, Installations and Structures on the continental shelf") because Mischief Reef is a low-tide elevation

how the Chinese authorities were in fact protecting and failing to stop their fishermen from illegally fishing in areas within the PHL's EEZ at Mischief Reef and the Second Thomas Shoal. It also noted the illegal construction of facilities as well as land reclamation on the reef without Manila's permission, thus violating the PHL's "sovereign rights with respect to its exclusive economic zone and continental shelf." In relation to the "Aggravation of Dispute" issue, the Tribunal made a finding on whether Chinese activities since 2013 (when arbitration had started) had aggravated South China Sea-related disputes between China and the Philippines (breaching UNCLOS Articles 279, 296, 300, and "general international law").[90] It also declared:

> China's recent large-scale land reclamation and construction of artificial islands was incompatible with the obligations on a State during dispute resolution proceedings, insofar as China has inflicted irreparable harm to the marine environment, built a large artificial island in the Philippines' exclusive economic zone, and destroyed evidence of the natural condition of features in the South China Sea that formed part of the Parties' dispute.[91]

On the harm caused to the marine environment[92] by China's island building activities around features such as Mischief Reef, the tribunal found that the PRC had seriously damaged the coral reef around related features, and had "violated its obligation to preserve and protect fragile ecosystems and the habitat of depleted, threatened, or endangered species".[93] The Tribunal found that China had breached UNCLOS Articles 123, 192, 194, 197 and 206.[94]

Regarding Article 206, the Tribunal also declared that the Chinese authorities knew their fishermen "have harvested endangered sea turtles, coral, and giant clams on a substantial scale in the South China Sea (using

(LTE) within the EEZ and continental shelf (CS) of the PHL and these activities had occurred without permission from the Philippines.

[90] Permanent Court of Arbitration, Press Release.

[91] Ibid.

[92] For damage caused to Mischief Reef and its environs, see Chapter 6.

[93] Permanent Court of Arbitration, Press Release.

[94] For full details of what the articles cover, see https://www.un.org/Depts/los/convention_agreements/texts/unclos/unclos_e.pdf.

methods that inflict severe damage on the coral reef environment)" and thus China had failed to honor its obligations to prevent these activities.[95] Research by Robles, for example, reveals that some extraction activities by PRC fishermen were "extremely destructive to the reef habitat" with extensive propeller damage to the reef flats at Mischief Reef. Giant clam fishing is especially destructive with explosives being used at times resulting in permanent damage to the reef, the killing of fish, and the destruction of their habitat. In response, the PRC has issued only one statement by the State Oceanic Administration (SOA), of a mere 500 words. Both the short released statement and a longer SOA report are "thoroughly contradicted by the evidence." Robles also asserts that the evidence of China co-operating to agree on environmental protection has been scant, and has not conducted an environmental impact assessment (EIA) as requested by UNCLOS' Article 206. Likewise, there has been no evidence of the PRC's legal system punishing Chinese fishermen for their unlawful and environmental destructive actions despite assurances in the past. This includes those engaged in the poaching of endangered species. The SOA's very brief statement declared that the ecological impact of China's land reclamation activities on reefs like Mischief Reef would be "partial, temporary, controllable, and recoverable." However, expert opinions and incontrovertible evidence point to long lasting if not permanent damage to "corals that have accumulated over centuries or millennia and stand meters above the substrata". According to Robles, "rejuvenation of these areas will take decades, and for the large massive colonies, centuries."[96]

There were additional violations regarding the Convention on International Trade in Endangered Species of Wild Fauna and Flora (CITES) and to which China was a party, when sea turtles, listed under CITES as endangered, were discovered on Chinese fishing boats, and giant clams, also listed under CITES as protected, were being collected by Chinese civilians as well. This was compounded by Chinese vessels destroying coral (also protected) with their propellers when collecting the clams.[97]

[95] Permanent Court of Arbitration, Press Release.

[96] Robles, "The South China Sea Arbitration," 178–186.

[97] Permanent Court of Arbitration Case No. 2013–19, §860; 335; §953, 955; 380–381. See also *The Ferse Report*. https://www.pcacases.com/web/sendAttach/1809.

Tribunal Findings in Relation to Mischief Reef

|Some of the key details and findings by the Tribunal in relation to Mischief Reef are summarized and provided below. For the full details, see §1203, 471 to 477.

On Fisheries:

1. May 2013: PRC flagged vessels which had engaged in fishing inside the Philippines' EEZ at Mischief Reef (and Second Thomas Shoal).
2. The PRC was aware of, tolerated, and failed to exercise due diligence to prevent these fishing activities by PRC flagged vessels near the feature. China's marine surveillance vessels in the area would have known about these vessels and had the means to stop them.
3. As such, the PRC "has failed to exhibit due regard" for the PHL's "sovereign rights" inside its EEZ in relation to fisheries.

On the Construction of Artificial Islands, Installations, and Structures:

1. The PRC had "engaged in the construction of artificial islands, installations, and structures at Mischief Reef without the authorization of the Philippines."
2. Recalled: (i) its finding that the reef is a low-tide elevation, (ii) its declaration that such elevations are "not capable of appropriation", and (iii) its declaration that the reef is within the EEZ and continental shelf of the Philippines.
3. Declared that the PRC has breached UNCLOS' Articles 60 and 80 in relation to the PHL's "sovereign rights" in its EEZ and continental shelf.
4. Found that (i) China constructed a large artificial island on the reef during a time when dispute resolution proceedings were ongoing; (ii) has, as a result of its extensive land reclamation and construction activities, caused "severe, irreparable harm to the coral reef ecosystem at Mischief Reef" and other features; and (iii) has "permanently destroyed" .... "evidence of the natural condition of Mischief Reef" and other features.

On the Aggravation of the Disputes

1. The PRC "has aggravated the Parties' dispute concerning their respective rights and entitlements in the area of Mischief Reef."
2. The PRC "has aggravated the Parties' dispute concerning the protection and preservation of the marine environment at Mischief Reef."[98]

PRC Response to July 2016 Arbitration Findings

The significance of the PHL's initiation of legal action and the subsequent Tribunal and its findings in the 2013 to 2016 period for the Spratly disputes should not be underestimated. China's reaction was to further reinforce their position on features like Mischief Reef and to engage in an unprecedented island reclamation campaign that has once again brought the South China Sea disputes to the forefront of regional diplomacy in recent years.

In response to the Arbitral Tribunal's findings in July 2016, the PRC's Foreign Ministry released a statement outlining its reasons for rejecting the verdicts. Most notably, the Chinese repeated their view that the Philippines had breached the commitment set out in the 2002 Declaration on the Conduct of Parties in the South China Sea "to resolve the relevant disputes through negotiations by states directly concerned." The PHL had thus acted "out of bad faith". The Foreign Ministry asserted that the arbitration was not about maintaining peace and stability but about denying China's territorial sovereignty and maritime rights and interests in the South China Sea. The arbitration, they claimed, "infringes upon China's right as a state party to UNCLOS to choose on its own will the procedures and means for dispute settlement." They also again referred to an optional exceptions declaration to the UN made by the PRC in 2006 in which "pursuant to Article 298[99] of UNCLOS, China excluded from the compulsory dispute settlement procedures of UNCLOS disputes concerning, among others, maritime delimitation, historic bays or titles, military and law enforcement activities" (Foreign Ministry of the People's

[98] Permanent Court of Arbitration Case No. 2013–19, §1203; 476.

[99] UNCLOS Article 298; see https://www.un.org/Depts/los/convention_agreements/texts/unclos/unclos_e.pdf.

Republic of China, July 12, 2016).[100] In addition to governmental statements, the Chinese have also provided detailed explanations for why the arbitration and its tribunal (and thus Filipino claims vis-à-vis Mischief Reef) should not be recognized. In advance of the findings' publication, the Chinese were also making their displeasure known. In June 2016 for example, the Chinese Society of International Law, a body that in its own words "strongly supports the positions of the Chinese Government" published an article on why the Tribunal's first award of October 2015 was "groundless in both fact and law" and "null and void" as well as why the Tribunal "manifestly has no jurisdiction". The award is "an essentially political award" and the Tribunal, which is "neither objective nor impartial", exercises jurisdiction "ultra vires, beyond the authorization of the UNCLOS", "impairs the integrity and authority of the Convention" and "deviates from the object and purpose of the dispute settlement mechanism of the UNCLOS." The law society's article is very technical, and cites an exhaustive number of international legal cases to reinforce its points.[101]

The article does not deny disagreements between the PRC and the PHL in the South China Sea. These relate to territorial sovereignty over "certain features" as well as maritime delimitation. These are the true "essence" of the disagreements. It also emphasizes the importance of "historic rights" that have existed long before UNCLOS. The Society was dismissive of claims by both the Tribunal and the Philippines that the proceedings were not about determining territorial sovereignty. To decide on the PHL's UNCLOS-related submissions without ascertaining territorial sovereignty was impossible.

The Tribunal "put the cart before the horse and acted contrary to the UNCLOS, by determining that it had jurisdiction over the claims, with the sovereignty over the features undetermined." This betrays the fact that "the real object of the Philippines in initiating the South China Sea Arbitration is to deny China's territorial sovereignty over Huangyan Dao (Scarborough Shoal) and the Nansha Islands" and "to legitimize its [the Philippines'] unlawful seizure and occupation of some of China's maritime features in the Nansha Islands." Assertions that the proceedings are unrelated to sovereignty are "nothing but an outright lie." The true

100 Foreign Ministry of the People's Republic of China, Statement on the Award.

101 Chinese Society of International Law, "The Tribunal's Award."

essence of the "unlawfully" initiated proceedings, they state, is not about settling bilateral disagreements in "good faith" but to "obtain bargaining chips in its quest for unlawful interests in the South China Sea." This Trojan Horse strategy, they declared, is evident in statements made by the Filipinos since they first commenced legal proceedings against China. On January 22, 2013 for instance, the article stated that the PHL Secretary of Foreign Affairs, Albert del Rosario, published a Questions and Answers statement regarding the arbitral proceedings. Phrases included: "to protect our national territory and maritime domain", not "surrendering our national sovereignty" and that "our action is in defense of our national territory and maritime domain".[102] In the State of Nation Address (SONA) Technical Report in 2014, which the Office of the President of the Philippines published in July of that year, the arbitration proceedings were discussed under the title "Protected Territorial Integrity through the Promotion of the Rule of Law."[103] The SONA Technical Report of July 2015, discussed the proceedings under the title "Protected our National Territory and Boundaries."[104] According to the Society, the language used in various PHL statements proved that the arbitration was very much about the one issue it claimed not to be about. For all these reasons, the Arbitration would not help to settle the disputes but rather "can only intensify the conflicts and further complicate the situations." As a "vicious precedent", it could open a "floodgate of abuse lawsuits" that would adversely impact the settlement of maritime disputes throughout the world. After all, the end goal of UNCLOS' dispute settlement mechanism is to resolve such disputes peacefully. The article also emphasized the importance of "consensus" as a foundation stone to any resolution, and a value that "is inherent in the centuries-long Chinese cultural tradition that advocates "harmony" being the most precious" and well as "non-litigation." This has been reiterated to the Philippines over many years and through numerous bilateral understandings and agreements, and yet Manila proceeded with litigation.[105]

More detailed criticisms by "more than 60 experts in the fields of law, international relations, history, geography etc." of the findings were

[102] *Official Gazette of the Government of the Philippines*, "DFA: Guide Q & A."

[103] Ibid., "State of Nation Address," 64–65.

[104] Ibid., 61–62.

[105] Chinese Society of International Law, "The Tribunal's Award."

included in an in-depth study of the PHL's fifteen arbitrational submissions in the "Chinese Journal of International Law" (in association with the aforementioned Chinese Society of International Law) in June 2018. Here the tribunal findings are repeatedly described as "null and void", "failed" and "erred", having "no basis in fact and law", and that "these awards threaten the international rule of law." These criticisms pertained to six issues: (1) jurisdiction; (2) admissibility; (3) historic rights; (4) the status of the Spratly Islands ("Nansha Qundao") and the Macclesfield Bank and Scarborough Shoal area ("Zhongsha Qundao"); (5) the legality of China's activities in the SCS; and (6) due process and evidence. In its conclusion, the 541-paged article declared that "the Tribunal's many errors deprive its awards of validity and threaten to undermine the international rule of law." Specifically referring to Mischief Reef, the study presented the assertions of a former Vice-Foreign Minister of the PRC, Tang Jiaxuan (1998–2003) (made during post-occupation bilateral consultations in 1995), who argued that one cannot discuss Mischief Reef alone. It must be discussed with the entire Spratly Islands archipelago in mind. In his assertions, Tang claimed that the PRC, from the international legal and historical perspective, has indisputable sovereignty over the Spratlys "of course including Mischief Reef" and that disputes such as Mischief Reef must be resolved through patient and bilateral negotiations. Given that there does not appear to be a solution at the present time, he stated that the PRC was willing to shelve the dispute and to explore the possibilities for joint development and other co-operative activities.[106] Some of the key criticisms made of the tribunal by the study include the following:

1. In the 2002 DoC and other talks on a possible CoC in the SCS, the PRC and ASEAN member states addressed "territorial and jurisdictional disputes" and not disputes that emphasized a tribunal's interpretation of or application of UNCLOS. For example, they contended that the question of whether low-tide elevations can be "appropriated as territory" is a sovereignty-related question. The study referred to a 2001 judgment where the ICJ declared that "International treaty law is silent on the question whether low-tide

[106] Ibid., 13, 218, 219, 382, 383.

elevations can be considered to be 'territory'."[107] Articles 74 and 83 of UNCLOS also declare that maritime delimitation between States with opposite or adjacent coasts "shall be effected by agreement on the basis of international law, as referred to in Article 38 of the Statute of the International Court of Justice, in order to achieve an equitable solution." The PHL's selective approach destroys "the integrity and indivisibility of maritime delimitation and contravene the principle that maritime delimitation must be based on international law as referred to in Article 38 of the ICJ Statute and that "all relevant factors must be taken into account."[108]

2. The study also complained that in some of the Philippines' 2013 submissions (8 to 14), the PHL had formerly raised issues without factoring crucial SCS developments or selectively ignoring others. New claims for example were "parasited" on already inadmissible new submissions. This caused China to question the professionalism of the tribunal's procedures (and its impartiality) as well as the PHL's submissions.[109]
3. The Chinese took particular issue with the tribunal submissions 4 to 6 "dismembering" "low-tide elevation" "submerged landmass" features such as Mischief Reef and separating it and others from the wider Spratly Islands (Nansha Qundao) archipelago (as well as the Paracel Islands (Xisha Islands]) in their investigations and findings. A feature's status, the journal claimed, "can only be determined within the bigger framework of the archipelago" and "relevant features" within the said area. The "low-tide elevations" findings were also "not well founded in fact" with "no support in either the Convention or customary international law." The phrase "submerged landmass" they contend "is a creature of the tribunal's invention". The use of satellite imagery by the PHL was also "insufficient" in determining a feature's status as was utilizing outdated survey materials by the British, Japanese, and US navies. Likewise, it criticized the tribunal for failing to give

[107] I.C.J. Reports 2001, Qatar v. Bahrain, §205; 101–102.

[108] Chinese Society of International Law, 383; 671–672.

[109] Ibid., 419.

proper weight to important historical documents that proved the long-term presence of Chinese fishermen in the Spratly Islands.[110]

4. They rejected the term "submerged landmass" for such features as Mischief Reef, arguing that the term does not appear anywhere within the contents of UNCLOS. The study's authors cite Paragraph 26 of a 2012 ICJ Judgment in a territorial dispute between Nicaragua and Colombia which stated: "rather they [low-tide elevations] form part of the submerged landmass of the State and fall within the legal regimes for the territorial sea and continental shelf, as the case may be." As such, these "component features" of the Spratlys, whether high-tide or low-tide features, "cannot be appropriated." The PRC's sovereignty extends beyond individual features. Despite this, the Tribunal's findings do "violence to international jurisprudence" and run counter to customary international law which they claim recognizes the territorial status of "China's outlying archipelago" and related maritime entitlements as well-established.[111]
5. The study accused the Filipinos of hypocrisy over the "submerged landmass" claim because the PHL has "persisted in claiming sovereignty" over various features "whatever nature those features possess" since the 1970s. This was cited in the December 2014 Position Paper. Presidential Decree No. 1596 (promulgated on June 11, 1978) for example publicized the Philippines' "unlawful claim to sovereignty over some maritime features" in the Spratlys (including Mischief Reef).[112] Both the study and the Position Paper stated that the Philippines claimed such features "together with the adjacent but vast areas of waters, sea-bed, subsoil, continental margin and superjacent airspace, and constituted the vast area as a new municipality of the province of Palawan, entitled Kalayaan." They continue by arguing that even though the Philippine Republic Act No. 9522 (March 10, 2009) asserted the status

[110] Ibid., 475, 511, 519.

[111] Ibid., 512–514. The authors also accused the PHL of gravely violating the One China Principle and infringing China's sovereignty and territorial integrity in their statements regarding the Taiwan-administered but PRC-claimed Itu Aba (Taiping Dao), the largest island in the Spratlys.

[112] Foreign Ministry of the People's Republic of China, "Position Paper of the Government."

of a number of KIG features, such as Mischief Reef, be designated in accordance with UNCLOS Article 121. This purpose of this act, they declare, was to allow the PHL to adjust its claims "based on those features" inside the KIG; "The Act did not vary the territorial claim of the Philippines to the relevant maritime features, including those it alleged in this arbitration as low-tide elevations."[113] The study also presented Note Verbale No. 000228 as proof of double standards by the PHL and argued:

> In Note Verbale No. 000228, addressed to Secretary-General of the United Nations on 5 April 2011, the Philippine Permanent Mission to the United Nations stated that, "the Kalayaan Island Group (KIG) constitutes an integral part of the Philippines. The Republic of the Philippines has sovereignty and jurisdiction over the geological features in the KIG." The Philippines has maintained, to date, its claim to sovereignty over 40 maritime features in the Nansha Islands, among which are the very features it now labels as low-tide elevations. It is thus obvious that the only motive behind the Philippines' assertion that low-tide elevations cannot be appropriated is to deny China's sovereignty over these features so as to place them under Philippine sovereignty.[114]

6. The Chinese also criticized the apparent failure of the tribunal to thoroughly and carefully review past cases of similar nature throughout the world and how international courts and tribunals dealt with such questions. Rather, they claimed that the "erroneous" tribunal "rendered a groundless [and "erroneous"] decision by picking an obiter dictum[115] as its basis."[116]
7. The tribunal's application of the vague and ambiguous Part 3 of Article 121 to certain Spratly Island features like Mischief Reef was also "erroneous". Article 121 (3) states that "rocks cannot

[113] Chinese Society of International Law, "The South China Sea Arbitration Awards," 661.

[114] Ibid.

[115] "|Latin for 'something said in passing.' A comment, suggestion, or observation made by a judge in an opinion that is not necessary to resolve the case, and as such, it is not legally binding on other courts but may still be cited as persuasive authority in future litigation." https://www.law.cornell.edu/wex/obiter_dictum.

[116] Chinese Society of International Law, 518.

sustain human habitation or an economic life of their own shall have no exclusive economic zone or continental shelf." The selective interpretation of Article 121 (3), they say, "flagrantly violated the rules of treaty interpretation." Here again the Chinese cite the ICJ and provide numerous examples of states claiming EEZ and CS areas on the basis of tiny and sparsely populated or unpopulated features. These include Johnston Atoll (USA), which originally had no people living on it and which, due to dredging and island building activities, expanded from a mere 0.1861 square kilometers to 2.4119 square kilometers. In 1983, the US claimed a 200 nm EEZ around the feature. Other notable examples they cite include Jan Mayen (Norway), Bouvet Island (Norway), Clipperton Island (France), Tromelin Island (France), Wake Island (USA), Jarvis Island (USA), Trindade and Martin Vaz (Brazil), and Isla de Aves (Venezuela).[117]

8. The study also criticized the tribunal for apparently attempting to "confuse the public" by pointing to an alleged double standard in the PRC's diplomatic protests (particularly from 2009 to 2011) against Japanese land reclamation activities and extensive claims to the sea and ocean floor around the tiny and almost completely submerged Okinotorishima atoll in the western Pacific. The scholars stridently rejected any comparison with what the PRC is doing on features like Mischief Reef as well as with UNCLOS Article 121 (3).[118] In April 2004, the PRC first declared that it did not recognize Okinotorishima as an island but merely a collection of rocks in its natural state undeserving of EEZ and continental shelf rights in accordance with UNCLOS.[119] The journal article referred to the feature as "the rock of Oki-no-tori" (not the Japanese title "Okinotorishima" which means the island of Oki-no-tori). It also contended that Okinotorishima is "not remotely comparable to component features of the archipelagos of Nanhai Zhudao" [the South China Sea] and that "the natural conditions of components features of Nansha Qundao [the Spratly Islands] are much better than those of the rock of Oki-no-tori". The Spratly

[117] Ibid., 532–538.

[118] Ibid., 551.

[119] Yoshikawa, "The US-Japan–China Mistrust Spiral."

Islands they claim, are a unit in their own right, and thus entitled to a considerable EEZ and CS area.[120]

9. Regarding Submissions 8 to 14, and their focus on the legality or otherwise of the PRC's various activities in the South China Sea, the publication addressed issues such as environmental protection relating to fishing as well as construction activities, and law enforcement activities in maritime areas by China. These submissions also addressed activities that contributed to an aggravation and extension of the dispute. Mischief Reef was dealt with specifically in places. On these issues, the authors repeated that it is not permissible for "Meiji Jiao" to be treated as an individual case, but rather each of the two SCS archipelagos are units over which China enjoys sovereignty. When Chinese marine surveillance vessels patrol around and visit Mischief Reef and elsewhere or when the PRC declares a fishing moratorium, these are affirmations of China's sovereignty and jurisdiction in the area and of the right to "manage and exploit resources". The controversial fishing moratorium, it argues, is evidence of the PRC's commitment to manage resources, to contribute to the sustainable development of fisheries, and to the preservation of the ecological environment. In fact, the study asserts that "it is only natural that China would not accept such actions" when referring to the Philippines who, it is claimed, forced China to respond by first taking unilateral actions such as petroleum explorations in disputed areas and trying to "carry out its own understanding of its rights" and imposing its own interpretations on China.[121] PRC marine surveillance vessels thus reacted to discourage the PHL from unilaterally "carry[ing] out its own understanding of its rights." In this regard, the study declared:

> it is incredible that the Tribunal turned a blind eye to the Philippines' failure in fulfilling its due obligation, and to the fact that it was the Philippines who first took unilateral actions. The Tribunal's logic, by which China was not allowed to take any response actions other than protest against the Philippines' unilateral action, is ridiculous.[122]

[120] Chinese Society of International Law, 551.

[121] Ibid., 557.

[122] Ibid., 396.

The scholars also rejected the claim that the PRC had breached UNCLOS Article 77 ("Rights of the Coastal State over the continental shelf") since the areas in question "are far from being the ascertained continental shelf of the Philippines." As for the claim by the PHL that their fishermen had been prevented from fishing at Mischief Reef and Second Thomas Shoal, it was asserted that the Philippines had failed to prove this claim with evidence, and stated that the Tribunal had acknowledged this failure. As for Articles 60 and 80, which relate to "Artificial islands, installations and structures" in the exclusive economic zone and on the continental shelf, the tribunal "erred" in its finding because the construction activities on Mischief Reef and other features are "within its [the PRC's] territory" and are "an act of exercising sovereignty". The construction activities at the reef are related to the Overall Urban Plan of Sansha City, Hainan Province. In relation to Submission No. 14, the authors were steadfastly opposed to the PHL's alleged attempt to bring the issue of "territorial sovereignty" into the equation and lamented that the tribunal had disregarded this reality. According to the study, this attempt "is the root of all its erroneous findings on this submission." They therefore claim it is incorrect to state that China had aggravated or extended the dispute. Here again the study cited a previous ICJ declaration that "maritime rights derive from the coastal State's sovereignty over the land, a principle which can be summarized as 'the land dominates the sea'." If sovereignty over such features as Mischief Reef is not decided upon then "it is impossible to decide whether maritime claims based on that feature are consistent with the Convention."[123]

10. The claims regarding the preservation of the maritime environment and damage caused by China's construction activities were also dismissed as non-existent, with the authors stating "there is no dispute in this respect to be aggravated. The alleged aggravation of a non-existent dispute is a fake issue." They declared China had never caused "permanent" and "irreparable" damage to the maritime environment.[124]

[123] Ibid., 558, 609, 658, 659.

[124] Ibid., 610.

11. The study was also deeply critical of the Tribunal's apparent lack of regional, cultural, legal, and diplomatic diversity and representativeness. For example, no Asians were on the Tribunal, and four out of the five tribunal members were from Europe. As such, it "lacked meaningful cognizance of and thus took little account of Asian civilization, diplomatic and legal traditions, and other regional factors which should have informed its decision-making in the Arbitration." This reality, they asserted, contributed to many errors later when making its findings.[125] The study also accused the tribunal of partiality with bias and inconsistencies apparent in some of its procedural arrangements. For example, some states were "improperly allowed" to attend the proceedings as observers. Insufficient evidence was also used to detail fishing locations and related activities.[126]

Closing Comments

The legal complexities of disputes like those over Mischief Reef as well as the stipulations and articles contained within UNCLOS III provide insights into the behavior of the PRC and the PHL over the years. At the same time, UNCLOS regulations have resulted in little or no reward for China and its centuries-long proof of links to the features of the South China Sea, albeit sporadic. Considering the limitations of maritime law and to provide a more comprehensive picture in which to examine the occupation issue, other key factors between China and the Philippines need to be considered as well, specifically national security and defense. However, it might be worthwhile ending this chapter with a comment by legal scholar Daniel Guilfoyle, writing on the same day the Tribunal released its findings:

> ...international tribunals normally bend over backwards to avoid findings of bad faith against a state. That is, one cannot act in bad faith without violating some other substantive right. So most tribunals consider it sufficient to stop at determining that a right or duty has been violated. This

[125] The PRC's criticisms of the Tribunal (well in advance of July 2016), included bias selection from the Japanese judge who had helped to select four of the Tribunal's five members in 2013; Johnson, "Beijing turns on Japanese judge."

[126] Chinese Society of International Law, 647–648.

tribunal has found China violated Article 300 of UNCLOS: the duty to act in good faith. This is an extraordinary rebuke and a clear indication that the law of the sea dispute resolution system will not be cowed by the posturing of the superpower. As a matter of principle, it takes a principled stand on the supremacy of the rule of law. As a matter of pragmatism, it flies in the face of the conventional wisdom that angering China over this dispute could jeopardize the stability of the law of the sea system.[127]

References

Banlaoi, Rommel C. "Security Aspects of Philippines-China Relations: Bilateral Issues and Concerns in the Age of Global Terrorism." Rex Book Store, Quezon City, Philippines, 2007.

Batongbacal, Jay. "Arbitration 101: Philippines V. China." *Asia Maritime Transparency Initiative*, January 21, 2015. https://amti.csis.org/arbitration-101-philippines-v-china/.

Buszynski, Leszek. "ASEAN's New Challenges." *Pacific Affairs* 70, no. 4 (1997): 555–578.

Callar, Michaela de. "For Having Pinay Wife, Sri Lankan Judge in PHL Arbitral Proceedings vs China Resigns." *GMA Network*, June 7, 2013. https://www.gmanetwork.com/news/news/nation/311870/for-having-pinay-wife-sri-lankan-judge-in-phl-arbitral-proceedings-vs-china-resigns/story/.

Chinese Society of International Law. "The South China Sea Arbitration Awards: A Critical Study." *Chinese Journal of International Law* 17, no. 2 (June 2018): 207–748. https://doi.org/10.1093/chinesejil/jmy012.

Chinese Society of International Law. "The Tribunal's Award in the 'South China Sea Arbitration' Initiated by the Philippines Is Null and Void." *Ministry of Foreign Affairs of the People's Republic of China*, June 16, 2016. https://www.fmprc.gov.cn/mfa_eng/zxxx_662805/t1371363.shtml; https://www.chinadaily.com.cn/china/2016-06/10/content_25666477.htm.

Dacanay, Barbara Mae. "China Builds on Five More Reefs Near Philippine-Claimed Island." *Gulf News*, May 24, 2011. http://gulfnews.com/news/world/philippines/china-builds-on-five-more-reefs-near-philippine-claimed-island-1.812272.

Dzurek, Daniel J. "China Occupies Mischief Reef in Latest Spratly Gambit." *International Boundaries Research Unit (IBRU) Boundary and Security Bulletin*, April 1995, 65–71.

[127] Guilfoyle, "Philippines v China: First Thoughts."

Emmers, Ralf. "Maritime Disputes in the South China Sea—Strategic and Diplomatic Status Quo." In *Maritime Security in Southeast Asia*, edited by Kwa Chong Guan and John K. Skogan. Oxford: Routledge, 2007.

Foreign Ministry of the People's Republic of China. "Jurisprudential Evidence to Support China's Sovereignty over the Nansha Islands". November 17, 2000. https://www.fmprc.gov.cn/mfa_eng/topics_665678/3754_666060/t19234.shtml.

Government of the People's Republic of China. "Position Paper of the Government of the People's Republic of China on the Matter of Jurisdiction in the South China Sea Arbitration Initiated by the Republic of the Philippines." December 7, 2014. https://www.fmprc.gov.cn/nanhai/eng/snhwtlcwj_1/t1368895.htm.

Government of the People's Republic of China. "PRC's Declaration on the Territorial Sea." Appendix 18, September 4, 1958. *Peking Review* 1, no. 28 (September 9, 1958). https://www.eapasi.com/uploads/5/5/8/6/55860615/appendix_18_--_prcs_declaration_on_the_territorial_sea__1958___.pdf.

Government of the People's Republic of China. "Summary of the Position Paper on the Matter of Jurisdiction in the South China Sea Arbitration Initiated by the Republic of the Philippines, the State Council, the People's Republic of China." December 7, 2014. http://english.www.gov.cn/archive/press_briefing/2014/12/07/content_281475020440060.htm.

Guan, Ang Cheng. "The South China Sea Dispute Re-visited." *Institute of Defence and Strategic Studies*. Singapore, Working Paper Series. Working Paper No. 4, August 1999. http://www.rsis.edu.sg/publications/WorkingPapers/WP04.pdf.

Guilfoyle, Daniel. "Philippines v China: First Thoughts on the Award in the South China Seas Case." *European Journal of International Law: Talk* (July 12, 2016). https://www.ejiltalk.org/philippines-v-china-first-thoughts-on-the-award-in-the-south-china-seas-case/.

Heydarian, Javad. "The West Philippine Sea?" *The Diplomat*, December 15, 2011. https://thediplomat.com/2011/12/the-west-philippine-sea/.

Hong, Nong. *UNCLOS and Ocean Dispute Settlement: Law and Politics in the South China Sea*. Abingdon: Routledge, 2012.

Johnson, Jesse. "Beijing Turns on Japanese Judge as Hague Tribunal Ruling Over South China Sea Nears." *Japan Times*, July 8, 2016. https://www.japantimes.co.jp/news/2016/07/08/national/politics-diplomacy/beijing-turns-japanese-judge-hague-tribunal-ruling-south-china-sea-nears/.

Klare, Michael T. *Resource Wars—The New Landscape of Global Conflict*. New York: Owl Books, 2001.

Kotani, Tetsuo. "The South China Sea Arbitration, No, It's Not a PCA Ruling." *Maritime Issues*, November 17, 2016. http://www.maritimeissues.com/south-china-sea-arbitration-ruling/the-south-china-sea-arbitration-no-its-not-a-pca-ruling.html.

Ministry of Foreign Affairs of the People's Republic of China. "Award of 12 July 2016 of the Arbitral Tribunal in the South China Sea Arbitration Established at the Request of the Republic of the Philippines." July 12, 2016. https://www.fmprc.gov.cn/nanhai/eng/snhwtlcwj_1/t1379492.htm.

Ministry of Foreign Affairs of the People's Republic of China. "Basic Stance and Policy of the Chinese Government in Solving the South China Sea Issue." November 17, 2000. https://www.fmprc.gov.cn/mfa_eng/topics_665678/3754_666060/t19230.shtml.

Ministry of Foreign Affairs of the People's Republic of China. "Historical Evidence to Support China's Sovereignty Over Nansha Islands." November 17, 2000. https://www.fmprc.gov.cn/mfa_eng/topics_665678/3754_666060/t19231.shtml.

Ministry of Foreign Affairs of the People's Republic of China. "International Recognition of China's Sovereignty Over the Nansha Islands." November 17, 2000. https://www.fmprc.gov.cn/mfa_eng/topics_665678/3754_666060/t19232.shtml.

Ministry of Foreign Affairs of the People's Republic of China. "Statement of the Award of 12 July 2016 of the Arbitral Tribunal in the South China Sea Arbitration Established at the Request of the Republic of the Philippines." July 12, 2016. https://www.fmprc.gov.cn/nanhai/eng/snhwtlcwj_1/t1379492.htm.

Official Gazette of the Republic of the Philippines.. "Presidential Decree No. 1596." June 11, 1978. https://www.officialgazette.gov.ph/1978/06/11/presidential-decree-no-1596-s-1978/.

Official Gazette of the Republic of the Philippines.. "Statement: The Secretary of Foreign Affairs on the UNCLOS Arbitral Proceedings against China, January 22, 2013." January 22, 2013. https://www.officialgazette.gov.ph/2013/01/22/statement-the-secretary-of-foreign-affairs-on-the-unclos-arbitral-pro ceedings-against-china-january-22-2013/.

Permanent Court of Arbitration, Case No. 2013–19. "In the Matter of the South China Sea Arbitration Before An Arbitral Tribunal Constituted Under Annex VII to the 1982 United Nations Convention on the Law of the Sea between the Republic of the Philippines and the People's Republic of China." https://docs.pca-cpa.org/2016/07/PH-CN-20160712-Award.pdf.

Permanent Court of Arbitration, Case No. 2013–19. Press Release. July 12, 2016. https://docs.pca-cpa.org/2016/07/PH-CN-20160712-Press-Rel ease-No-11-English.pdf.

"Philippines Renames Coast 'West Philippine Sea'." *South China Morning Post*, September 12, 2012. https://www.scmp.com/news/china/article/103 5119/philippines-tags-coast-west-philippine-sea.

Raditio, Klaus Heinrich. *Understanding China's Behaviour in the South China Sea—A Defensive Realist Perspective*. London: Palgrave Macmillan, 2019.

Ramos-Mrosovsky, Carlos. "International Law's Unhelpful Role in the Senkaku Islands." *University of Pennsylvania Journal of International Law* 29, no. 4 (2008): 903–946.

Robles, Alfredo C., Jr. *The South China Sea Arbitration: Understanding the Awards and Debating with China*. Eastbourne, UK, Sussex Academic Press, 2019.

"South China Sea Arbitration Decided by Biased Arbitrators." *Xinhua*, July 20, 2016. http://www.china.org.cn/opinion/2016-07/20/content_38920677.htm.

"Sovereignty Over the Spratly Islands." *China Post*, June 22, 2009. http://www.chinapost.com.tw/commentary/the-china-post/joe-hung/2009/06/22/213223/Sovereignty-over.htm.

Storey, Ian James. "Creeping Assertiveness: China, the Philippines, and the South China Sea Dispute." *Contemporary Southeast Asia: A Journal of International and Strategic Affairs* 21, no. 1 (April 1999): 95–119.

Tiglao, Rigoberto, Andrew Sherry, Nate Thayer, Michael Vatikiotis. "Tis the Season." *Far Eastern Economic Review* 161 (December 24, 1998).

Tordesillas, Ellen. "Bring China's 9-Dash Line to UN: Justice Carpio." *Malaya Business Insight*, November 7, 2011. http://www.malaya.com.ph/nov07/edtorde.html.

Ubac, Michael Lim. "It's Official: Aquino Signs Order on West Philippine Sea." *Philippine Daily Inquirer*, September 13, 2012. https://globalnation.inquirer.net/50012/its-official-aquino-signs-order-on-west-philippine-sea.

UNCLOS III (United Nations Convention of the Law of the Sea). https://www.un.org/depts/los/convention_agreements/texts/unclos/unclos_e.pdf.

Valderama, Tito C. "Speaker Urges Speedy Trial of Sino Fishers." *Philippine Journal* (16 April 1995).

Valencia, Mark J., Jon M. Van Dyke, and Noel A. Ludwig. *Sharing the Resources of the South China Sea*. Honolulu: University of Hawai'i Press, 1997.

Wu, Shicun. "Competing Claims Over the South China Sea Islands and the Way Forward: A Chinese Perspective on the Philippine-China Arbitration Case." In *Arbitration Concerning the South China Sea: Philippines Versus China*, edited by Shicun Wu and Keyuan Zou, 13–22. Contemporary Issues in the South China Sea Series. Routledge, 2016.

Yoshikawa, Yukie. "The US-Japan-China Mistrust Spiral and Okinotorishima." *Asia-Pacific Journal* 5, no. 10 (2007). http://apjjf.org/-Yukie-YOSHIKAWA/2541/article.htm.

Zhen, Liu, and Catherine Wong. "China Intensifies Lobbying of Other Nations Ahead of South China Sea Court Ruling." *South China Morning Post*, April 28, 2016. https://www.scmp.com/news/china/diplomacy-defence/article/1939446/china-intensifies-lobbying-other-nations-ahead-south.

CHAPTER 3

Security Context

Abstract This chapter provides the security context to the occupation and introduces the reasons why China calculated that Mischief Reef's occupation was feasible and sustainable. This includes how the Philippines was perceived as being weak and incapable of a concerted response. It positions the occupation in a post-Cold War security environment context when the USA was scaling down on defense spending and disengaging from Southeast Asia. Washington's strategic position prior to the occupation as well as the complicated nature of US-Philippine security ties before 1994 is also discussed. The chapter covers Beijing's strategy in the SCS at that time, and shows how PLAN had a growing naval advantage over rival claimant states. It also presents the complications attached to China's strategy of challenging any attempts by ASEAN states to internationalize the SCS disputes. The chapter concludes with a look at the current strategic situation related to China's twenty plus years of occupation. The PRC's extensive land reclamation activities and the construction of military facilities including a runway on a once submerged atoll are also presented. These activities may provide insights into why a Chinese presence on Spratly features on the eastern border of the SCS became a more pressing objective.

Keywords ASEAN Regional Forum (ARF) · Militarization · People's Liberation Army Navy (PLAN) · Sino-Philippine maritime disputes · South China Sea disputes · Spratly Islands disputes

S. Fox, *Mischief Reef*,
https://doi.org/10.1007/978-981-16-3884-8_3

Prior to the Occupation

Understanding the current security situation vis-à-vis Mischief Reef requires some contextual information regarding the occupation before delving more deeply into the issue of security. Prior to China's silent take-over of Mischief Reef in 1994–1995, the question of the feature's rightful ownership was not a major issue between the two countries. Rather, the matter was incorporated more generally into Filipino concerns from the late 1980s onwards about China's intentions in the Kalayaan area. Thereafter, the opening sequence of events which led to the occupation of Mischief Reef can arguably be discerned. For example, in April 1988, during a state visit to China, both Deng Xiaoping, the PRC's paramount leader from 1978 to 1992, and the then PHL President Corazon Aquino (1986–1992) discussed the Philippines' heightened anxiety over China's objectives in the eastern Spratlys. Deng's response was to address Aquino's concerns with assurances that the Chinese would deal with any disputes peacefully, that both states should initiate joint-development projects, and that the sovereignty question should be set aside for the time being for the sake of the two countries' mutual interests.[1]

The years immediately prior to the Mischief Reef incident, however, witnessed a flurry of activity by virtually all the disputants in the Spratly group. These developments considerably strained tacit and non-binding understandings between the various disputants. Activities at sea were often focused on the seizure of as much uninhabited territory as possible in advance of the ratification of UNCLOS. By the early 1990s, for example, China had already taken control of eight additional features. Vietnam, its main rival in the Spratlys at that point, increased its own presence on some twenty features. In 1992, China and Vietnam clashed again near the Paracel Islands with the PRC prevailing to consolidate its control over the area. The Philippines, as well as all the remaining claimants, engaged in a rush to "militarily garrison" as many features within their perceived EEZ area as their capabilities would allow, and aspired to strengthen their military presence in contested areas.[2]

[1] "Aquino Returns from China." *Kyodo International News*, 1988.

[2] Clifton et al., "Mischief in the China Seas," 17. See also Meyer, "Incident at Mischief Reef," 5–6.

The context of the pre-occupation years merits comment to how China views the South China Sea outside of purely physical strategic considerations. Chen Jie explains the Chinese have asserted their control over the SCS for centuries and as such hold long standing and strong emotional ties to the area that cannot be easily discarded even if modern international law undermines their position. The Chinese did not suddenly begin to stake their claims in the final years of the Cold War. Writing in late 1994, Chen reminded people: "it is embedded in the Chinese national psyche that the Spratly archipelago has been part of the motherland's territory since ancient times." He also described why issues like Mischief Reef and other features are so sensitive: "In their [China's] eyes, the nature of the dispute is crystal clear: initially taking advantage of China's turbulent domestic policies and its preoccupation with superpower threats, regional countries have occupied China's islands and reefs, carved up its sea areas, and looted its marine resources." The PRC's more assertive approach to the Spratly Islands since the late 1980s were thus perceived within China as a "long overdue and legitimate action to protect its territorial integrity." Until Chinese sovereignty over the entire archipelago is recognized, he argued, then the country will continue to "regard itself as a victim of regional countries' aggression and encroachment." In this context, the PRC sees itself in a transitional phase wherein the take-over of features should be seen more as some recovery of territorial losses and not territorial gains.[3] Commenting in 2016, security and defense analyst David Wroe lamented how the Chinese leadership had "really backed itself into a corner in drumming up a very strong, nationalist line", and observed how PRC citizens understand the disputes as the result of humiliating theft by other states over many years when their country was weak.[4]

Worryingly for Beijing, the deadly March 1988 clash with Vietnam had not dented Hanoi's resolve to consolidate "its" territory within the Spratly group. From 1988 until 1991, the Vietnamese had taken control of an extra seven features, out of a total of twenty-five SRV features all together, and considerably strengthened its position in the area as a result.[5] For China's fellow disputants, uncertainty was fed by the seeming

[3] Chen, "China's Spratly Policy," 892–893.

[4] Wroe, "Making Mischief in the South China Sea."

[5] Fravel, "Strong Borders," 296–299.

mismatch between Beijing's words versus deeds in the area. During visits to Singapore in August 1990 and Malaysia in December 1990, the PRC Premier Li Peng announced that his country wished to open discussions on joint development in the area and urged disputants to shelve the sovereignty issue in the interest of mutual benefits. When China's President Yang Shangkun expressed similar sentiments on a trip to Thailand and Indonesia in early 1992, it was followed shortly afterwards by the aforementioned controversial "Territorial Sea Law" of February 25, 1992. Outwardly, this seemed to make a mockery of Chinese claims of wanting a sincere and fair resolution of the disputes. From late June until early July 1992, PRC representatives attended the third Indonesian-sponsored workshop on "Managing Potential Conflicts in the South China Sea." Within days however, PLAN occupied the Vietnam-claimed Da Lac reef in the western Spratlys.[6] In the years immediately prior to 1994, it was apparent that there was a distinct disconnect between Beijing's words and its actions. However, in a context where it seemed as if nearly all the disputants were engaged in feature-grabbing and claim strengthening, Manila must have assumed that its defense ties with the US would provide a sufficient obstacle to any Chinese designs towards a grab of Mischief Reef.

May 1994: Manila's Energy Deal Upsets Beijing

The early 1990s also saw the Spratly neighbors attempt to strengthen their respective legal positions by "economic internationalization" of the disputes via the pursuance of joint ventures with foreign energy companies. This, they hoped, would see powerful vested interest groups from the world's leading states holding expensive energy claims within the Spratly area, broadening the scope of the disputes. It could also serve as a strong legal counterclaim to competing claims or occupations already carried out by a rival. Even Beijing, despite its aversion to multilateralism on the issue of its own sovereignty, understood the usefulness of this approach when challenging Vietnam's claims. In 1992, for example, the PRC's Chinese National Offshore Oil Corporation (CNOOC), finalized a contract with the US oil company, Crestone to explore for resources

[6] Guan, "The South China Sea Dispute," 10.

in the vicinity of Vanguard Bank,[7] a western Spratly feature which had been occupied by the Vietnamese in 1989. In 1993, Brunei stepped into the ring by formally outlining its EEZ area. In the same year, Hanoi responded to Beijing's Crestone move by granting exploration rights to a collective of energy firms which included Mobil in an area west of Crestone's designated concessions. In May, this tit-for-tat exchange continued, with PRC and Vietnamese survey vessels being sent into the area in question. Vietnam upped the ante in May of the following year, when it authorized an oil company to begin drilling within the Crestone exploration area. In June, Beijing responded by announcing plans to conduct seismic surveys within the area.[8]

A little less than a year later, in May 1994, the Philippines' Department of Energy granted a six-month oil exploration permit for a desktop study to Vaalco Energy of the US and its Filipino subsidiary Alcorn Petroleum and Minerals. This allowed them to explore near Reed Bank, to the north-east of the eastern Spratlys. Beijing bitterly protested against this move, declaring it to be a violation of PRC sovereignty and a disrespectful rejection of the spirit of the Deng-Aquino joint-development talks in 1988. In response, Manila tried unsuccessfully to soothe China's rage by belatedly inviting the Chinese to also participate in the venture. Wang Mingfan, the PRC's Assistant Foreign Minister, issued an official protest with the PHL, and the Chinese Ministry of Foreign Affairs immediately released a statement asserting China's sovereignty over the Spratly Islands.[9] According to one source, Beijing's diplomatic response may have been influenced by fears that the PHL would proceed to allow exploration at the site, placing the Filipinos in a stronger position in which to defend their claim to effective control and authority in the area. If this insight is accurate, it bears similarities to the PRC's 1992 response to the Vietnam and US Crestone deal off the SRV's coast.[10] On July 6, 1994, Manila announced that Alcorn Petroleum would conduct preliminary research for oil in the Kalayaans. Media reports stated that the area in question would be near

[7] The area is located between Vanguard Bank and Prince of Wales Bank, 160 nms off the coast of Vietnam and in an area which lay within the SRV's claimed continental shelf zone.

[8] Fravel, "Strong Borders," 296–299.

[9] Tiglao, "Troubled Waters." See also Meyer, "Incident at Mischief Reef," 6; Storey, 96–97.

[10] Chung, "The Spratly Islands Dispute," 290–291.

Lawak (Nanshan) and Patag (Flat) islands, the closest PHL features to Mischief Reef. According to Dzurek, even though the Philippines asserted that the oil company agreement would not involve on-site exploration, the Chinese may also very well have seen it as a violation of the 1992 Manila Declaration.[11] Despite this setback in relations, from Manila's perspective, Beijing's protestations and responses were, on the surface, and with the exception of its dealings with Vietnam, overwhelmingly verbal rather than physical. However, as shown at the start of Chapter 5, "The Occupation of Mischief Reef", this Alcorn move by the Filipinos in May 1994 was to prove a decisive factor in the Chinese decision to take over the feature.

Strategic Calculations and Circumstances

The PRC's 1994–1995 occupation of Mischief Reef threw open a whole series of questions about the rising dragon's intentions in the region. It also seemed to confirm fears regarding the objectives of PLAN following its strategic shift further out to sea after the mid-1980s. During that period, the PRC's Central Military Committee decided to re-focus its defense planning away from an increasingly unlikely all-out conflict with the USSR on its western borders, and instead turn towards China's southern and eastern peripheries. Inspired by PLAN's Commander-in-Chief from 1982 to 1987, Admiral Liu Huaqing, the Chinese set themselves on a strategy of "offshore active defense" aimed at strengthening their ability to engage in military activities on the high seas for sustained periods. This sought to address PLAN's relative weaknesses in terms of asserting its maritime power within and beyond the so-called "first island chain", an area which included the East China Sea and the South China Sea.[12] This military goal may provide another insight into why a Chinese presence on a Spratly feature on the eastern border of the SCS became a more pressing objective. John W. Garver also commented in 1992 on the motivations for the PRC's more assertive behavior in the area by observing how a consolidated and extensive presence in the South China Sea would allow China to "become a Southeast Asian nation in the

[11] Dzurek, "China Occupies Mischief Reef," 68.

[12] Klare, *Resource Wars*, 128.

same sense that the United States is both an Atlantic and Pacific Nation or Russia both a European and Far Eastern one."[13]

However, observers should not overplay the military significance of the occupation of tiny features such as Mischief Reef which, due to their size and characteristics, do not bestow automatic rights to maritime jurisdiction to waters surrounding it. At best, such activities in general only grant the occupier a very small maritime area around the feature in question. In reality, while occupation does enhance one's position if only slightly, the means through which to control the vital Sea Lines of Communication (SLOCs) and strategically key waters which pass near the Spratly group and through the SCS would require considerable military and naval superiority. This would have to apply in terms of power projection, technology, and military capabilities, something which the Chinese did not yet possess in the mid-1990s. That being said, if the US is not factored into the equation, then in relative terms and by regional standards, PLAN had a considerable and growing naval advantage over East Asian states such as the Philippines in the early to mid-1990s. In the 1994–1995 occupation period, for example, the Philippines possessed rather inadequate naval capabilities in which to observe and fend off Chinese vessels within the PHL's EEZ.[14] It is apparent that from a Chinese military planning perspective, the take-over of the reef was thus feasible because the PHL was weak and incapable of a concerted response. Crucially, the US had disengaged from the immediate area in the early 1990s, and remained non-adversarial in terms of competing Spratly claims. Both, therefore, would be unlikely to react aggressively to a non-violent and covert occupation which at the very least would place the PRC in a relatively stronger position in the area.

The US Prior to Occupation

The approaches adopted by the US in relation to the SCS are a critical influence on how rival claimants might choose to address their grievances. As the main counterweight and guarantor of security against the rising China, the US has generally been successful in the wider strategic sense of constraining and discouraging any Chinese designs on expansionism.

[13] Garver, "China's Push," 1028.

[14] Emmers, "Maritime Disputes," 53–54.

The position of the US in relation to the South China Sea disputes prior to the mid-1990s had also been generally consistent with its stance since the 1970s. A key problem for the PHL in its response to the Mischief Reef occupation, however, was that Washington disagreed with Manila on the parameters of the commitments outlined in the 1951 Mutual Defense Treaty. This bilateral US-Philippines pact was signed before Manila had formally annexed the Kalayaan area in the late 1970s. As such, the Americans argued that Mischief Reef did not apply to the 1951 treaty.[15]

In the years immediately preceding the 1995 Mischief Reef incident, the US Department of Defense issued four reports on US approaches to East Asia. In the 1990 report, the focus was on the potentially volatile Northeast Asia region in the context of communist regimes collapsing in Eastern Europe and the Soviet Union pulling out of Afghanistan. Little if anything was said about the South China Sea except the oft-stated commitment to the safety and stability of SLOCs. In October 1991, at a meeting in Malaysia, the Commander-in-Chief of US Pacific Command, Admiral Charles Larson, summed up Washington's position on the SCS with a number of points. The first of these was that the US was non-committal and had no interest in intervening. Secondly, he declared that the SCS disputes were a regional issue and that the US had no plans in place to deal with an outbreak of conflict in the Spratlys. Thirdly, he pressed the point that it was the duty of the relevant states and their regional groups such as ASEAN to co-operate and manage their problems peacefully rather than militarily. Finally, since at that stage the SCS disputes were still an exclusively a Vietnam-China issue, he asserted that the US might take a role alongside ASEAN, the former USSR, and other states to ensure that whoever behaved aggressively in the dispute be persuaded to obey internationally agreed rules. In a February 1995 report compiled before the Mischief Reef incident came to light, the US Department of Defense barely mentioned the Spratly Islands.[16]

[15] Meyer,"Incident at Mischief Reef," 7–8.

[16] Guan, "The South China Sea Dispute," 13–15.

US-Philippine Security Before 1994–1995

In the years immediately prior to the occupation, Chinese defense planners may have seen the strategic environment in regard to a feature such as Mischief Reef as one favorable to strengthening the PRC's position through occupation without suffering a high cost for the action. This was also at a time of increased activities by virtually all the rival claimants. In 1991 and 1992, US forces ended their presence at Subic Bay Naval base and Clark Air Force base, two facilities which had been understood to be acting as a deterrent against Chinese adventurism in the area.

As explained by Storey, from 1947 until 1992 the defense of the Philippines fell largely upon the shoulders of the United States, the former colonial master. Security, it seemed, was assured via agreements such as the 1947 Military Bases Agreement, the 1951 Mutual Defense Treaty, and the 1954 Manila Pact. By the early 1990s, however, domestic political calls for a reduction in the US military's presence and influence in the Philippines placed these defense arrangements under significant pressure. These pressures included increasingly vocal calls from Filipino nationalists to end the US military presence on their territory and thus remove one of the most obvious symbols of the Philippines' weak post-colonial status and continued reliance upon the US. The early 1990s was also a context which appeared favorable to a major defense shift by Manila. Most notably, the termination of the Cold War brought an end to the Soviet threat in the region, and with it a major setback for pro-US supporters who argued for a continued US military role in the Philippines.[17]

Numerous Filipino political representatives also felt assured that the Soviet danger had passed and that the increasingly stronger Chinese dragon was too far away to represent a serious threat. The PHL's relations with other ASEAN states were solid, and US-Japan ties, as a bedrock of regional security, were as strong as ever. As such, the opinion of many within the Filipino political class was that their country faced no major external threats or danger. Crucially, many also felt that even though the US military presence on Filipino soil had come to an end in 1992, past military treaties with the US remained, and these could be relied upon to address any threat to the Philippines. The 1951 Mutual Defense Treaty, for example, whose parameters both Manila and Washington would argue over after February 1995, declared that the US military

[17] Storey, "Creeping Assertiveness," 102.

would come to the country's rescue in the event of an "armed attack" on "the metropolitan territory of either of the Parties or on the island territories under its jurisdiction in the Pacific Ocean, its armed forces, public vessels or aircraft in the Pacific".[18] Manila's confidence in the US assisting in its defense in a crisis could be seen in a 1992 statement by then PHL Defense Secretary Renato de Villa when he said: "We still have a mutual defense treaty with the US. If we are attacked from the outside – which is not likely to happen in the first place – if the Philippine government invoked this treaty, then the US will have to come to our aid in defending us."[19] This atmosphere in the early 1990s alongside powerful anti-military sentiments within the country meant that Filipino planners also lacked the means, the will, and the ability to address its defensive weaknesses.[20]

It would be a mistake, however, to declare that prior to Mischief Reef's occupation, the Filipino leadership held a complacent and careless attitude towards their defense capabilities. The aforementioned 1992 Territorial Sea Law passed by the PRC sent alarm bells ringing throughout the region about China's intentions in the Spratlys and elsewhere. For example, PLAN had also taken control of the Vietnam-claimed Da Lac reef on July 4, 1994. The scaling-down of both US and Soviet forces from the region, such as Russia having sharply cut down on personnel and equipment at their Cam Ranh Bay military base in Vietnam in the early 1990s, likewise begged questions about whether the non-transparent and often ambiguous Chinese military would try to fill the "power vacuum" in areas such as the South China Sea. Indeed, the West Point trained Fidel V. Ramos, who was the PHL's President (June 1992–June 1998) at the time of the Mischief Reef incident, had previously warned against the folly of ending the US military presence in the Philippines. However, by the time he came to power, the decision had already been made. Appreciating the urgent need to upgrade his country's military forces, he tried to make the best of a bad situation by lobbying hard to secure this objective in

[18] 1951 Mutual Defense Treaty, Article V; https://avalon.law.yale.edu/20th_century/phil001.asp.

[19] Storey, "Creeping Assertiveness," 109.

[20] Ibid., *passim*.

the years prior to 1994–1995. At each turn, however, he was stalled from moving forward by political opposition and budgetary constraints.[21]

This was also in a context where Washington was seeking ways to scale down on defense spending and adjust to a new security environment. Spewing volcanic ash from the Philippines' Mount Pinatubo in 1991 made the surrounding skies unsafe for aviation, and was a decisive factor in convincing Washington to close down Clark Air Force Base shortly afterwards, despite it being one of the most important US military facilities in the region. In addition, although there was some interest on the part of the US to maintain a naval presence in Subic Bay, they were compelled to leave after the Philippines' Senate voted in September 1991 to end their decades long lease to operate from Filipino bases. The PHL formally took over Subic Bay the following September, and by November, all US military personnel had departed.[22] A key problem with this shift, however, was that while the Philippines had exercised its right to request an American departure, they were now left in a much more vulnerable security position. Unfortunately, it was not until the occupation of Mischief Reef less than three years later that the Filipino leadership realized just how vulnerable they were. At a time in which the PHL voluntarily rid itself of a US presence on land, sea, and air, the Armed Forces of the Philippines (AFP) were in a compromised state and in dire need of substantial upgrading and modernization. Their standing as one the ASEAN states' weakest military players was exemplified by their relatively low military spending, and the very limited capabilities of their naval forces. The entire Filipino navy, for example, which was tasked with defending the state's interests in areas such as Kalayaan, was made up of eleven World War Two era US-built corvettes, thirty-two small patrol craft, and a handful of amphibious landing vessels. The state's air force consisted of a mere seven very old F-5 jet planes, of which only five were airworthy.[23] Given these statistics, China must have surmised that a quiet and non-belligerent occupation of Mischief Reef was feasible, and one which the strengthening PLAN could sustain into the foreseeable future.

[21] Ibid., 101, 104.

[22] Chung points out that alongside the withdrawal from bases, the downturn in ties between the two countries witnessed the US cutting development aid to PHL by two-thirds, an estimated 10 billion US dollar 'US-Japan Multilateral Assistance Initiative' was postponed, and the number of staff at the US embassy reduced; Chung, 245.

[23] Storey, 102–103.

Beijing's Diplomatic Strategy Leading Up to Occupation

Alongside their extensive historical claims to virtually all of the South China Sea, one of Beijing's main strategies vis-à-vis the Spratly Islands was to challenge any attempts by ASEAN member states to internationalize the disputes. This was for the primary purpose of keeping the US and Japan out of what they viewed as the PRC's back yard. It also permitted the regional giant to negotiate from a position of relative strength at any bilateral talks table. Despite this, the Chinese were careful not to isolate themselves from their regional neighbors. In 1992, for example, China as well as Russia accepted invitations to attend as "guests" a meeting of ASEAN foreign ministers. This meeting in Manila, the first ever for China in ASEAN's twenty-five year history, declared the SCS to be a high priority matter. From this stemmed the previously mentioned "Manila Declaration on the South China Sea."[24] The PRC was not a member of the regional grouping, but nonetheless published a separate statement claiming that it "recognized and welcomed" the declaration.[25] On a similar note, China's Foreign Minister Qian Qichen stated that China was in agreement with the declaration's "principles".[26]

Following the Mischief Reef incident, however, the Chinese denied that the Manila Declaration applied to them.[27] As contended by one scholar, the declaration suffered from a clear lack of external support, particularly from the US. Vietnam lent its support but the PRC only paid lip service to it, and never officially complied with its principles, and reiterated its position that bilateral rather than multilateral talks were the way forward. Washington was unsupportive and stuck to its decades-long position of neutrality vis-à-vis the SCS disputes. At the first ever ASEAN Regional Forum (ARF)[28] in July 1994, as PRC personnel were apparently in the opening stages of building structures on Mischief Reef, China's Foreign Minister Qian Qichen reiterated his country's commitment to a peaceful resolution of any disagreements over the Spratly group,

[24] Formally "ASEAN Declaration on the South China Sea (22 July 1992)". See *Documents on ASEAN and the South China Sea*, 35.

[25] Salcedo as quoted in Meyer, "Incident at Mischief Reef," 15.

[26] Severino, "ASEAN and the South China Sea," 42.

[27] Meyer, "Incident at Mischief Reef," 10, 15.

[28] The ARF, a regional security institution, was established as a response to the US military's withdrawal from the PHL in 1991–1992. For its creation and the role it has played see Zha and Valencia, "Mischief Reef: Geopolitics," 94.

and condemned the use of force to address any grievances. At the same time, the Chinese persisted in their refusal to multilaterally engage in any discussion of sovereign jurisdiction.[29] Bilateral talks between disputants continued apace nonetheless. In 1994, for example, China engaged in discussions with Vietnam with the aim of resolving their various land and sea disagreements. The Chinese also continued its negotiations with the Philippines over possible joint development projects in the eastern Spratly Islands.[30] In the lead-up to the occupation, the PRC's diplomatic behavior did little to suggest that their military were making plans to upset the normally smooth relations with the PHL by taking control of Mischief Reef. As Manila saw it, up to that stage, military actions were reserved for Vietnam while other claimants only suffered diplomatic protests and physical but largely unremarkable expressions of sovereignty in contested areas which could be responded to without much trouble.

Developments in recent years would appear to justify the long-held fears and suspicions expressed regarding China's occupation of Mischief Reef. The initial 1994–1995 structure built on stilts, described by Beijing as a mere "fishermen's shelter" has now been replaced by an extensive artificially constructed island of some 1380 acres with its own military base with anti-aircraft and missile defense capabilities, a 2.7 km runway, and a harbor. All this has happened despite repeated protests by Manila throughout the twenty-five plus years since the atoll's takeover. These realities, along with potentially substantial energy resources in surrounding waters, indicate in stark terms the military and economic security value which the Chinese attach to the atoll. The seeming irreversibility of the take-over in terms of military and diplomatic pressure has also reminded the Filipinos both of their loss and of their relative weakness. Even the South China Sea Arbitration tribunal ruling in July 2016, which found that the feature was within the PHL's EEZ and on its continental shelf, and was submerged at high tide in its natural state, thus nullifying the PRC's island building efforts, could not change facts on the ground. However, this prompts the need to examine the developments which may have influenced the Chinese decision to act, and crucially, who lay behind it.

[29] Emmers, "Maritime Disputes," 55–56.

[30] Meyer, "Incident at Mischief Reef," 10.

References

"Aquino returns from China." *Kyodo International News*, April 17, 1988.

Chen Jie. "China's Spratly Policy—With Special Reference to the Philippines and Malaysia." *Asian Survey* 34, no. 10 (October 1994): 893–903.

Chung, Christopher. *The Spratly Islands Dispute: Decision Units and Domestic Politics*. Canberra: Australian Defence Force Academy: School of Humanities and Social Science, 2004. https://www.unsworks.unsw.edu.au/primo-explore/fulldisplay/unsworks_3198/UNSWORKS.

Clifton, Tony, Marites D. Vitug, Greg May, Ron Moreau, and Matt Forney. "Mischief in the China Seas." *Newsweek*, March 20, 1995.

Documents on ASEAN and the South China Sea. http://www.assidmer.net/doc/Documents-on-ASEAN-and-South-China-Sea-as-of-June-2011.pdf.

Dzurek, Daniel J. "China Occupies Mischief Reef in Latest Spratly Gambit." *International Boundaries Research Unit Boundary and Security Bulletin* (April 1995): 65–71.

Emmers, Ralf. "Maritime Disputes in the South China Sea—Strategic and Diplomatic Status Quo." In *Maritime Security in Southeast Asia*, edited by Kwa Chong Guan and John K. Skogan. Oxford: Routledge, 2009.

Fravel, M. Taylor. *Strong Borders, Secure Nation—Co-operation and Conflict in China's Territorial Disputes*. Princeton: Princeton University Press, 2008.

Garver, John W. "China's Push Through the South China Sea: The Interaction of Bureaucratic and National Interests." *The China Quarterly* 132 (December 1992): 999–1028.

Guan, Ang Cheng. "The South China Sea Dispute Re-visited." Institute of Defence and Strategic Studies (IDSS). Working Paper Series, Working Paper No. 4. Singapore, August 1999. http://www.rsis.edu.sg/publications/WorkingPapers/WP04.pdf.

Klare, Michael T. *Resource Wars—The New Landscape of Global Conflict*. New York: Owl Books, 2001.

Meyer, Stanley E. (Lt.Col.). "Incident at Mischief Reef: Implications for the Philippines, China, and the United States." United States Army War College, Strategy Research Project, January 1996.

Mutual Defense Treaty. Article V, 1951. https://avalon.law.yale.edu/20th_century/phil001.asp.

Severino, Rodolfo C. "ASEAN and the South China Sea." *Security Challenges* 6, no. 2 (Winter 2010): 37–47.

Storey, Ian James. "Creeping Assertiveness: China, the Philippines, and the South China Sea Dispute." *Contemporary Southeast Asia: A Journal of International and Strategic Affairs* 21, no. 1 (1999): 95–119.

Tiglao, Rigoberto. "Troubled Waters." *Far Eastern Economic Review*, June 30, 1994: 20–21.

Wroe, David. "Making Mischief in the South China Sea." *Sydney Morning Herald*, July 15, 2016. https://www.smh.com.au/politics/federal/making-mischief-in-the-south-china-sea-20160715-gq6knp.html.

Zha, Daojiong, and Mark J. Valencia. "Mischief Reef: Geopolitics and Implications." *Journal of Contemporary Asia* 31, no. 1 (2001): 86–103.

CHAPTER 4

The Decision to Occupy

Abstract Here, the dynamics behind the decision to occupy are examined more closely, with China's strategic motivations and the timeline of events first presented. It postulates why the Chinese acted when they did, and why Mischief Reef was selected. The murky question of who among the Chinese elite sanctioned the risky operation is tackled, describing the key actors and agencies behind the move as well as the likely factors that led to the takeover. The chapter shows how China increasingly felt that rival claimants, especially Vietnam, were irreversibly undermining its relative claims in the area, and that action was urgently needed. It also discusses how China's presence might have helped prevent an entente between the Philippines and Vietnam. At the very least, it ensured the Philippines did not occupy the reef first. An examination of the influence of PRC domestic politics and political circumstances of the time are undertaken, including competing interests which impacted on the country's Spratly Islands' policies. The influence of uncertain post-Tiananmen post-Cold War circumstances in China is also brought up. The chapter shows how stresses between the civilian leadership, the moderate Ministry of Foreign Affairs, and hardliners within the military influenced approaches to the Spratly disputes.

Keywords Chinese Domestic Politics · Jiang Zemin · Sovereignty · Spratly Islands disputes · US-Philippine security ties

S. Fox, *Mischief Reef*,
https://doi.org/10.1007/978-981-16-3884-8_4

Strategic Motivation

There are conflicting reports of when exactly the Chinese first placed structures on Mischief Reef and of when the Filipinos first became aware of these. The Chinese, using the distraction of a comparatively active typhoon season, especially at its most intense from May to November 1994, has been mentioned.[1] There is also a dearth of data for when the occupation became an official directive. The available data cites June 1994 as the earliest date of construction activities (see below) whilst most sources emphasize the period from late 1994 to early 1995. Alongside the strategic considerations discussed below, a decisive push factor was the decision by Manila to grant a six month "desktop" oil exploration permit to the US oil company Vaalco and its PHL subsidiary company Alcorn Petroleum and Minerals Corporation in May 1994. Another important factor that may have hardened Chinese resolve vis-à-vis Mischief Reef might have been the highly publicized September 1994 detention of fifty-five PRC fishermen by PHL armed forces. According to Valencia, the men had been attempting to set up habitable shelters on one PHL-claimed feature in the Spratlys group, and were charged with illegal entry and the possession of explosives. As a result, Beijing felt compelled to respond.[2] This occurred within a wider context of growing competition for features and resources in the area, and may have persuaded the Chinese to act more swiftly in late 1994 (at the latest) in order to pre-empt other claimants.

Prior to Mischief Reef, virtually every military confrontation in the South China Sea was exclusively confined to China and Vietnam. The PHL was not the only state in the region strongly believing that the PRC would restrict its use of military force to Vietnam – a regional pariah before the 1990s because of its invasion of Cambodia in 1979 and its strategic alignment with the USSR. Observers also believed that Beijing would avoid serious clashes with less maligned SCS states which could draw powerful external players such as Japan and the US into the Spratlys debate.[3] Given the risks involved, it raises questions regarding why the Chinese chose to take control of the feature when they did. While the contexts in which China's 1974 and 1988 confrontations with Vietnam

[1] "Tropical Cyclones in 1994", Royal Observatory of Hong Kong, 12–14.

[2] Valencia et al., *Sharing the Resources*, 79.

[3] Klare, *Resource Wars*, 125.

in the SCS are more transparent in terms of available documentation, and point to behavior sanctioned at the highest level with the Chinese Communist Party (CCP), the Mischief Reef occupation is considerably murkier and thus needs to be deduced with circumstantial evidence.

The crux of Fravel's argument on China's motivation to occupy the reef was that in the lead-up to 1994, virtually all of the Spratly disputants rushed to grab features. This activity applied to Vietnam in particular, who also had a claim to Mischief Reef. As a result, China increasingly felt that its relative claim strength in the area was being irreversibly undermined and that action urgently needed to be taken in order to prevent further losses. In the years prior to the 1994–1995 takeover for example, all three of the main claimants to the features in the Spratlys—the PRC, Vietnam, and the Philippines—had intensified their efforts at capturing and controlling as many features as possible. China's taking control of the strategically well-placed reef was thus an attempt to act before others did, in keeping with practices by other countries in the Spratly Islands in the months beforehand. A map demonstrates that Mischief Reef is located to the extreme east of the Spratly group and serves as a type of Chinese outpost in the area. As Fravel argues, "as China's other features are all in the far west, occupation of this reef broadened the scope of the waters over which China could claim effective control." He also contends that the Chinese occupation of the reef may have helped to prevent an entente or alliance between the Philippines and Vietnam. Such an outcome would have significantly undermined the breadth of China's claim to the eastern Spratlys. The reef's occupation and proximity to the PHL meant that Manila was now far more anxious about its security interests in the Spratlys, and compelled them to find a *modus vivendi* favorable to the Chinese within a matter of months following the incident.[4] It also arguably prevented the possibility of a relatively stronger Vietnam from occupying it from under Manila's nose, and at the very least ensured that the Filipinos did not occupy it for themselves, which, given the tendency by the disputants, would probably have happened sooner or later. Dzurek also contends that the occupation may have been fed by fears of plans for increased military co-operation between the Philippines and Vietnam.[5]

[4] Fravel, *Strong Borders*, 296–299.

[5] Dzurek, "China Occupies Mischief Reef," 68.

On December 4, 1994, the SRV's Defence Minister Doan Khue visited Manila on a five-day trip focused on Spratly-related discussions. The country's Foreign Minister Nguyen Manh Cam was also scheduled to travel to the PHL for talks. These high-level meetings, especially between defence ministers, may have suggested to Beijing that Hanoi and Manila were possibly close to an anti-China Spratly Islands security treaty which threatened to encircle or contain their presence. Strategically, the PRC take-over of Mischief Reef would place the Chinese military between the PHL island of Palawan and the SRV-occupied Sin Cowe East Island, and ensure a PRC presence further east of the Vietnamese.[6]

The May 1994 Vaalco/Alcorn US-Philippines energy deal at Reed Bank in the eastern Spratlys would also certainly have raised Chinese concerns about a weakening of its position in the area, and may have convinced PRC planners that Manila was moving away from the 1988 Deng-Aquino understanding on joint development. For these reasons, it was perhaps not coincidental that PRC construction activities on Mischief Reef are reported to have commenced during the following month: June 1994. Another factor which should be considered was the policy orientation of the PHL President since 1992, Fidel V. Ramos. From the start of his tenure, Ramos made no secret of his desire to exploit the full potential of the Philippines, not just terrestrially but also in often untapped maritime areas of the archipelagic state. This was reflected in Executive Order Number 186 of July 12, 1994, in which he changed the name of the "Cabinet Committee on the Law of the Sea" to the "Cabinet Committee on Maritime and Ocean Affairs (CCMOA)". On November 8, 1994, this committee published its "National Marine Policy" which called for action on maritime-related security, economic, technological, and resource issues.[7] For the PRC's South China Sea policy advisers, they may have estimated that it was a question of when and not if the Filipinos would begin to further consolidate their presence on unoccupied features.

The incident is also viewed by some scholars as a classic case of China once again capitalizing on opportunities at a time when potential adversaries were restricted in their ability to react or at least were reluctant to do so. This was certainly a key factor in 1974 and 1988 in the PRC's two major clashes with Vietnam over the Paracels and the western Spratlys. As

[6] Ibid.

[7] Chung, "The Spratley Islands Dispute," 280–281.

discussed in the previous chapter, the early 1990s was also a time when the once solid Washington-Manila relationship began to show cracks as the Philippines sought to emphasize its independence from the US. The US military had likewise scaled down its joint military operations with the PHL in this period and did not appear interested nor willing to take sides in the South China Sea disputes. In addition, the capabilities of the AFP to make an effective and sustained response at the time were lamentable. As such, it was a period when the risks would have been at their lowest in years, should China decide to surreptitiously assert its claims and display its enhanced naval capabilities in the Spratlys. Valencia likewise notes how US surveillance over the reef area using P3 Orion marine reconnaissance aircraft for example was scaled back in the period in question because, among other reasons, the Americans did not perceive a threat to their forces there. The collection and analysis of aerial surveillance data by the US had also been scaled back and in some cases suspended. The Philippines was incapable of such surveillance due to a dire lack of aerial and marine resources, particularly in regard to radar equipment and facilities.[8]

Fravel, however, warns against perceiving Chinese activities in the area as expansionist. He notes, for example, that they were reluctant to physically assert their control of more features after the March 1988 clash with Vietnam and the occupation of six Spratly features. Attractive windows of opportunities existed in the years immediately prior to 1995 for the PRC to make the most of the US disengagement from the region, and yet China's behavior was very controlled and reactive rather than proactive. In the rush for features in 1993 and 1994, for example, the Chinese did not exploit the situation to the extent they could have in an improved relative power position and where the capabilities now existed to maintain a constant presence in the eastern Spratlys. With regards to Mischief Reef, Fravel asserts that the People's Liberation Army Navy (PLAN) did occupy the reef, which was unoccupied and permanently submerged. However, Beijing "did not take any stronger actions that a preference for offensive uses of force might predict when faced with reduced constraints."[9] This is a moot point likely to draw agreement and disagreement from scholars and observers in equal measure. It could be argued, however, the Chinese did not require any offensive use of force in this case, and have taken to a

[8] Valencia et al., "*Sharing the Resources*," 80.

[9] Fravel, *Strong Borders*, 313.

policy of patiently reinforcing their position on the feature over the years whenever favorable strategic circumstances permitted it. The domestic political circumstances within the PRC in the early to mid-1990s also shed some light on the inter-relationship between security behaviour and elite power in China.

Beijing's Unofficial Explanation

As discussed earlier, in terms of the South China Sea, the early 1990s witnessed seeming contradictions between what the Chinese government said and promised as opposed to what actually transpired. This has raised some pertinent questions about decision-making responsibility for the country's military forces, and in this case, the issue of who sanctioned the occupation of Mischief Reef. Storey, for example, in his examination of the affair, looks at the possible explanations for the incident, and then through a process of elimination attempts to pinpoint the players who were most likely to have sanctioned the occupation. One view is that it was carried out exclusively by PLAN. This then raises the issue of whether the take-over was supported by senior high-level officers or, as PRC officials would later claim, by "low level functionaries without the knowledge and consent of the Chinese government"[10] who took the initiative to act without the approval or knowledge of their senior commanders. At first glance, two factors suggest that the latter was a possible explanation. The story provided by Chinese officials and the PRC's embassy in Manila in the days following the discovery of structures on the reef, if accepted as true, point to genuine surprise by the civilian leadership, and to the fact that the activities had indeed taken place. The other factor was the knowledge that rogue elements within PLAN were engaging in unauthorized activities such as smuggling and piracy activities in the waters of the SCS.[11] In the case of the Mischief Reef occupation however, these explanations are, according to Storey, flawed. Blaming the incident on rogue or even "over-zealous" and nationalistic lower-level PLAN commanders does not stand up to scrutiny. Rogue elements, for one, would stand to make no monetary benefit from building structures on a submerged reef. It is also apparent that the construction of even small facilities on a submerged

[10] "China Nibbles, ASEAN Dithers." 1995.

[11] "Hye Mieko Attack Triggers," 1995.

reef over the course of a number of months and at a considerable distance from the PRC's coastline would have necessitated financial, logistical, and military support on a scale which certainly would have required the sanction of top-level PLA officers. The fact that Manila was so swift in its rejection of this "low level functionaries" explanation by PRC officials also suggests that their story does not stand up to scrutiny.[12] Dzurek surmises his own view on who sanctioned the actions when he states:

> This Chinese effort at deniability is poor, there is no possibility that a low-level Chinese bureaucrat had the authority to dispatch seven naval vessels to set up an outpost over 1000 kilometers from mainland China.[13]

It is apparent also that while the Chinese officials initially denied authorization of the move, they later defended it with words suggesting approval of the act. On March 10, 1995, for example, the PRC Foreign Minister, Qian Qichen, made a statement declaring:

> Ours is not a military activity and will pose no threat to other countries. Chinese fishermen have been traditionally fishing in the region and shelters have been built to protect them. China has had sovereignty over the islands since ancient times and there were no disputes. Just in the late 70s, some countries made claims over the islands. China has shown restraint and is willing to develop the region in a co-operative way, setting aside disputes.[14]

Some scholars have expressed a certain degree of sympathy for Beijing's explanation that the occupation took place without the approval of the Politburo Standing Committee (PBSC) or the Central Military Commission (CMC). Alongside the "low-level functionaries acting without the knowledge and consent of the Chinese government" statement made by the PRC Embassy in Manila in early February 1995, Fravel for example, cites interview data which suggests that Standing Committee elites were genuinely "surprised" by the actions. This response, if accepted as sincere, indicates that the key body in charge of formulating foreign and security policy in the PRC did not sanction it and was not aware of what was going on in the months prior to Manila's publication of the discovery

[12] Storey, 100. See also Guan, 11; Chung, 269.

[13] Dzurek, "China Occupies Mischief Reef," 67.

[14] Raman, "Chinese Territorial Assertions".

in February 1995. Also mentioned is an "internal circulation bulletin" which discusses frictions over policy between the Politburo and military hard-liners in relation to the Spratly Islands throughout the early to mid-1990s.[15] Given these various views, it is apparent that even though the operation may or may not have been officially sanctioned by the PRC's ultimate decision-making body, the PBSC, then at the very least, it certainly would have required the tacit approval of top elites such as the CCP's General Secretary, Jiang Zemin (1989–2002). In order to examine the influence of PRC domestic politics on the decision-making behind the 1994–1995 occupation, we need to discuss the political circumstances of the time in more detail and the competing interests which impacted on the country's Spratly Islands' policies.

Decision-Making in the PRC and PLA-Civilian Leadership

The informal and intimate features of PRC politics mean that factional and bureaucratic politics often play a powerful role in decision-making. The importance of behind-the-scenes manoeuvring, manipulation, and compromise, particularly between the top two dozen or so elites on the twenty-five member Party Political Bureau (Politburo) and its nine member PBSC also sheds some light on why the decision-making process remains so dynamic, unpredictable, and enigmatic to outside observers. This uncertainty in the decision-making process is especially apparent during periods of political succession from one top leader to the next. At the apex of this decision-making structure is the top political leader.[16] The General Secretary is officially though not always actually the most powerful figure in China. Since the 1990s, a leader is not perceived to have fully consolidated his leadership unless he officially holds three positions. These are: (a) General Secretary of the Central Committee of the Communist Party of China; (b) President of the PRC; and (c) Chairman of the CMC. When a new leader assumes his role as General Secretary, the time period needed to assume all three roles can be a matter of months and years or in some cases never at all. As discussed below, in PRC President Jiang Zemin's case, while he had secured all three positions

[15] Fravel, *Strong Borders*, 296–299.

[16] Martin, "Understanding China's Political System," 4–5, 19.

prior to the Mischief Reef Incident, his leadership position was certainly not assured with rivals from within the elite indirectly challenging his power. This scenario was to have an impact on events which led to the 1994–1995 take-over of the feature.

A key institution in China is the PLA, where structurally the lines between military and civilian leadership are often blurred, and at times difficult to differentiate.[17] This has created a lot of unease amongst China's neighbors and the United States in terms of who exactly is in charge of China's military forces and who has the final say with regards to military activities and manoeuvres. Evidence in China points to the fact that when political relations are strained with a neighbor, or when the leadership is weak, then this can strengthen the hand of military elements within the PRC's decision-making elite who would support a more assertive approach to foreign policy issues. According to Bush, evidence exists that "the PLA, which wants to preserve as much freedom and flexibility for the navy as possible, has been a key actor behind the scenes in shaping China's tough negotiating position" in maritime areas.[18] The power of the party leaders to hold rival elements together and speak with one voice in influencing PLAN is similarly a factor that has affected courses of actions in the East and South China Seas. During a major downturn in ties with Japan over the Pinnacle Islands (*Senkaku Shoto / Diaoyu*) and Taiwan in 1996, for example, major military periodicals in the country, the PLA Daily (*Jiefangjun Bao*) and the China Defence News (*Zhongguo Guofang Bao*) contained numerous articles warning that Japanese activities were indicative of a larger conspiracy and condemned the revival of militarism. Dissatisfaction over the Party leadership's moderate approach to Japan was also demonstrated within the PLA when a group of thirty-five army generals reportedly submitted a signed letter to the Party top brass insisting on a tougher stance in the East China Sea (ECS) to "resist Japanese militarism and recapture the Diaoyu Islands, and criticizing the government's relaxed stand on the issue."[19] CCP officials and military figures also used the opportunity to condemn Foreign Minister Qian Qichen, with one Chinese military expert stating that the purpose of exercises carried out by the PLA and PLAN off the

[17] Ibid., 2.

[18] Bush, "China-Japan Tensions," 30.

[19] Lo, Ping, "Jiang Zemin Seen," 138.

Chinese coast near Liaoning Province in September 1996 was not only to warn Japan to be sensitive in the ECS, but was also to send an implicit message to "government officials preoccupied with economic ties to Japan who apparently ignore the nationalist sentiments among soldiers."[20] Even before the Mischief Reef incident, stresses between the civilian leadership, the moderate Ministry of Foreign Affairs, and hardliners within the PLA over approaches to the Spratly disputes were also increasingly evident.

Who Decides?

South China Sea issues fell under the responsibility of at least three government agencies within the PRC. These are as follows: (1) the Hainan Island Marine Office; (2) PLAN; and (3) the PRC's Foreign Ministry. The first of these oversees "dual central and local leadership with an emphasis on local initiative."[21] According to Chinese law, PRC jurisdiction over the SCS falls under Hainan Province's remit, where that province's authorities have been tasked by Beijing with the duty of developing and managing the central leadership's strategies and policies towards the SCS.[22] The second of these agencies is PLAN, which constantly lobbies the Party leadership for a more assertive stance in terms of defending China's sovereign claims in the area. According to Lu Ning, the traditionally more hawkish PLAN is engaged in a never-ending head-to-head with moderates in the PRC's Ministry of Foreign Affairs who oppose calls for tougher action in areas such as the Spratly Islands.[23] The third and most important of these agencies is the aforementioned Foreign Ministry, which on paper has the final say on the Spratlys issue and how the state deals with it.[24] The struggle for power and favor among the three agencies within the CCP elite means that for leaders such as Jiang during the Deng-Jiang succession period of the early to mid-1990s, there was a difficult juggling act between reinforcing his position and supporting the military, whose good will he depended upon in his quest to consolidate his still volatile position as the country's leader.

[20] "Party Leaders, Generals," *Hong Kong Standard*, 1.

[21] *Ming Pao*, Hong Kong.

[22] Ibid.

[23] Lu, *The Dynamics of Foreign-Policy*, 11.

[24] Guan, "The South China Sea," 11.

Jiang, PLA Commander, and Domestic Politics

The undermining of the "low level functionaries" explanation points the finger at influential military commanders within the highest echelons of the PLA authorizing the occupation with the unofficial acknowledgement of the civilian leadership. According to Storey, while the Chinese military may have acted alone and without "formal" authorization from Jiang, the PRC's domestic political circumstances in the lead-up to 1994–1995 might provide a more convincing explanation for the Mischief Reef occupation.[25] In the years prior to the occupation, Jiang had been in the midst of an ongoing and unresolved process of leadership consolidation since 1989. He came to power following the upheaval of the Tiananmen Square massacre and amid deep uncertainty concerning China's future in the new and dynamic post-Cold War world. These were years of gradual and uncertain power shifts in a country which does not have a pleasant history of smooth and peaceful transfers of power.[26] The state was thus making a volatile adjustment from the era of Deng Xiaoping (1978–1992) to the era of Jiang Zemin (1989–2002), Deng's protégé, whose future and whose ability to ride the storm of Chinese politics as yet remained undecided. On the domestic political front, Jiang sought to consolidate his position and personal authority in the shadow of an aging Deng, and struggled to find the center ground between the more apparent competing left and right wing groups who were pushing and pulling for influence. This required Jiang to define a "new center" between the different forces of reform, liberalism, conservatism, and nationalism. The 1994 Fourth Plenum (Fourth Plenary Session) of the Fourteenth Central Committee that gathered in Beijing on September 25–28 saw the symbolic passing of the leadership torch from the Deng era to the 'Third Generation' of Chinese leadership under Jiang, who was eager to secure his authority amongst other elites within the leadership.[27] According to Chung however,

> While the September 1994 Communist Party plenum formally marked the start of the post-Deng era, any claim by Jiang as paramount leader was premature. His support by the military was uncertain, his edge over rivals

[25] Storey, "Creeping Assertiveness," 101.

[26] Fewsmith, *China Since Tiananmen*, 239–240.

[27] Ibid., 240.

to succeed Deng was thin and his longevity as leader independent of the patriarch's patronage was questionable.[28]

In this context, it is very possible that the quiet sanctioning of the occupation of Mischief Reef may have been attributable to Jiang's desire to win over support from senior military figures within the Chinese elite who were lobbying for assertive action in the South China Sea. In the summer of 1994, when activities on Mischief Reef had commenced or were about to, the aging Deng, though retired and in the political background, still commanded a great deal of respect and loyalty. People also questioned whether Jiang could successfully lead the country after Deng's death. In this dynamic context, Jiang worked hard to consolidate his own position, and to convince others of his patriotic credentials and of his ability to be tough when necessary. The PLA, as one of the cornerstones of the Chinese polity, was an essential player to win over if Jiang's objectives were to be realized. In a period which saw more assertive approaches by Beijing from the early to mid-1990s on issues raising from Taiwan, the East China Sea, the South China Sea, and relations with the US, it is not difficult to imagine that the PRC President, though uninvolved with its implementation, may have given his off-the-record blessing to the Mischief Reef occupation. Such a move, though risky in terms of foreign relations, would no doubt have paid domestic political dividends for Jiang from neo-conservative members of the elite as well as the PLA.[29] This viewpoint is also given added credibility by virtue of the strong influence of the Chinese military on decision-making at the time. Chung, for example, states that the power of the PLA was at its highest in years during the post-Tiananmen massacre period as well as the Deng-Jiang leadership transition from the early to mid-1990s as Deng appeared close to death. The military also felt they had a mandate for a decisive stance on sovereignty following the Political Report of the Fourteenth Party Congress in 1992, which placed a special emphasis on territorial integrity. Potential rivals to the President's power within the Politburo Standing Committee who competed for the military's favor were also present in the background. These included elites such as Li Peng (Premier), Qiao Shi (Chairman of the Standing Committee of the National People's

[28] Chung, "The Spratly Islands Dispute," 265.

[29] Storey, "Creeping Assertiveness," 101.

Congress), and Li Ruihuan (Chairman of the National Committee of the Chinese People's Political Consultative Conference—CPPCC). In this context, Jiang may have tacitly approved the 1994–1995 occupation because to stand against the PLA amid the unfolding frictions over Taiwan would almost certainly have jeopardized his position as leader. All of his long-standing efforts to maintain the military's support could also have been seriously undermined. As Chinese leader, Jiang likewise appreciated that supporting a sovereignty and territorial integrity-related move would have bolstered his own nationalist and patriotic credentials. From the PLA perspective, the take-over of Mischief Reef would help them to defend their calls for extra funding while also outmanoeuvring their rivals for influence on South China Sea policy, the Ministry of Foreign Affairs (MFA), by displaying their resolve to defend China's claims. As such, the decision to occupy the feature was arguably heavily influenced by a convergence of interests between Jiang and the PLA.[30] While evidence proving this is not available or non-existent, the circumstantial evidence makes a compelling case for a mutual understanding between the PLA and Jiang Zemin, which manifested itself in the take-over of Mischief Reef in the second half of 1994.

References

Bush, Richard C. "China-Japan Tensions, 1995–2006—Why They Happened, What to Do." Foreign Policy at Brookings Policy Paper Number 16. Brookings Institution, Washington, DC, 2009.

"China Nibbles, ASEAN Dithers." (Editorial) *Asian Wall Street Journal*, March 10–11, 1995.

"Chinese Navy Detains Filipino fishermen in the Spratlys." *China News Digest*, January 24, 1995.

Chung, Christopher. "The Spratly Islands Dispute: Decision Units and Domestic Politics." *Australian Defence Force Academy, School of Humanities and Social Science,* Canberra, 2004. https://www.unsworks.unsw.edu.au/primoexplore/fulldisplay/unsworks_3198/UNSWORKS.

Dzurek, Daniel J. "China Occupies Mischief Reef in Latest Spratly Gambit." *Boundary and Security Bulletin* 3, no. 1 (1995): 65–71.

Fewsmith, Joseph. *China Since Tiananmen—From Deng Xiaoping to Hu Jintao.* Cambridge: Cambridge University Press, 2008.

[30] Chung, 273, 290–291, 300–301.

Fravel, M. Taylor. *Strong Borders, Secure Nation—Co-operation and Conflict in China's Territorial Disputes*. Princeton: Princeton University Press, 2008.

Guan, Ang Cheng. "The South China Sea Dispute Re-visited." Institute of Defence and Strategic Studies (IDSS). Working Paper Series, Working Paper No. 4. Singapore, August 1999. http://www.rsis.edu.sg/publications/WorkingPapers/WP04.pdf.

"Hye Mieko Attack Triggers Upsurge in Piracy." *South China Morning Post*, June 28, 1995.

Klare, Michael T. *Resource Wars—The New Landscape of Global Conflict*. New York: Owl Books, 2001.

Lo Ping. "Jiang Zemin Seen Facing Crisis Over Diaoyutai Issue." *Cheng Ming*, October 1, 1996.

Lu, Ning. *Decision Making in China*. Boulder, CO: Westview Press, 1997.

Martin, Michael F. "Understanding China's Political System." Congressional Research Service (CRS) Report for United States Congress 7–5700, R41007, April 2010. http://www.fas.org/sgp/crs/row/R41007.pdf.

Ming Pao, Hong Kong, July 4, 1994.

"Party Leaders, Generals to Discuss Diaoyu Issue at Plenum." *Hong Kong Standard*, September 23, 1996.

Raman, Bahukutumbi. "Chinese Territorial Assertions: the Case of Mischief Reef." Warfighter (blog), January 14, 1999. http://www.warfighter.org/mischief.html.

Storey, Ian James. "Creeping Assertiveness: China, the Philippines, and the South China Sea Dispute." *Contemporary Southeast Asia* 21, no. 1 (April 1999): 95–119.

"Tropical Cyclones in 1994." *Royal Observatory of Hong Kong*, May 1995, Government of Hong Kong, https://web.archive.org/web/20061230231319/www.weather.gov.hk/publica/tc/tc1994.pdf.

Valencia, Mark J., Jon M. Van Dyke, and Noel A. Ludwig. *Sharing the Resources of the South China Sea*. Honolulu: University of Hawai'i Press, 1997.

CHAPTER 5

The Occupation of Mischief Reef

Abstract Here the occupation's various stages are discussed, detailing the immediate responses of the Philippines and other regional players as well as the USA. It includes the Second Mischief Reef Incident in 1998 when China further consolidated its gains. The chapter provides contrasting opinions of the occupation, most notably Beijing's initial claim of its non-military character. Manila's hopes of halting further Chinese activities were also dashed, describing the psychological shock and erosion of trust, and the limited attempts by the poorly equipped Philippines to physically respond. Scholarly opinions on the apparent Chinese dual strategy of negotiating while consolidating the take-over are also reviewed. The chapter then looks at US-Philippine security ties and alliance provisos in its aftermath. Following this, the after-effects are discussed. It shows how the occupation sent ripples through ASEAN and represented a watershed. While the organization denounced the take-over, its words were not matched with substantial punitive actions. The affair nonetheless led to calls for more binding agreements in the SCS. Despite these developments, China could not be dislodged from the reef. With military and economic retaliation off the table as feasible options, the Philippines had little choice but to adopt a three-pronged diplomatic strategy, discussed herein.

Keyword ASEAN · Code of Conduct (CoC) · First Mischief Reef Incident (Mischief Reef I) · Occupation of Mischief Reef · Occupation's

S. Fox, *Mischief Reef*,
https://doi.org/10.1007/978-981-16-3884-8_5

After-Effects · Philippines Armed Forces · People's Liberation Army Navy (PLAN) · Second Mischief Reef Incident (Mischief Reef II) · US-Philippine security ties

China's First Moves

Sometime between June and December 1994, the Chinese began to place structures on stilts on Mischief Reef. This was at a time when the relatively weak and under-funded PHL's naval forces had been restricted from patrolling the area as a result of the monsoon season and adverse weather conditions. These construction efforts are believed to have taken place over the course of a few months.[1] Observers have different opinions on why the PRC acted when it did. Numerous experts point to Manila's covert granting of a six month "desktop" oil exploration permit to the US oil company Vaalco and its PHL subsidiary company Alcorn Petroleum and Minerals Corporation in May 1994. This followed the collapse of Sino-Filipino talks in relation to exploration and production near the Reed Bank area. As a result, the Chinese decided that occupying a feature within the neighboring Kalayaan Island Group (KIG) was the most effective way by which to strengthen their claims.[2] Tiglao also contends that another purpose of the occupation was to send an unspoken message to the PHL President Fidel V. Ramos that if his country mistakenly believed that the PRC was too far away to defend its interests in the Reed Bank area then they would construct fortifications nearby which could act as supply depots for Chinese vessels. Ramos was apparently advised to proceed with the ill-fated Alcorn move by his chief legal adviser, Antonio Carpio, a fierce critic of China and its South China Sea policies.[3]

As mentioned earlier, September 1994 has also been cited as significant in the dispute due to the detention of fifty-five PRC fishermen by PHL armed forces that month. The men were caught trying to build habitable shelters on one unnamed PHL-claimed feature in the Spratlys group.

[1] McCarthy, "Reef Wars"; Guan, "The South China Sea," 11.

[2] Lim, "Tempest," 85–86; Storey, "Creeping Assertiveness," 97; Tiglao, "Troubled Waters"; Dzurek, "China Occupies Mischief Reef," 30.

[3] Tiglao, "Bold Move."

The Filipinos charged them with illegal entry and the possession of explosives. In addition to developments on Mischief Reef, the Chinese would later avenge September 1994 by detaining thirty-five PHL fishermen in January of the following year.[4]

This Chinese gamble of stealthily occupying a feature claimed by a member of ASEAN must have been predicated on the belief that once occupied, the PHL navy would not have the will to re-occupy it by force, nor would they be willing to risk a dangerous conflict which could spiral into something much larger. Manila's decision not to re-occupy the reef or at least destroy the PRC installations there almost certainly prevented the outbreak of potential conflict. The Filipinos must also have known, as illustrated in clashes between Vietnam and the PRC in 1974 and 1988, that China was willing to use force and kill if necessary to defend what they considered to be their sovereign territory in the South China Sea.[5] The occupation itself was a surreptitious affair which apparently took Manila by complete surprise and involved as many as seven to nine Chinese naval ships, of which only two remained once the construction activities were completed.[6] The reef was the seventh Spratly feature to be occupied by the PRC in nearly as many years, but as stated earlier, this was the first time that a state other than Vietnam had one of its own features furtively occupied by the PRC.[7]

Up until that time, the majority of Philippine citizens viewed China as a giant but distant neighbour. While physical Chinese quarrels with the Vietnamese were well-known, Manila felt confident that the PRC would not risk regional alienation or US animosity by stealthily occupying a feature within the Philippines' EEZ and for reasons that did not include serious provocation as the Filipinos saw it. This all changed in late January

[4] Swanstrom, "Conflict Management and Negotiations," 98. See also "Chinese Navy Detains Filipino," *China News Digest*.

[5] McCarthy, "Reef Wars"; Guan, "The South China Sea," 11.

[6] Dzurek, "China Occupies," 67; the seven vessels travelled over 1100 kms to the reef, and brought with them building materials, construction workers, and communications equipment. According to Valencia, et al., *Sharing the Resources*, there were nine PRC vessels involved, 81. Lim in "Tempest" cites eight, 85.

[7] Fravel, *Strong Borders*, 296–299.

1995[8] when a Filipino fishing boat captain informed the Manila authorities that he had been fishing near Mischief Reef when PLAN personnel, who by then had taken control of the reef, held him against his will in detention for a week before releasing him. The PHL government sought to verify the story by sending the mayor of Thitu (Pagasa) Island to the reef. The mayor reported back that he had indeed gone to the feature, but that his vessel was driven out of the area by PLAN ships anchored nearby. On February 2, Manila dispatched a naval vessel and a military plane to the area to confirm the previous accounts given and report that PLAN appeared to be close to completing a type of military facility with living quarters on the reef with a large satellite dish. Chinese flags were also seen flying over the reef.[9]

A PHL Department of National Defense report found that a number of PLAN vessels were moored close to the feature. These included an amphibious warship and a submarine support vessel. The Filipinos also published aerial photographs of a recently constructed and elevated building upon stilts on the atoll.[10] Reviewing these images, Baker and Wiencek noted how each of these three hut-like buildings were constructed in an octagonal configuration atop of steel pylons. A small storage hut that stood separate from the main newly built area could also be seen. Armor shields, they state, were also evident on the outside of each of these huts. Perhaps due to the unclear images, they also mentioned inconclusively that an armed individual may have been standing behind at least one of these shields and was observing aircraft flying overhead.[11] For the Filipinos, such findings made a mockery of Chinese assertions that the structures were mere shelters for fishermen rather than markers of PRC sovereignty and control.[12]

On February 8, President Ramos publicly announced in a televised press interview that the PRC had "illegally occupied" the feature, that the

[8] Lim cites a Filipino navy spokesperson who claimed his office started receiving reports of the Chinese presence as early as January 22; see Lim, "Tempest," 125; and "Military Finds No Trace," *The Philippine Star*.

[9] Odgaard, *Maritime Security*, 73–74; Severino, "Southeast Asia in Search," 185; Valencia et al., *Sharing the Resources*, 80.

[10] Branigin, "China Takes Over."

[11] Baker and Wiencek, *Cooperative Monitoring*, 94.

[12] Valencia et al., *Sharing the Resources*, 80.

incident was harmful to positive bilateral ties, and that it was incompatible with international law.[13] He also declared that China's actions were contrary to the spirit of the 1992 Manila Declaration noting that although the PRC was not a signatory, it had pledged to respect the declaration's provisions. The Filipino Department of Foreign Affairs also stated at the time that even though Vietnam, Malaysia, and Taiwan had also previously taken over features claimed by the Philippines, these occupations had happened before the 1992 declaration. The purpose of this statement was to counter any possible PRC attempt to use these occupations by other states as leverage to remain on Mischief Reef.[14]

It was through the PHL's Department of Foreign Affairs, a strongly worded *aide memoir* was delivered to the PRC Embassy in Manila protesting the structures on Mischief Reef and the detention of Filipino citizens.[15] The PRC's reaction was to both defend its actions on the reef and to reject the allegations made by Manila. A spokesperson for the PRC Foreign Ministry, Chen Jian, declared:

> Structures had been built on the reef by China to ensure the safety and lives as well as the production operations of the fishermen who work in the waters of the Nansha (Spratly) Islands. The Chinese side never detained nor arrested any Filipino ship nor established any military base on the Meiji (Mischief) Reef.[16]

Immediate Responses

As China's main rival in the South China Sea, Vietnam also used the opportunity to wade into the issue. Ramos' announcement on the reef's occupation was made during an official visit to the Philippines by Nguyen Manh Cam, Vietnam's Foreign Minister. On February 6, the two countries issued a carefully worded joint statement which did not specifically mention Mischief Reef, but called for restraint in disputed areas. In a

[13] According to a 1995 issue of *Far Eastern Economic Review*, PHL patrol vessels first noticed the structures on Mischief Reef as early as November 1994, but Manila chose not to admit this until the following February; "Who Knew What?" *Far Eastern Economic Review*.

[14] "U.S. Stays Neutral," *Japan Times*; "Indonesia Calls for Peaceful," *Japan Times*.

[15] "China Nibbles, ASEAN Dithers," *Wall Street Journal Asia*.

[16] *Indian Defence Review* 14 (1999): 60.

later press interview during the trip, Nguyen expressed his view that the incident could be resolved without further trouble but that "no one should do anything to make the situation more complex."[17] The PHL Foreign Secretary, Roberto Romulo, also declared in this tense period that whoever resorts to force or aggression in that area is the first one who "loses all moral and legal right to make a claim."[18] On February 14, the *Japan Times* reported that the Philippines was considering taking the issue to the United Nations and the International Court of Justice (ICJ) but relented when it realized that China, as a United Nations Security Council (UNSC), could veto any resolution and that the ICJ could not act if the Chinese refused to recognize its jurisdiction.[19] Just over one week after making the occupation public, Ramos ordered his military forces to increase their aerial surveillance in the Mischief Reef area and also to remain extremely vigilant to any encroachment upon any other PHL territory in the Kalayaan area.[20] A squadron of five aging fighter planes was deployed to the area and Filipino military personnel and a patrol ship were ordered to destroy a number of PRC sovereignty markers within PHL-claimed zones.[21] Ramos also met with the Filipino National Security Council (NSC) in mid-February, after which he stated that his country would explore all diplomatic options, declaring:

> As part of this diplomatic effort, the Philippines has put forward as an interim measure the concept of stewardship. Each disputed island should be placed under the stewardship, meaning the primary responsibility, of the claimant country closest to it geographically, on the understanding that the steward country accommodates the other claimants' need for shelter, anchorage and other peaceful pursuits.[22]

Ramos told the PHL National Security Council in February that the Chinese were trespassers, and that the structures were part of a new outpost through which the PLAN could operate within the heart of the

[17] Ibid.

[18] Ibid.

[19] "Philippines Says Spratlys Dispute," *Japan Times*.

[20] *Journal of the United Service Institution of India* 12, 564.

[21] Song, "Managing Potential Conflicts," 5; "U.S. Stays Neutral," *Japan Times*; "Indonesia Calls for Peaceful," *Japan Times*.

[22] *Journal of the United Service Institution of India* 12, 564.

Philippines' EEZ. The Council concurred that the take-over was a physical demonstration of China's SCS claims.[23] Following this, Ramos called on the "foreign" trespassers to peacefully leave the area, promised to stand firm in defending his country and, in a display of resolve, ordered the deployment of an additional twenty-eight patrol ships, one cargo vessel, five F-5 fighter planes, two Huey helicopters, and four Italian-made S-211 jet trainers to Palawan Island, headquarters of AFP's Western Military Command and the nearest undisputed PHL territory to Mischief Reef.[24]

The PHL leader continued by asserting that what happened at Mischief Reef was a development which all parties interested in the peace and stability of the SCS and the entire East Asian region should be worried about. The PRC's decision to build "military structures" on the reef, he claimed, was a dangerous attempt to change the status quo in the area and to secure a fait accompli by stealth and then to defend that act by force. Interestingly, Ramos also disclosed the fact that in conciliatory talks with the PRC leadership, they had asserted that the occupation was "ordered by low-level functionaries acting without the knowledge and consent of the Chinese Government." The Chinese also denied the involvement of the PLAN in the detention of Filipinos in the Spratlys or the building of military-related facilities and stated that the structures were put on the reef by a department of the PRC's fisheries administration.[25] On March 10, 1995 for instance, the PRC's Foreign Minister Qian Qichen stated that "there is no tension in that region. I don't think any crisis will occur ..." He also asserted that the building of shelters in the Spratly Islands by local Chinese fishing authorities should not be viewed as a sign of aggression.[26] The Chinese also reportedly stated that fishermen from other claimant states including the Philippines and not just China could use the new facilities on the atoll.[27]

Perhaps to de-escalate the situation or simply because their work was done, the Chinese moved seven of their nine vessels in the reef area to

[23] "Philippines to Boost Forces," *Japan Times*.

[24] "Beijing Extends Envoy's Term," *Foreign Broadcast Information Service* EAS-95-032, 64.

[25] Fravel, *Strong Borders*, 297; the author also suggests the Chinese sought to financially compensate the Philippines for the occupation.

[26] "China Calms Regional Fears," *Associated Foreign Press*; Lim, "Tempest," 86.

[27] Lim, "Tempest," 86.

a location outside the PHL's EEZ, however, they did not dismantle the structures.[28] The Filipinos remained unconvinced about China's reassurances. Manila set up a "Marine and Archipelagic Development Policy Task Force" during this time with the purpose of developing the Kalayaan Island Group (KIG) area. The Filipinos also declared that they would commence building lighthouses in the area.[29] Other announcements included the running of naval patrols close to the occupied reef.[30]

On March 18, ASEAN foreign ministers released a joint statement to express "serious concern about recent developments which affect peace and stability in the South China Sea." They also called on all parties to "remain faithful to the letter and spirit of the Manila Declaration" which was supported by other countries throughout the world. The March 18 statement reminded observers of the importance of resolving differences by peaceful means and to "refrain from taking actions that de-stabilize the situation." It specifically called "for the early resolution of the problems caused by recent developments in Mischief Reef."[31]

The PHL President dispatched his Under Secretary in the Foreign Office, Rodolfo Severino, to the PRC to discuss the issue with talks beginning on March 19 and lasting three days. The talks achieved nothing and Severino returned to Manila complaining that "the Chinese continued to maintain their position that these structures are wind shelters for their fishermen. We believe that this has set back the moves towards confidence-building since 1990."[32] According to Valencia et al., prior to the meeting, Manila had been hesitant about bilateral negotiations over joint development for example because they feared being bullied by China and because these negotiations did not address the issue of sovereignty.[33] In general, while the Filipinos viewed the March negotiations as a failure,

[28] "Philippines to Boost Forces," *Japan Times*.

[29] Dzurek, "China Occupies," 67; he writes that alongside these moves, the Filipinos acknowledged that Vietnam also had forces and weaponry on four PHL-claimed features. However, they were quick to distinguish between Vietnamese occupations that took place before the 1992 Manila Declaration and the 1994–1995 Chinese occupation of Mischief Reef.

[30] Valencia et al., *Sharing the Resources*, 81.

[31] "Statement by the ASEAN Foreign Ministers," March 18, 1995. See also Severino, "ASEAN and the South China Sea," 42–43.

[32] *Indian Defence Review* 14 (1999), 60.

[33] Valencia et al., *Sharing the Resources*, 80–81.

the Chinese stated that they were a success because the two countries had come to understand each other's positions.[34]

After the talks ended, the PHL made its most dramatic response when it destroyed Chinese facilities and markers on Half Moon Shoal, Jackson Atoll, First Thomas Shoal, Second Thomas Shoal, Pennsylvania Reef, and Sabina Shoal. These were discovered a day before the Beijing talks began, further eroding trust. Filipino patrol vessels also detained four PRC fishing boats and sixty-two crew members on charges of illegal fishing near Alicia Anne Shoal, close to Mischief Reef, and took them to a military base on Palawan Island. In the period from March 20 to 28, the Filipinos also detained Chinese fishing vessels and their crew members in the Mischief Reef area and destroyed PRC markers.[35]

In response, Beijing stated that the destruction of the markers would not help to resolve the dispute nor undermine the PRC's sovereign rights.[36] In a positive move, March 1995 also saw the Filipinos releasing the fifty-five Chinese fishermen who had been detained since September of the previous year.[37] On March 28, the PHL military protested that Chinese personnel were still present on the reef's structures.[38]

Following the first ever China–ASEAN Forum, initiated by the PRC and taking place in early April (3–5) in the Chinese city of Hangzhou, Severino would later claim that PRC negotiators indicated that they were considering altering the extent of their sovereign claims in order to operate within the parameters of international law in the SCS. ASEAN made it clear in their pronouncements that the Mischief Reef affair had damaged confidence and trust in China's assurances. Severino expressed his satisfaction that the regional grouping had stood behind Manila and had aired its protests in "unusually forceful terms". Filipino Foreign Minister Roberto Romula similarly declared his "gratification"

[34] BBC/FE/2260/B3, March 24, 1995. BBC/FE/2260/G1, March 24, 1995; cited from Swanstrom, "Conflict Management and Negotiations," 111.

[35] Kim, "Naval Strategy," 20; Dzurek, "China Occupies," 67; Severino, "Southeast Asia in Search," 185; Song, "Managing Potential Conflicts," 5; Mackerras, *The New Cambridge Handbook*, 55; Valencia et al., *Sharing the Resources*, 81; "Philippine Navy Seizes Vessels," *Associated Press*; "Philippine Navy Holds Chinese Fishermen," *Reuters*.

[36] "Ramos Welcomes U.S. Bilateral," *Foreign Broadcast Information Service*, 70.

[37] Valencia et al., *Sharing the Resources*, 82.

[38] "Manila Charges China," *Honolulu Advertiser*, A7; "Ramos Stresses Peaceful Spratlys Solution," *Foreign Broadcast Information Service*, 60.

that ASEAN had stood up to the PRC "with one voice."[39] It was on April 4 that Foreign Minister Qian Qichen used words which underlined a shocked Beijing's desire to put the occupation issue behind them without standing down from its position on the reef, and to work on proposals for cooperative projects in the SCS. To this end, Qian stated: "China's standpoint is that we want to abandon the controversy and manage the islands together. China has built on these islands civilian structures with no military character at all. They were built only to accommodate the work of our fishermen."[40] In another ASEAN meeting on Sentosa Island in Singapore that same month, Mischief Reef was also placed on the agenda with six foreign ministers from ASEAN member states reaffirming the 1992 Manila Declaration.[41]

The Philippine government continued to accuse the Chinese of constructing a permanent military installation on the reef and to demand that all PRC vessels and personnel be removed from the area. The Chinese repeatedly rejected the claims by arguing that the structures were for peaceful purposes as shelters for Chinese fishermen, and that their presence on the reef was valid and would continue because it was within Chinese sovereign territory. The Philippines sought to display their resolve by sending some PHL naval ships into the area to investigate. These, however, were promptly warded off by PLAN warships. These reactions were seen by Manila as Chinese determination to maintain its presence in the area by force if necessary.[42]

The Philippines' response to the seeming diplomatic failure to resolve the issue was to assert its claims and presence more decisively in the Kalayaan area. In April, the government informed global media outlets that they had arrested sixty-two Chinese fishermen in waters off Mischief Reef (discussed earlier). Manila also claimed that the men possessed markers and materials for the purposes of claiming the area for the PRC. In addition, the PHL stated that the men had said that they wanted to protect an endangered species of sea turtles in the area. In the coming weeks, more Chinese markers were found on PHL claimed features and

[39] "Why China Is Creating," *Straits Times*; Storey, "Creeping Assertiveness," 106; "Philippines Says ASEAN Has," *Reuters*.

[40] *Indian Defence Review* 14 (1999), 62.

[41] Lim, "Tempest," 86.

[42] Klare, *Resource Wars*, 125.

were subsequently destroyed by Filipino authorities. In response to this chain of events, the Filipinos intensified their own demarcation efforts and intensified the construction of navigational aids such as lighthouses and beacons.[43] In response to these activities, a spokesperson for the PRC's Foreign Office declared "this action will do no good to a settlement of the issue nor will it harm China's sovereignty"[44] On April 6, Ramos, in spite of the poor state of his country's armed forces, warned: "I will not hesitate to take the necessary protective measures for our territory."[45] The Filipinos hoped to pressure the ARF into more decisive action against China. In advance of the ARF's first working session in Brunei in May 1995, Severino declared "….if the [ARF] is a forum for consultation worthy of the name, I don't see how it can avoid discussing the issue". China, however, had stated its unwillingness to discuss the issue at the meeting. Despite Manila's efforts, ARF showed a reluctance to face a possible diplomatic showdown with Beijing over the affair at a time when the body was still only in its formative stages.[46]

Nevertheless, in appreciation of the ongoing fallout from the occupation, the Chinese sought desperately to calm the waters. To this end, PRC President Jiang Zemin had sent a letter to Manila on May 13 via his new ambassador to the PHL, Guan Dengming, aimed at reconciling the two neighbours. The letter, which was presented by Guan to President Ramos on May 15, proposed a number of confidence-building joint measures in the areas of fisheries, research, the joint development of resources, disaster prevention, rescue missions, and environmental protection. Ramos responded to the letter by arguing that any joint projects should be multilateral in nature. On May 15, however, the day on which Jiang's letter was sent, the Filipinos invited a group of just under forty local and international journalists to the reef area aboard an AFP naval vessel, the MV Benguet, described by Lim as an "amphibious assault craft" which was escorted by two PHL warships.[47] The purpose of the trip was a "news-gathering" activity to allow the media to witness what

[43] Meyer, "Incident at Mischief Reef," 7.

[44] "Manila Removes Markers," *Foreign Broadcast Information Service*, 23.

[45] "Who Knew What?" *Far Eastern Economic Review*, 14; Raman, "Chinese Territorial Assertions."

[46] "Why China Is Creating," *Straits Times*.

[47] Lim, "Tempest," 86.

was happening on the reef. It was also aimed at discrediting PRC claims that the recently built structures were not of a military nature and to show that they were in fact almost identical to military installations constructed by PLAN on other Spratly features such as Johnson Reef and Subi Reef. However, when the ship came within ten kilometers of the feature, two PLAN frigates arrived from the direction of Johnson Reef and prevented it from coming any closer. According to one source, the group were eventually able to fly over the reef in helicopters.[48] The Chinese leadership also responded furiously to the Filipino move. On May 16, the Foreign Ministry officially declared that "any similar action could result in serious consequences. We advise the other side not to misinterpret China's restraint, but, instead, to return to the correct path of negotiations to resolve the dispute."[49] Other sources claim that the MV Benguet was obstructed for over seventy minutes by two fishing vessels; one with the markings "China Fishing Administration 34". According to Wroe, this represented the first physical confrontation between the PRC and the PHL in the disputed area. This incident happened just three days after the release of a Spratly Islands policy statement by the US (discussed subsequently).[50]

In addition to the above warning, the PRCFM continued with the admonition: "the Philippine side had better return to the correct course of settling the relevant dispute through peaceful talks. If the Philippine side continues to act willfully and recklessly, it should be responsible for all consequences arising therefrom."[51] China also reminded the Philippines: "it does not have limitless tolerance for encroachment on China's

[48] Ibid.

[49] *Indian Defence Review* 14 (1999), 60, 62; see also *Journal of the United Service Institution of India* 129, 565; Raman, "Chinese Territorial Assertions"; "Philippine Leader Defends Spratlys Tour," *Reuters*; Marso, "Manila Denies Provoking China"; "Manila, Beijing Agree," *Reuters*; Lim, "Tempest," 86.

[50] Wroe, "Making Mischief." Another source mentioned a "vintage" World War II "tank landing vessel" that had been carrying journalists to Mischief Reef in mid-1995. The vessel, however, broke down and needed to be towed back to Palawan. It is unclear from the source if the incident refers to the MV Benguet or not. See Fisher, "Rebuilding the US-Philippine Alliance," *The Heritage Foundation*, 8.

[51] "The Spratly Islands," Congressional Record—Senate, 104th Congress, 1st session, Congressional Records, 141: S7386, May 24, 1995, at S7386.

sovereignty and dignity" and that the PHL "must bear full responsibility for any serious consequences."[52] The US released a statement that criticized the harsh language used by the Chinese.[53]

On the home front, Ramos had to delicately balance powerful domestic forces who exploited the issue to attack him as an opportunist or as an indecisive leader. Filipino nationalists and political opponents, for example, complained that their President was exploiting the "Chinese bogeyman" and the reef's takeover to "lure the Americans back". Other players demanded that the 1951 Mutual Defense Treaty be upgraded to ensure that the pact's obligations included all features within the Philippines' EEZ.[54] With military and economic retaliation off the table as feasible options however, there was little choice but to continue down the diplomatic route and to emphasis their claims without engaging in direct confrontation with the Chinese. In June 1995 for example, Manila announced the construction of lighthouses on Reed Bank (also known as Reed Tablemount), Nares Bank (inside the same area), and Seahorse Shoal. These would serve as a legal basis for new PHL baselines, activities destined to anger Beijing.[55] With the PHL navy persisting in destroying PRC markers in disputed areas, the Chinese cautioned them in early July that their forbearance had been tested to its limits.[56]

US-Philippine Security

The discovery of Chinese structures on a reef claimed and administered by the Philippines had a sobering and invigorating influence upon that country's perception of its own security. Within a matter of weeks, the Filipino Congress introduced a 50 billion pesos (US $1.23 billion) defense modernization bill, modeled upon suggestions provided by Ramos in 1989, but rejected at the time, which they planned to implement over the

[52] "Spratlys Dispute Flaring." *Voice of America*; "China Asked to Cool Rhetoric," *Associated Press*.

[53] "U.S. Asks China to cool Rhetoric," Associated Press, May 17, 1995.

[54] "Ramos Trying to Get," *Straits Times*; "Philippines Security Based On," *Asia Times*.

[55] "Philippines to Build Lighthouses," *Reuters*.

[56] Lim, "Temptest," 86.

course of fifteen years.[57] At the time, PHL Senator Orlando S. Mercado was reported as saying: "We're not modernizing because of the Spratlys, but maybe it gave our bill a bit of a push."[58] Mercado continued by observing how decrepit his country's military had become after decades of depending on the Americans to protect them. The occupation showed, amongst other examples, how badly the PHL air force needed new fighter jets and the navy missile-equipped patrol craft. The acquisition of radar systems in particular was a pressing issue because without them "we don't even know who is flying over us."[59] Although the radar systems risked being viewed by Beijing as retaliation for their take-over of Mischief Reef, there were no alternatives: the Filipinos found themselves in the midst of a "damned if we do and damned if we don't" conundrum.

The refusal of the US to get involved, and to argue that the incident lay outside the remit of the 1951 Mutual Defense Treaty was a bitter pill to swallow. It was made painfully clear to Manila that the Kalayaans would not be protected in the event of a clash and that, from Washington's perspective, the 1951 pact only referred to situations where the national interests of "both" states were placed in danger.[60] Washington also contended that the 1951 Treaty did not refer to the area in which Mischief Reef is located. The Treaty only covered the "metropolitan" areas of the Philippines. This, they claimed, was likewise stipulated in the Paris Treaty of 1899 and the Philippine Constitution of 1939. The Kalayaan area was also only claimed by Manila after the 1951 Treaty further negating any obligation on the US to respond.[61]

Since the occupation was not an "armed attack", had taken place within the Kalayaan area, and arguably only really affected the contestable sovereignty claims of the Philippines, the US was able to argue against intervention and resist diplomatic pressure to undo the Chinese action. Storey observes two precedents which, arguably, Manila should have noted in any expectation of US military intervention on issues which did

57 The PHL's defense modernization project was, however, dogged by delays and obstacles throughout the late 1990s and early 2000s; see Chung, "The Spratly Islands Dispute," 247–250.

58 Tasker, "A Line in the Sand," 14–16.

59 Ibid., 28.

60 Storey, "Creeping Assertiveness," 108.

61 "Ramos Orders More Troops," *Foreign Broadcast Information Service*, 50.

not directly affect the interests of Washington. In 1974, the US stood by as China forcefully consolidated its control over the Paracel Islands which its ally, South Vietnam, administered. Washington had also consistently refused to aid the Filipinos in their conflict against Islamic separatists.[62]

Aside from the US appearing to abandon its "ally" on the reef issue, as Filipinos saw it immediately afterwards, another point of contention was the question of whether or not the US military knew about the PRC's construction activities on the reef long before Manila did. PHL suspicions are reflected in the views of a senior unnamed AFP official interviewed by Storey, who noted the six month time period from June to December 1994 when these activities took place. The official contended that the Americans would almost certainly have been aware of what PLAN was doing on the reef months prior to the Filipino coastguard finding out about it, and yet they did not alert their ally in Manila. Though impossible to prove, he argues this failure of disclosure was due to a US decision to withhold that intelligence data so as to reprove the Filipinos for expelling the Americans from Subic Bay in 1992, and to remind them that a consequence of such actions was less flexibility in the sharing of intelligence. What made matters worse was that the US Navy at first denied they knew anything about these activities before they became public knowledge in February 1995. This claim, however, was undermined in March 1995 by public responses to the incident given by Commander-in-Chief of the US Pacific Command, Admiral Richard Macke. When he was asked how it could happen that the activities of PLAN could continue unnoticed by the US military for six months, he defended himself by stating "I didn't say we didn't know anything about it .... We don't get surprised an awful lot." Manila's frustration with Washington only increased after they sought more information about what the US military had known, only to be refused.[63]

Despite this breach of trust, as the Filipinos saw it, the incident did intensify fears in the US and amongst China's neighbors with regards to the threat posed by PLAN to the freedom of navigation and passage by air and sea in the South China Sea. The PRC's state news agency, Xinhua, sought to calm nerves by publishing an article in mid-May 1995 which

[62] Storey, "Creeping Assertiveness," 108.

[63] "For Our Eyes Only," *Far Eastern Economic Review*.

quoted a statement made by their Foreign Ministry spokesperson, Shen Guofang, where he declared:

> ...on the issue of the navigation rights in the South China Sea, the Chinese Government holds a definite and clear-cut position, namely, China's action to safeguard its sovereignty over the Nansha (Spratly) Islands and the relevant maritime rights and interests will not affect navigation through and the freedom and safety of flights over the international waterway of the South China Sea in keeping with the international laws.[64]

Shortly after the occupation became public in February 1995, the United States, while sticking to its traditional "neutral" line on the SCS disagreements, announced how it "strongly opposes the threat or use of military force to assert any nation's claim. The US takes no position on the legal merits of the competing claims and is willing to assist in the peaceful resolution of the dispute."[65] The Filipinos, believing that the US might react more decisively to the occupation of PHL territory, pressed politicians in Washington to support a response which might help Manila to attain its objectives vis-à-vis Mischief Reef.

A product of this pressure was the introduction of a Congressional resolution on March 10, 1995 (House Resolution 114) which was sponsored by Republican Congressman Benjamin A. Gilman. The resolution tabled those allied with the Philippines in Washington and cautioned the PRC against using threats or force within the Spratly group. It also reiterated the American stance that the "right of free passage through the South China Sea is in the national security interests of the US and its friends and allies." It likewise warned: "any attempt by a nondemocratic power to assert its claims to territory in such Sea is a matter of grave concern to the United States", that the PRC "must adhere faithfully to its commitment under the Manila Declaration of 1992", and that the US "should review the defense needs of democratic countries with claims to territory" in the South China Sea.[66] In addition, Congressman Gilman warned: "in order to avoid a future confrontation that we might lose, we had better shore up the defenses of our democratic friends and allies in the region." Gilman also referred directly to Mischief Reef when he

64 *Summary of World Broadcasts*; Raman, "Chinese Territorial Assertions."

65 United States Congressional Serial Set, 262; Raman, "Chinese Territorial Assertions."

66 Gilman, "Peace and Stability."

said that the Spratlys issue had come to a head "principally because last month Chinese military forces kidnapped Filipino citizens and planted the PRC flag on territory claimed by the Philippines." These "acts of aggression committed by the armed forces of the PRC against citizens of the Philippines are contrary to both international law and to peace and stability in East Asia." Progress at resolving the issue had been hampered primarily by "Beijing's intransigence", and by the fact that the Chinese leadership were "turning the South China Sea into their own lake." At home, the Clinton administration, he complained, appeared "to be absent without leave on the strategic issue of the South China Sea" and warned of scenarios in which US naval vessels and their allies might be "denied free passage during a time of emergency" thus hindering the ability of the USA to "expeditiously come to the aid of our allies" throughout the world.[67] In spite of this strongly worded appeal, a Senate Resolution of March 30, 1995 (agreed to on June 22, 1995) was more subdued than the House Resolution just three weeks earlier. It reminded "the claimants in the South China Sea that the United States does not take a position on any individual claim." It also repeated the US' "active support" for ASEAN's 1992 Manila Declaration while asking "all the claimants" to respect the declaration and to "refrain from using military force to assert or expand territorial claims in the South China Sea." Again, referring to developments on Mischief Reef, it called on all the disputants to "scrupulously observe the January 1995 status quo ante pending any negotiations or resolution of the conflicts between such claimants over such claims."[68]

Notwithstanding the Senate Resolution's diplomatic language, the US government showed signs of greater assertiveness on the issue. On May 10, 1995 its State Department made one of its strongest statements to date on the Spratly disputes when it declared.

> the US would view with serious concerns any maritime claim, or restriction on maritime activity in the South China Sea that was not consistent with international law, including the 1982 United Nations Convention on the Law of the Sea.[69]

[67] Ibid.

[68] US Senate Resolution 97, March 30, 1995.

[69] "Spratlys and the South China Sea," *US Department of State*; see also "US Warns Against Restriction."

The frictions which followed in the months after the Mischief Reef incident also spurred renewed debate within the US about the South China Sea disagreements. When scholars and researchers at the government-financed US Institute of Peace conducted a number of discussions on the disputes, they came up with five conclusions concerning the PRC's activities and objectives in the area. These were:

a. that energy resources were not the main driving force behind China's actions, but a desire to display its sovereignty in the area;
b. for historic and strategic reasons, the Chinese appreciated the vulnerability that an undefended SCS posed to the nation's southern coast, and PRC control in the SCS would constitute a key ring of defense against attack emanating from the south-east;
c. contrary to some perspectives, the PRC's SCS strategy was backed by the CCP leadership and should not be dismissed as rogue behavior by recalcitrant factions or elements within PLAN;
d. for the foreseeable future, the rising PRC's reliance on foreign investment would prevent a trend of "adventurist action" to strengthen China's claims position; and
e. the Chinese felt that time and circumstances were in their favor in the long-run and that other priorities existed, such as Taiwan. As such, it would be prudent to wait.[70]

With the benefit of hindsight, it appears as though many of these conclusions were accurate. The issue of motivations and objectives are discussed later.

The heightened level of US-China tensions was also evidenced in statements made by Joseph Nye, the Assistant Secretary of Defense for International Security Affairs, to a group of Japanese journalists on June 16, 1995. Nye asserted that if military activities in the Spratlys resulted in the interruption of freedom of navigation (FON) then Washington would take the necessary action to restore normality.[71] The Pentagon tried to downplay Nye's comments. However, defense analysts interpreted them as "the first time there's been mention of the physical involvement of

[70] *Indian Defence Review* 14 (1999), 60; Raman, "Chinese Territorial Assertions."

[71] "Jolt from the Blue," *Far Eastern Economic Review*, 22.

America in a possible conflict" in the Spratly Islands and wider South China Sea.[72]

In July 1995 and in advance of a late July ARF meeting, the visit of Indonesia's Foreign Minister, Ali Alatas, to Beijing for discussions on the aggravated situation in the Spratlys, impressed further in the minds of the PRC's decision makers the seriousness with which the region was taking the incident. This was the first visit by a high profile Indonesian political figure to China since the restoration of diplomatic ties in 1990. Later that same month, Washington finally turned its assurances of help into action when US Navy commandos visited the headquarters of the PHL's Western Military Command in Palawan, the nearest undisputed Filipino territory to Mischief Reef, for the purposes of training Filipino military personnel.[73] US military forces and PHL navy special task forces also participated in joint exercises to the west of Palawan.[74] They were tasked with defending Spratly features which were still administered by the Philippines. The two countries also engaged in a joint study on how best to protect PHL territory and how the US could be of assistance. Within the Filipino Parliament, a number of politicians, including the Speaker of the House of Representatives, Jose de Venecia, pondered on the question of reinviting US naval vessels to utilize the Subic Bay port for repairs and refitting. While the Filipinos sought American assistance, there was still internal resistance to luring US forces back to a pre-1992 security arrangement. The response of the government at that time to the idea was thus a polite refusal.[75]

When the Chinese carried out naval exercises in the Yellow Sea in late October 1995, President Ramos used the occasion to once again condemn the take-over of Mischief Reef and to emphasize his country's displeasure with the PRC by declaring: "The Philippines cannot be put completely at ease in our bilateral relations with China until the situation in the Panganiban Reef (Mischief Reef) in our Kalayaan group of islands is completely normalized."[76]

[72] Ibid.

[73] *Far Eastern Economic Review* 157, 87; Raman, "Chinese Territorial Assertions."

[74] "Manila Terms Spratly Exercises."

[75] *Far Eastern Economic Review* 157, 87; Raman, "Chinese Territorial Assertions."

[76] "Manila Sees China as Threat," *Reuters*; "Ramos Wary," *United Press International*.

China's Response

Both the Indonesian visit and the stepping up of US-Filipino cooperation as well as the possibility of a return to the region by the US military spurred the Chinese to intensify their efforts at reassuring their neighbours. During a meeting of the Second ARF Forum in late July (July 28–August 1) in Bandar Seri Begawan in Brunei, the group's Foreign Ministers found Qian Qichen, the PRC Foreign Minister, more flexible and eager to calm the waters. Notably, the PRC representative stated that China was willing to approach the SCS disagreements multilaterally. However, the Foreign Minister also repeated his country's "indisputable sovereignty" in the area and stood against any interference from non-ASEAN members or other external players. On a positive note, he declared in his opening remarks that Beijing was open to accepting international law, including UNCLOS, as the starting point for negotiations. This opened up the possibility of resolving or at least managing the disputes. China's insistence on indisputable sovereignty over the Spratly group did, however, beg the question of how sincere its words were, or its willingness to make concessions in the interest of a peaceful resolution. In subsequent discussions, the Chinese stated that their willingness to use international law such as UNCLOS as a guideline for negotiations should not be misconstrued as an acceptance of the EEZ and continental shelf claims of the other claimants.[77]

Nonetheless, the Chinese and the Filipinos displayed their ability to move forward following two rounds of bilateral discussions (on August 9 and 10) with the setting up of an agreed code of conduct (CoC), the *Joint Statement on PRC-RP Consultations on the South China Sea and On Other Areas of Cooperation*, which was signed on August 11, 1995.[78] The code asked that the two neighbours settle their disputes in a "peaceful and friendly manner through consultations on the basis of equality and mutual respect." They also announced plans to explore the possibility of joint developments and joint management of disputed features in the area.[79] In addition, the code saw Beijing and Manila agree to support approaches in accordance with UNCLOS. This helped to de-escalate the situation and

[77] Buszynski, "ASEAN's New Challenges," 573; "ASEAN-China: South-East Asia Hopes," *Inter-Press Service*.

[78] *Joint Statement PRC and RP*.

[79] "Mischief Reef and 'Love Me Tender'," *Philippine Daily Inquirer*.

took the heat out of the dispute which had dominated relations over the previous six months.[80] Key points in the CoC included the following commitments: (a) the dispute should not destabilize normal relations between the two countries; (b) to refrain from using or threatening force to resolve the dispute; (c) a progressive and gradual process of cooperation leading to a settlement; (d) to find a resolution based on international law including UNCLOS; (e) both sides should keep an open mind in relation to multilateral cooperation; (f) to the promotion of safe navigation and the prevention of piracy; (g) to the protection of the marine environment and the conservation of resources; and (h) that Spratly disputes should be directly resolved by the claimants concerned without affecting freedom of navigation.[81] Following a conversation between PHL President Ramos and the PRCFM's Wang Yingfan after the code was signed, Ramos expressed his belief that the negotiations had been a success and that consultations in the future were possible.[82]

From the Filipino perspective, the code was viewed as a step in the right direction because it included assurances on no further changes to the status quo in the Kalayaans, a non-binding suspension of any further constructions or upgrades on contested features, and prior notification with regards to naval activities in the area. Central to the code was the non-use of force, confidence-building bilateral cooperation, and the freedom of navigation. As observed by Storey, for Manila, even though PRC structures remained on the reef, they nonetheless were now content that China's activities had been contained and tensions had been significantly reduced.[83] Commenting at the conclusion of the negotiations, Severino conceded that despite progress, the Philippines had failed to persuade the PRC to dismantle the structures on the reef.[84] As later events would show, Manila's hopes of putting a halt to any further Chinese activities on the reef were to be dashed.

[80] Emmers, "Maritime Disputes," 52–53.

[81] "China Assures RP," *Manila Bulletin*, 6.

[82] Swanstrom, "Conflict Management and Negotiations," 111.

[83] Storey, "Creeping Assertiveness," 105.

[84] "Manila, Beijing Agree," *Reuters*.

The Occupation's After-Effect

Manila's constrained reaction to what was in effect a quiet occupation of a feature within its own EEZ was no doubt influenced by military and strategic realities. As one of the most poorly-equipped and poorly-funded naval forces among the Spratly disputants, the Philippines simply did not have the means with which to force the Chinese to withdraw from Mischief Reef and its surrounding waters. As such, it chose to adopt a three-pronged diplomatic strategy based on: (a) bilateral talks with the PRC; (b) petitioning regionally through ASEAN and ARF; and (c) encouraging international support with particular emphasis on the US, the UN, and Japan.[85] Valencia et al. observed that despite shows of force, in reality Manila's basic strategy was to portray the dispute as a multilateral rather than a bilateral issue and to garner international support for their position. Other proposals by the Filipinos included the demilitarization of the area, and that, as an interim solution, a disputed feature be placed under the stewardship of the claimant state that is geographically closest to it. This latter idea would also see the steward permitting other claimant states to utilize a feature for shelter, anchorage, or other peaceful activities.[86] Beijing completely rejected the proposals. Manila also proposed that the waters around disputed features should be designated a marine reserve.[87]

The country similarly soon realized that as far as Washington was concerned, as mentioned, the 1951 US-Philippines Mutual Defense Treaty did not extend to the Kalayaan area, which had been annexed in the 1970s but was located outside the main PHL islands. US forces therefore would not involve themselves in any attempted removal of PLAN ships and personnel from the area. The US did, however, condemn the use of military force against the Philippines (without actually naming China), and provided succor to Manila with assurances of extra military aid and training.[88] It also made a declaration on the freedom of navigation in the South China Sea. Nonetheless, such assurances could not undo the fact that Mischief Reef was now lost, with the Chinese showing no signs of moving from it.

[85] Chung, "The Spratly Islands Dispute," 242.

[86] "Demilitarization of Spratly Islands," *Foreign Broadcast Information Service*, 51.

[87] "Marine Reserve Status Proposed," *Foreign Broadcast Information Service*, 60.

[88] Klare, *Resource Wars*, 125.

Storey argues that the feature's takeover was part of a dual strategy of negotiation and occupation[89] adopted by China, which was influenced by domestic political realities within the PRC. Militarily, the timing was favorable because the AFP was too weak to make an effective response, and with the non-committal US having disengaged from the Philippines, the possibility of an armed confrontation over the sovereignty of a submerged reef—not directly tied to US national interest and backed up by questionably weak claims on both sides—would have been low. Under such circumstances and with a rush on occupation and exploration activities elsewhere in the Spratly Islands, military planners within PLAN may have felt that the summer of 1994 was a suitable time in which to quietly grab Mischief Reef.[90]

Following the incident, the Filipinos had no choice but to resort to pressuring and condemning China at the courts of regional and international opinion. ASEAN was an obvious choice by virtue of the fact that the Philippines was a member state, and because a number of its members had claims to sections of the Spratly Islands, many had serious concerns about PRC activities and intentions in the area. At a meeting in July 1995, ASEAN collectively denounced the use of military force in the South China Sea, and declared that all disputants should resolve their disagreements by diplomacy. Beijing tried to ease concerns amid a downturn in ties with its neighbours, as well as with Japan and the US, by assuring regional states that it would strive for a resolution of the issue with Manila and would, to the best of its ability, eschew military force in the future. The Chinese, however, remained steadfast on the issue of sovereignty and would not countenance any talk of surrendering Mischief Reef or any other occupied feature.[91] This position essentially remains the same today.

The occupation's effect on ASEAN was also apparent. The PRC's bold and seemingly unprovoked occupation of a feature claimed by a member state sent ripples through the organization. Before 1995, the regional grouping tended to steer clear of agreeing to anything concrete

[89] Fisher refers to this apparent pattern of behavior by China as "grab and talk" whereby the Chinese engaged in an act of territorial acquisition and then followed with prolonged diplomatic activity. See Fisher, "Rebuilding the US-Philippine Alliance," *The Heritage Foundation*, 6.

[90] Storey, "Creeping Assertiveness," 95.

[91] Klare, *Resource Wars*, 125–126.

or binding on the South China Sea. The incident forced a change of heart, at least temporarily, within ASEAN about its hitherto overly cautious approach towards Beijing. For example, just over a month since Manila publicly disclosed the PRC presence on the reef, and two days in advance of a bilateral Sino-Filipino meeting in Beijing (March 18, 1995), ASEAN issued a unanimous declaration asking that all disputants in the SCS should adhere to the spirit and the letter of the 1992 Manila Declaration. The occupation represented a watershed for observers such as ASEAN because, as noted by Raman, it was the first occasion in which a rising China had "unilaterally changed the status quo at the expense of a claimant other than Vietnam and covertly established its presence in waters and in an area claimed by the Philippines as falling within its Exclusive Economic Zone."[92] Contrary to Beijing's strategic objectives in the area, the occupation also attracted a number of powerful outside players into the South China Sea equation. The most notable of these were the US, Japan, and the European Union (EU). The strong and unified response by ASEAN to the incident surpassed the expectations of those few who sanctioned the occupation and later the wider Chinese leadership, who imagined a limited response or none at all. On a positive note, this collective response compelled the Chinese to do more to engage and reassure ASEAN and to rethink how it approached the regional group.[93]

As a result of the occupation, southeast Asian states as well as the US and Japan and other interested players in the region began to think more carefully about how they viewed the rising China's objectives in the Spratlys. This was particularly the case with the PHL, who up until then generally felt no immediate threat from the "distant" PRC. When the Chinese took control of Mischief Reef by stealth and then held it with force, they destroyed the myth that the military element of the disputes were an exclusively China–Vietnam affair. The PRC's action sent a clear signal that China would assert its sovereignty against any claimant in the disputes, and not just Vietnam. The build-up of China-related maritime frictions over Taiwan, the East China Sea, and the South China Sea represented by incidents such as seen on Mischief Reef and the Taiwan Crisis in 1995 likewise pushed the US and its ally, Japan,

[92] Raman, "Chinese Territorial Assertions."

[93] Meyer, "Incident at Mischief Reef," 19.

towards eventually strengthening their ability to protect vital interests in the region. Most notable of these is the freedom of navigation and the security of vessels which pass through the maritime areas and vital SLOCs connecting Northeast Asia with the Middle East. This is a key strategic issue for an island state such as Japan, dependent upon seaborne supplies of essential goods and resources. As argued by Klare, both Washington and Tokyo thus placed a higher priority on their capabilities to respond to incidents, to project force, and to manage problems in key maritime areas. This was exemplified in the year after the Mischief Reef incident when the Japanese published the 1996 "National Defense Program Outline", which represented the first major revision of Japan's security policy in two decades, and which greatly alarmed the Chinese. The US was, throughout the 1970s and up until 1995, largely uninvolved and non-committal in terms of the SCS disputes. Mischief Reef however, while not altering the US position of neutrality vis-à-vis the competing claims, did convince American policymakers to review their once comfortable view of China in the SCS. A product of this was, as mentioned earlier, Washington's first ever official statement on May 10, 1995 on the Spratly disagreements, which declared that the US "strongly opposes the use of force to resolve competing claims" and "unilateral actions" by any of the various disputants.[94] Crucially, a central plank of the statement was the US commitment to maintaining the freedom of navigation and referring to this as a fundamental interest for Washington. No longer just spinning its old line about neutrality with regards to rival claims, the Americans were now tacitly declaring that they would physically resist any moves by the Chinese or any other player that could threaten freedom of navigation in the area.[95]

The incident also painfully illustrated how the PHL was now the most vulnerable of all the Spratly claimants and of how once the US had disengaged from the Philippines, a major deterrent against the use of force by the PRC in the eastern Spratly Kalayaan area had been removed. Manila had little choice but to resort to limited diplomatic pressure and symbolic retaliatory actions such as the removal of PRC territorial markers and the arrest of Chinese fishermen in the spring of 1995. Forced to act after

[94] "Spratlys and the South China Sea," *US Department of State*; see also "US Warns Against Restrictions," *Straits Times*.

[95] Klare, *Resource Wars*, 126, 131–133.

the horse had already bolted from the barn, the Filipinos commenced a defense modernization program aimed at addressing its security weaknesses.[96] Given the initial negative ramifications caused by the occupation of a relatively minor submerged reef repeatedly raises the question of why China chose to take control of the feature when it did.

It is also important to consider the implications of developments after the 1994–1995 occupation. Following a bilateral code of conduct (CoC) agreement in August 1995, it shows how Manila and Beijing attempted to stabilise ties. This code of conduct, however, did not herald a new beginning: evidence emerged of China disobeying the CoC, and both sides persisted in claims and counter-claims with occasional clashes. It explains how problems arose over selective interpretations of UNCLOS, frustrating other claimants, and placing doubts on Beijing's commitment to resolving the dispute. Despite this, both states eventually sought to reduce tensions, resulting in a conflict-prevention agreement in June 1997, and a China-ASEAN joint statement on the SCS in December 1997. In February 1998, Manila reversed a 1992 decision and signed a "Visiting Forces Agreement" (VFA), with the USA (ratified by the PHL Senate in May 1999), signaling a hedging strategy. The failure of this strategy was reflected in the "Second Mischief Reef Incident" (also known as "Mischief Reef II") in late 1998 when the PRC began to construct much more extensive structures on the reef. Manila's suspicions of a deceitful "creeping invasion" and empty gesturing were also noted and elucidated, and the weaker PHL's limited options are also considered. China's decision to reinforce its presence on the reef did not go unnoticed, nor did the relatively tame response by the US and ASEAN member states despite Manila's calls for concrete measures. This demonstrates how this second incident brought home to the Philippines the bitter reality of Mischief Reef's irretrievable loss and its sense of being like "an orphan" in its campaign to elicit outside involvement. The cautious optimism that followed an ASEAN-led "Declaration on a Code of Conduct" for maritime disputes in November 2002 is also interesting, including its shortcomings. Contrasting scholarly arguments regarding the PRC's strategic objectives are also worth considering, as well as the incentives and restraints that influenced its behaviour, and related Spratly Island developments since the late 1990s. Also of interest is the Philippines'

[96] Emmers, "Maritime Disputes," 52–53.

international arbitral tribunal case against China at the Hague (initiated in January 2013), China's extensive island building activities on Mischief Reef in subsequent years, and the tribunal's landmark findings against China's presence and behaviour on the reef in July 2016.

Life After Occupation

Following the August 1995 signing of a code of conduct between the two countries, the dangerous tit-for-tat pattern following the initial Filipino discovery of PRC structures gradually died down, and both Manila and Beijing attempted to return the relationship to a more normal footing. A noteworthy consequence of the frictions that followed the first Mischief Reef incident was a warming in relations between Manila and Hanoi although these should not be overstated. This was reflected on November 7, 1995 when both countries published a Joint Statement on the Fourth Annual Bilateral Consultations at the end of three days of talks on how to manage disagreements in the Spratlys. On December 3, 1995 the Vietnamese President Le Duc Ahn expressed his agreement with PHL Speaker Jose de Venecia's appeal to reduce arms in the area.[97] Such endeavors by the Filipinos complemented President Ramos' later call at the ASEAN Summit in Bangkok, Thailand (December 14–15) to "demilitarize the Spratly Islands in the South China Sea as a matter of regional necessity."[98]

In 1996, the AFP stated that the facilities on Mischief Reef had been upgraded in the period from March to May and now included "electronic equipment."[99] Despite the occasional incident however, the year 1996 was one of relative calm in relation to Mischief Reef. This may have been attributable to the PRC being distracted with more pressing problems and crises involving Taiwan in the mid-1990s. The August 1995 code of conduct, however, did not herald a new beginning for Sino-Filipino ties. Both sides persisted in their pattern of claim and counter-claim, resulting in occasional clashes near features such as Mischief Reef. January 1996, for example, witnessed a minor skirmish between AFP and PLAN

[97] Lim, "Tempest," 88.

[98] "Demilitarize Spratlys," *Manila Bulletin*.

[99] "Military official Says China," *BBC Monitoring Service*; "Philippines Navy 'Not Alarmed'," *BBC Monitoring Service*.

warships in an area about 113 kms northwest of Manila.[100] Further frictions followed Beijing's ratification of UNCLOS in May 1996 because it also adopted a method for delineating its baselines and EEZ that is only reserved for archipelagic states such as the Philippines and Indonesia.[101] Manila angrily protested, claiming that the approach "disturbs the stability of the area and sets back the spirit of cooperation".[102] The move meant that China was expanding its baseline claim or the point at which a state can delineate its 12 mile territorial sea and 200 mile EEZ even further from the PRC mainland and beyond the Paracel Islands. By this action, Beijing formally increased its South China Sea territorial claims by a staggering 965,000 square miles.[103] Many criticized China for using what appeared to be a distorted interpretation of UNCLOS in order to emphasize its sovereignty over the South China Sea. It also placed serious doubts on the PRC's stated commitment to address the Spratly problems by using UNCLOS as a guideline. At the second China-ASEAN forum in Indonesia in June 1996, ASEAN aired its concerns about the move.[104] When Jiang Zemin made the first ever state visit by a PRC head of state to the Philippines in November 1996, President Ramos used the occasion to repeat the Filipino claim to Mischief Reef, following an Asia-Pacific Economic Cooperation (APEC) summit in Subic. Jiang's reply was to offer discussions on the possibility of joint development in the Spratlys.[105]

For the first two years after the occupation, the Philippines also still clung cautiously to Beijing's August 1995 code obligation that even though the structures on Mischief Reef would remain, it would not carry out any further unilateral actions within the Spratly group. Perhaps reflecting higher priorities elsewhere at the time involving Taiwan, in May 1996 Beijing reportedly instructed PLAN to keep its warships out of the Kalayaan area claimed by Manila. July saw the PHL's Defense Secretary Renato de Villa visit the PRC and agree on the exchange of defense

[100] The PHL navy reported on January 22, 1996 that one of their ships had been engaged in a 'gun battle' with PLAN vessels. Lasting about ninety minutes, it was later played down by Filipino President Ramos as relating to local smuggling activities by Chinese ships; see *Jane's Intelligence Review*, March 1, 1996.

[101] Guan, "The South China Sea," 2–3, 8–9.

[102] *Economist*, Issues 7964–7967, 37.

[103] "Manila Rebuffs Territorial Claim," *Financial Times*, 51.

[104] "China Backs Further Dialogue," *Bangkok Post*.

[105] Farolan, "Mischief Reef."

attaches for the first time since 1975, when the two countries established diplomatic ties. This was followed by a February 1997 visit to the PHL by the PRC's Defense Minister Chi Haotian in which the Chinese provided Manila with the equivalent of a three million US dollar military loan.[106] Tensions were raised in April 1997, however, when eight PLAN vessels were observed in waters close to the contested reef.[107]

In the same period, the Economist reported that three Chinese warships were spotted near the PHL administered islands of Lankiam Cay (also Panata; in Chinese Yangxin Shazhou) and Loaita (also Kota; in Chinese Nanyue Dao). The discovery of a "hut-like structure" on another nearby reef also raised concerns in Manila, and suggested that improved bilateral ties had not altered China's intentions in the area. In addition, it was clear that by 1997, the frequency of rival flags and markers being put up and pulled down on the disputed non-Spratly Scarborough Shoal (in Tagalo Kulumpol ng Panatag; in Chinese Huangyan)[108] only 220 kms off the main Filipino island of Luzon, had increased dramatically. Almost in tandem with the PRC warships sightings were reports of the Chinese State Oceanic Administration engaging in "joint international amateur radio exploration activities" and placing Chinese flags on the shoal. PHL naval vessels sailed toward the shoal and then replaced the hoisted flag with a Filipino one. Choosing not to clash with the Filipinos, the PRC ships left the area.[109]

When PHL military and congressional elites flew to Scarborough Shoal from May 17–18 to celebrate the ninety-ninth anniversary of the founding of the Filipino navy (May 20), they used the occasion to assert their claims with very publicized flag-waving. The Chinese protested the incident. The PRC's Foreign Ministry spokesman, Shen Guofang, for example, cautioned that the highly publicized trip was a "provocation against Chinese territorial sovereignty." To help prevent a further escalation in tensions, the two governments reached an agreement in June 1997 in which each side would notify the other in advance of any activity in

[106] "Warships Ordered," *South China Morning Post*; "Philippines to Sign Deal," *South China Morning Post*; "General Chi to Sign," *South China Morning Post*.

[107] Storey, "Creeping Assertiveness," 97; "Ramos Asserts Claim," *South China Morning Post*.

[108] For a concise account, see Zha and Valencia, "Mischief Reef: Geopolitics and Implications," 91.

[109] "Scraply Islands," *Economist*.

disputed areas. In December 1997, the Filipino parliament authorized the spending of 6.5 billion US dollars for the purpose of upgrading its still weak military capabilities, especially its naval power, which at that stage was simply no match to the increasingly stronger PLAN. In the same month, China and ASEAN also signed a joint statement on the South China Sea at the ASEAN Summit.[110] If anything, Chinese activities on and around contested features such as Mischief Reef and Scarborough Shoal after 1994–1995 pointed to an even stronger assertion of claims by the PRC, ones which Manila would have to counter if they hoped to defend "their" sovereign territory.

In early 1998, Washington and Manila signed a "Visiting Forces Agreement" (VFA) which permitted US naval vessels to anchor at PHL bases and to engage in exercises with the Philippine navy. This was a symbolic reversal of the decision made by the PHL Senate in 1992 to end the lease on the strategically placed Subic Bay Naval Base (and other facilities) to US forces. Despite the ramifications of the Mischief Reef affair, negotiations which led to this treaty were to be long and drawn out. In 1996, for example, the two countries had called a halt to all major military exercises until a more substantive and clearly defined agreement could be found. These talks would eventually bear fruit with the signing of the VFA on February 10, 1998. The treaty was then sent to the Philippine Senate for ratification in early October. It was only after the second major Mischief Reef incident of late 1998 and early 1999 that the agreement was finally ratified in late May 1999.[111] According to Swanstrom, this second incident, (commencing in late October[112] when construction activities began) was influenced in part by the detention of twenty-three Chinese fishermen by the Philippines in August 1998 on charges of intruding into the country's territorial waters (discussed below).[113]

[110] Ibid.

[111] Guan, "The South China Sea," 21.

[112] Joyner cites the beginning of the Second Mischief Reef Incident as late October 1998. See Joyner, "The Spratly Islands Dispute," 53. See also Tiglao et al., "Tis the Season."

[113] "Spratley Dispute Flares Again," *International Herald Tribune*.

The Second Mischief Reef Incident (Mischief Reef II)

Manila had decided in early 1998 to install more lighthouses on features in the Kalayaan area in order to emphasize its claims. Due to diplomatic wrangling and competition between government departments over funding, however, the proposal was scrapped at the last minute, and building work stopped. As pointed out by one observer, in doing so the Philippines lost an opportunity to maximize its archipelagic waters in accordance with UNCLOS.[114] Renewed tensions over the Spratlys in the autumn of 1998 also did not help. Despite occasional bilateral and multilateral talks aimed at resolving the Mischief Reef issue as well as other disputed features claimed by the two countries, the character of these discussions was that of general assurances to refrain from the use of military force and promote expressions of goodwill, but little else. Indeed, Filipino suspicions of empty gesturing by Beijing seemed to be confirmed in late October 1998 when the PRC began to reinforce its facilities and to add more structures on the reef.[115] Manila condemned the activities as a violation of the August 1995 CoC. The PRC, however, maintained that they had told the Filipinos in advance (via the PHL Embassy in Beijing) on October 15, 1998 about their plan to conduct work on the existing 1994–1995 structures on the feature. Filipino fears were confirmed on October 29 when one of the air force planes recorded a new and substantial structure next to the original octagonal huts on Mischief Reef. One PHL politician, Roilo Golez, assessed, based on photos of the new structure, that "Beijing is gearing up for military operations."[116]

On November 11, Manila demanded that the new structures be dismantled. Using language that was both escalatory and naïve, President Joseph Estrada (June 1998–January 2001) told journalists on the same day: "I have already instructed the Chief of Staff to block the entry and exit points so that intruders will not be able to enter any more." November 11 also saw General Joselin Nazareno, Chief of Staff of the AFP send out a command to naval vessels in the area to fire a warning shot across the bow of any PRC vessel that came within five nms of Mischief

[114] Tordesillas, "Bring China's 9-Dash Line."

[115] Klare, *Resource Wars*, 126.

[116] Clapano, "China Builds Five More," *The Philippine Star*; Lim, "Tempest," 92–93.

Reef. However, he also instructed the Philippine Air Force (PAF) to not fly below 5000 feet of the feature so as to prevent a possible exchange of fire.[117]

On November 12, a spokesperson for the President, Jerry Barican, sought to downplay Estrada's earlier comments by emphasizing that the PHL leader had not said "blockade" but rather "block" thus only referring to an increase in aerial and naval patrols by the Philippines near the reef. The country's Secretary of Foreign Affairs Domingo Siazon Jr. attempted to reassure the PRC's Ambassador Guan Dengming that Estrada was misquoted. He nonetheless pressed the ambassador for answers as to why the Chinese were building again on Mischief Reef. As perhaps was expected, Guan responded that they were only carrying out repairs to some structures and that "they are not military structures." Guan also rejected the now Secretary of National Defense Orlando S. Mercado's charge of a "creeping invasion" by the PRC. Fortunately, despite the raised temperatures, violence was averted and the two sides focused on resolving their disagreements diplomatically. The Chinese leader Jiang Zemin reassured the Sixth Leaders' Summit of APEC in Kuala Lumpur, Malaysia (November 14–18) that his country would resolve the disputes peacefully. Again, such seeming contradictions placed doubts regarding the sincerity of Chinese diplomacy, and confirmed PHL assertions that Beijing's strategy was one of "talk and take."[118] Siazon and the PRC's Foreign Minister Tang Jiaxuan met on November 16 and both agreed to bring together a group of experts on confidence-building measures (CBMs) the following January as well as to examine China's proposal of "joint use". When leaders Estrada and Jiang met the next day, they also agreed to resolve their difference via diplomatic channels.[119] As Lim points out, the Filipino reaction to Beijing's "joint use" of the facilities on Mischief Reef proposal has been mixed. For example, while top decision makers like Foreign Affairs Secretary Siazon agreed in principle to "joint use" of fishing facilities on the reef, other elites

[117] "Navy Told," *The Philippine Star*; see also Lim, "Tempest," 92–93; "Memo on Spratlys Mission," *South China Morning Post*; Tiglao et al., "Tis the Season," 18; Baker and Wiencek, *Cooperative Monitoring*, 94.

[118] Joyner, "The Spratly Islands Dispute," 74.

[119] "Talks with Jiang," *The Philippine Star*; see also Lim, "Tempest," 92–93.

like Defense Secretary Mercado viewed such offers as a ploy that would severely weaken the Philippines' claim to Mischief Reef.[120]

The Chinese decision to act in late 1998 once again begged questions about the country's intentions for the Spratly Islands and why Beijing reinforced its presence on the reef in spite of the obvious consequences for positive relations with the Philippines. Manila's suspicions appeared valid given that construction activities on Mischief Reef were already well underway when Jiang made his statement in Kuala Lumpur. The new building work (which had started in late October) was discovered by PHL reconnaissance aircraft in early November after the most powerful tropical cyclone of the year, Typhoon Zeb (October 10–20), had dissipated. The aircraft also observed a number of Chinese ships that the Filipino government said included four military supply vessels. As many as one hundred workers were observed several days afterwards. The workers were there mostly to lay concrete foundations for new buildings on the atoll.[121]

Commenting on the move, B. A. Hamzah, an analyst at the Malaysian Institute of Maritime Affairs (MIMA), also cited the presence of warships as a potentially serious escalatory issue. In regard to developments in late 1998, he complained:

> Beijing has been very mischievous in sending warships to disputed territory in open violation of the bilateral code of conduct it signed with Manila.... It was very irresponsible and intimidating. China's recent action does not bode well for confidence-building and regional security.[122]

He also postulated that Mischief Reef II was the product of a PRC government decision.[123] Tiglao, et al. also cited an unnamed Western diplomat based in Beijing who expressed the opinion that the move emanated from pressure from the PLA. This was perhaps a sweetener by the central government for the PLA after the latter took steps to fundamentally alter civil-military relations in China by dissolving the military-business complex. Jiang initiated the policy on July 22, 1998,

[120] Avendano and Nazareno, "RP Agrees to Joint Use"; see also Lim, "Tempest," 92–93.

[121] Tiglao et al., "Tis the Season," 18; Baker and Wiencek, "Cooperative Monitoring," 94.

[122] Cited from Tiglao et al., "Tis the Season," 19.

[123] Ibid.

at a session of the Central Military Commission (CMC) by calling on the military and armed police to cease commercial activities in the future.[124]

The November 1998 surveillance photographs showed that the Chinese had, in spite of highly publicized good-will talks between the leaders of both states, recently built and in a quite expeditious fashion,[125] a three hundred meter pier, new barracks, and a type of communications command and control center in areas next to the original 1994–1995 structures. Filipino officials denounced the activities as of a substantial military nature given the obviously more permanent and fortified characteristic of the structures and the sizeable logistical support and protection provided by the PLAN. Manila also condemned it as a violation of the Code of Conduct of August 1995. As mentioned, they also cited it as further evidence of the PRC's surreptitious attempts to control features in the Spratlys through a strategy of "creeping invasion."[126]

One senior Department of Foreign Affairs official lamented that his country had effectively lost Mischief Reef for good because occupation and building structures on the feature meant that the PRC held sovereignty over it. He also complained that as long as there was a Chinese presence on the reef, then nothing would change regardless of the various attempts at mediation.[127] The country's Secretary for National Defense, Orlando Mercado, responded to the development with the warning: "Now they've expanded one structure, and they'll be reclaiming land along the reef to link with another structure to build an airstrip" and that "it will be the farthest projection of China's power, and a dagger at our underbelly."[128]

On November 30, a PHL official informed the press that the Filipino Navy had impounded six PRC fishing vessels and twenty crew members the day before in waters within the Philippines' EEZ at Alicia Anne Reef.[129] Given the timing, it might be viewed as perhaps the PHL hitting

124 Tiglao et al., "Tis the Season," 18; Mulvenon, 1.

125 Tiglao et al., "Tis the Season," 19.

126 A term first coined by former Philippine Defense Secretary Mercado: Baker, 7; Baker and Wiencek, *Cooperative Monitoring*, 94.

127 "Mischief Reef and 'Love Me Tender'," *Philippine Daily Inquirer*.

128 Tiglao et al., "Tis the Season," 18.

129 Lim, "Tempest," 93; Klare, *Resource Wars*, 126; see also "Timing of China's Move," *International Herald Tribune*.

back at China for its recent activities on Mischief Reef. Estrada's government also turned down calls from Beijing for the men's release and declared that they would be prosecuted under Filipino law for trespassing and illegal activities inside the state's territorial waters. As a result of these developments, tensions between the two states in disputed waters raised, a development exemplified by the sinking of a Chinese fishing boat and the ramming of an AFP navy gunboat.[130] In November, Estrada also used the occasion of the APEC summit in Kuala Lumpur to express his dissatisfaction with China's behaviour on the reef. As a result, it was here the two sides reached the compromise that would see the issue put before a panel of Chinese and Filipino experts, and where the bilateral cooperative use of the reef's facilities might be considered.[131] Nonetheless, as with previous compromises, such progress was largely symbolic without any substantial or tangible movement on a workable resolution. The approximate first ten years after the Mischief Reef II incident were years of stability and promise most notably represented by the landmark "Declaration on the Conduct of Parties in the South China Sea" in November 2002. As the next chapter shows, what was to follow was quite different.

References

"ASEAN-China: South-East Asia Hopes on Spratlys Row Raised." *Inter-Press Service*, July 25, 1995.

Avendano, Christine, and Rocky Nazareno. "RP Agrees to Joint Use of Spratlys." *Philippine Daily Inquirer*, November 21, 1998.

Baker, Carl. "China-Philippines Relations: Cautious Cooperation." *Asia-Pacific Center for Security Studies*, October 2004. https://apcss.org/Publications/SAS/AsiaBilateralRelations/China-PhilippinesRelationsBaker.pdf.

Baker, John C., and David G. Wiencek (eds.). *Cooperative Monitoring in the South China Sea: Satellite Imagery, Confidence-Building Measures and the Spratly Islands Disputes*. Westport, CT: Praeger, 2002.

"Beijing Extends Envoy's Term." *Foreign Broadcast Information Service* EAS-95-032.

Branigin, William. "China Takes Over Philippine-Claimed Area of Disputed Island Group." *The Washington Post*, February 11, 1995, A18.

Buszynski, Leszek. "ASEAN's New Challenges." *Pacific Affairs* 70, no. 4 (1997): 555–578.

[130] Klare, *Resource Wars*, 126.

[131] "Estrada, Jiang discuss," *Philippine Daily Inquirer*.

"China Asked to Cool Rhetoric." *Associated Press*, May 18, 1995.
"China Assures RP on Spratlys." *Manila Bulletin*, August 12, 1995.
"China Backs Further Dialogue but Proves Wary About Change." *Bangkok Post*, June 14, 1996.
"China Calms Regional Fears on Spratlys." *Associated Foreign Press* (Beijing), March 11, 1995.
"China Nibbles, ASEAN Dithers." *Wall Street Journal Asia*, March 10–11, 1995.
"Chinese Navy Detains Filipino fishermen in the Spratlys." *China News Digest*, January 24, 1995.
Chung, Christopher. *The Spratly Islands Dispute: Decision units and Domestic Politics*. Canberra: Australian Defence Force Academy: School of Humanities and Social Science, 2004. https://www.unsworks.unsw.edu.au/primo-explore/fulldisplay/unsworks_3198/UNSWORKS.
Clapano, Jose Radel. "China Builds Five More Structures in the Spratlys." *The Philippine Star*, November 13, 1998.
"Demilitarization of Spratly.Islands Endorsed." *Foreign Broadcast Information Service* EAS-95-031, February 15, 1995.
"Demilitarize Spratlys." *Manila Bulletin*, December 15, 1995.
Dzurek, Daniel J. "China Occupies Mischief Reef in Latest Spratly Gambit." *International Boundaries Research Unit Boundary and Security Bulletin*, April 1995, 65–71.
Economist 339, nos. 7964–7967 (1996).
Emmers, Ralf. "Maritime Disputes in the South China Sea—Strategic and Diplomatic Status Quo." In *Maritime Security in Southeast Asia*, edited by Kwa Chong Guan and John K. Skogan. Oxford: Routledge, 2007.
"Estrada, Jiang Discuss Mischief." *Philippine Daily Inquirer*, November 18, 1998.
Far Eastern Economic Review 157 (1994).
Far Eastern Economic Review, June 1, 1995.
Fisher, Richard D., Jr. "Rebuilding the US-Philippine Alliance." February 22, 1999, No. 1255. Backgrounder Executive Summary, The Asian Studies Center, The Heritage Foundation, Washington, DC, USA. https://thf_media.s3.amazonaws.com/1999/pdf/bg1255.pdf.
"For Our Eyes Only." *Far Eastern Economic Review*, July 27, 1995.
Fravel, M. Taylor. *Strong Borders, Secure Nation—Cooperation and Conflict in China's Territorial Disputes*. Princeton: Princeton University Press, 2008.
"General Chi to Sign." *South China Morning Post*, 1997.
Gilman, Benjamin A. "Peace and Stability in the South China Sea—Hon. Benjamin A. Gilman of New York in the House of Representatives, Friday, March 10, 1995." Congressional Record—Extension of Remarks, E577-E578, March 10, 1995. https://www.govinfo.gov/content/pkg/CREC-1995-03-10/pdf/CREC-1995-03-10-pt1-PgE577-3.pdf and https://www.congress.gov/bill/104th-congress/house-resolution/114/text.

Guan, Ang Cheng. "The South China Sea Dispute Re-visited." Working Paper No. 4, Institute of Defence and Strategic Studies, Singapore, Working Paper Series, August 1999. https://www.rsis.edu.sg/wp-content/uploads/rsis-pubs/WP04.pdf.

Indian Defence Review 14 (1999).

"Indonesia Calls for Peaceful Solution to Six-Nation Dispute over Spratlys." *Japan Times*, February 18, 1995.

Jane's Intelligence Review, March 1, 1996.

"Joint Statement PRC and RP." https://www.scribd.com/document/61125477/Joint-Statement-PRC-and-RP.

"Jolt from the Blue." *Far Eastern Economic Review*, August 3, 1995.

Journal of the United Service Institution of India 12 (1999).

Joyner, Christopher C. "The Spratly Islands Dispute in the South China Sea: Problems, Policies, and Prospects for Diplomatic Accommodation." In *Investigating Confidence-Building Measures in the Asia-Pacific Region*, edited by Ranjeet K. Singh, 53–108. Report No. 28, Henry L. Stimson Center, Washington, DC, USA. May 1999. https://www.stimson.org/wp-content/files/file-attachments/Investigating%20Confidence-Building%20Measures%20in%20the%20Asia-Pacific%20Region.pdf.

Kim, Duk-ki. *Naval Strategy in Northeast Asia: Geostrategic Goals, Policies and Prospects*. Cass Series: Naval Policy and History. Oxford (UK): Routledge, First Edition, 2000.

Klare, Michael T. *Resource Wars—The New Landscape of Global Conflict*. New York: Owl Books, 2001.

Lim, Benito. "Tempest Over the South China Sea: The Chinese Perspective on the Spratlys." *Asian Studies* 36, no. 2: 69–132. http://www.asj.upd.edu.ph/mediabox/archive/ASJ-36-2-2000/lim.pdf.

Mackerras, Colin. *The New Cambridge Handbook of Contemporary China*. Cambridge, UK: Cambridge University Press, 2001.

"Manila, Beijing Agree on Spratlys Code of Conduct." *Reuters*, August 10, 1995.

"Manila Charges China Still Intruding in Spratlys." *Honolulu Advertiser*, March 29, 1995.

"Manila Rebuffs Territorial Claim by Beijing." *Financial Times*, May 18, 1996.

"Manila Removes Markers." *Daily Report: People's Republic of China*, Issues 58–62. Foreign Broadcast Information Service, 1995. https://babel.hathitrust.org/cgi/pt?id=mdp.39015033804884&view=1up&seq=23.

"Manila Sees China as Threat Despite Assurances." *Reuters*, October 28, 1995.

"Manila Terms Spratly Exercises Simply Routine." *Wall Street Journal Asia*, July 25, 1995.

"Marine Reserve Status Proposed for Spratlys." *Foreign Broadcast Information Service* EAS-95-041, March 2, 1995.

Marso, Ed. "Manila Denies Provoking China." *United Press International*, May 17, 1995.

McCarthy, Terry. "Reef Wars." *Time Magazine*, March 8, 1999. http://content.time.com/time/world/article/0,8599,2054240,00.html.

"Memo on Spratlys Mission Delayed." *South China Morning Post*, November 10, 1998.

Meyer, Stanley E. (Lt.Col.). "Incident at Mischief Reef: Implications for the Philippines, China, and the United States." *USAWC Strategy Research Project*, US Army War College, January 1996.

"Mischief Reef and 'Love Me Tender'." *Philippine Daily Inquirer*, July 18, 2011. http://opinion.inquirer.net/7987/mischief-reef-and-%E2%80%98love-me-tender%E2%80%99.

"Military Official Says China Upgrading Structures on Mischief Reef." *BBC Monitoring Service*, Asia Pacific, March 5, 1996.

"Military Finds No Trace of Chinese Naval Base." *The Philippine Star*, January 26, 1995.

Mulvenon, James. "PLA Divestiture and Civil-Military Relations: Implications for the Sixteenth Party Congress Leadership." December 2001. China Leadership Monitor, No. 1, Part 2. *Hoover Institution*, Stanford, CA, USA. https://www.hoover.org/sites/default/files/uploads/documents/clm2_JM1.pdf.

"Navy Told: Fire at Chinese Ships If..." *The Philippine Star*, November 12, 1998.

Odgaard, Liselotte. *Maritime Security Between China and Southeast Asia: Conflict and Cooperation in the Making of Regional Order*. Farnham, UK: Ashgate Publishing, 2002.

People's Republic of China Daily Report, Issue 58–62, *United States Foreign Broadcast Information Service*, 1995.

"Philippine Leader Defends Spratlys Tour to China." *Reuters*, May 15, 1995.

"Philippine Navy Holds Chinese Fishermen. *Reuters*, March 26, 1995.

"Philippines Navy 'Not Alarmed' by New Chinese Structures on Disputed Reef." *BBC Monitoring Service*, Asia Pacific, May 22, 1996.

"Philippine Navy Seizes Vessels." *Associated Press*, March 25, 1995.

"Philippines Says ASEAN Has One Voice on Spratlys." *Reuters*, April 5, 1995.

"Philippines Says Spratlys Dispute May Be Taken to the U.N., World Court." *Japan Times*, February 14, 1995.

"Philippines Security Based on US Presence—Francisco Tatad, Philippine Senate Majority Leader." *Asia Times*, June 6, 1997.

"Philippines to Boost Forces on Spratlys." *Japan Times*, February 16, 1995.

"Philippines to Build Lighthouses on the Spratlys." *Reuters*, June 14, 1995.

"Philippines to Sign Deal." *South China Morning Post*, July 1, 1996.

"Philippines Warns of Increased Chinese Military Acts on Disputed Islands." *Agence France-Presse ASIA*, January 19, 1999.

Raman, Bahukutumbi. “Chinese Territorial Assertions: the case of Mischief Reef.” Warfighter (blog), January 14, 1999. http://www.warfighter.org/mischief.html.

“Ramos Asserts Claim to Outcrop.” *South China Morning Post*, November 18, 1997.

“Ramos Orders More Troops to Spratlys.” *Foreign Broadcast Information Service* EAS-95-031, February 15, 1995.

“Ramos Stresses Peaceful Spratlys Solution.” *Foreign Broadcast Information Service* EAS-95-066, April 6, 1995.

“Ramos Trying to Get US Military Back, Say Lawmakers.” *Straits Times*, October 22, 1995.

“Ramos Welcomes U.S. Bilateral Naval Exercises.” *Foreign Broadcast Information Service* EAS-95-036, February 23, 1995/.

“Ramos Wary of Chinese Peace Promises,” United Press International, October 28, 1995.

“Scraply Islands.” *The Economist*, May 22, 1997. https://www.economist.com/asia/1997/05/22/scraply-islands.

Severino, Rodolfo C. “ASEAN and the South China Sea.” *Security Challenges* 6, no. 2 (Winter 2010): 37–47. https://www.jstor.org/stable/26459936.

Severino, Rodolfo C. “Southeast Asia in Search of an ASEAN Community—Insights from the Former ASEAN Secretary General.” *Institute of Southeast Asian Studies*, Singapore, 2006.

Song, Yann-huei. “Managing Potential Conflicts in the South China Sea: Taiwan’s Perspective.” East Asian Institute (EAI) Contemporary China Series: Occasional Paper 14, National University of Singapore (NUS), Singapore University Press, April 1999.

“Spratlys and the South China Sea.” US Department of State, Washington, DC, May 10, 1995.

“Spratley Dispute Flares Again.” *International Herald Tribune*, December 1, 1998.

“Spratlys Dispute Flaring.” *Voice of America*, May 11, 1995.

“Spratlys Tension Helps Push Forces Upgrade.” *Jane’s Defence Weekly*, February 25, 1995. http://articles.janes.com/articles/Janes-Defence-Weekly-95/SPRATLYS-TENSION-HELPS-PUSH-FORCES-UPGRADE.html.

“Statement by the ASEAN Foreign Ministers on the Recent Developments in the South China Sea, 18 March 1995.” *Association of Southeast Asian Nations*. http://www.aseansec.org/2089.htm.

Storey, Ian James. “Creeping assertiveness: China, the Philippines, and the South China Sea dispute.” *Contemporary Southeast Asia* 21, no. 1 (April 1999): 95–119.

Storey, Ian. *ASEAN and the Rise of China—The Search for Security*. Oxford: Routledge, 2011.

Summary of World Broadcasts: Asia Pacific, *BBC*, Volumes 2304–2317: 3373–3384.
Swanstrom, Niklas. "Conflict Management and Negotiations in the South China Sea: The ASEAN Way?" January 1999, 93–125. Institute for Security and Development Policy, Nacka, Sweden. https://isdp.eu/content/uploads/publications/2001_swanstrom_conflict-management-and-egotiations.pdf.
"Talks with Jiang Defuse Tensions Over Spratlys." *The Philippine Star*, November 19, 1999.
Tasker, Rodney. "A Line in the Sand." *Far Eastern Economic Review*, April 6, 1995, 14–16.
Tiglao, Rigoberto. "Bold Move, 'Insanity' or Stock Market Play?" *The Manila Times*, October 19, 2020. https://www.manilatimes.net/2020/10/19/opinion/columnists/topanalysis/bold-move-insanity-or-stock-market-play/782298/.
Tiglao, Rigoberto. "Troubled Waters." *Far Eastern Economic Review*, June 30, 1994.
Tiglao, Rigoberto, Andrew Sherry, and Michael Vatikiotis. "Tis the Season, Policy and Politics, South China Sea." *Far Eastern Economic Review*, December 24, 1998.
"Timing of China's Move on Spratleys Raises Asian Suspicions." *International Herald Tribune*, December 2, 1998.
Tordesillas. Ellen. "Bring China's 9-Dash Line to UN: Justice Carpio." *GMA News Online*, November 8, 2011. https://www.gmanetwork.com/news/opinion/content/237813/bring-china-s-9-dash-line-to-un-justice-carpio/story/.
"U.S. Asks China to cool Rhetoric." *Associated Press*, May 17, 1995.
United States Congressional Serial Set 262.
US House of Representatives Resolution 114. "Expressing the Sense of the House of Representatives that the United States should support peace and stability in the South China Sea." 104th Congress, introduced March 10, 1995. https://www.congress.gov/member/benjamin-gilman/G000212?searchResultViewType=expanded&q=%7B%22type%22%3A%5B%22joint-resolutions%22%2C%22resolutions%22%5D%7D&pageSize=100&page=2.
US Senate Resolution 97 (S.Res 97). "S.Res.97—A Resolution Expressing the Sense of the Senate with Respect to Peace and Stability in the South China Sea." 104th Congress, introduced March 30, 1995. https://www.congress.gov/bill/104th-congress/senate-resolution/97/summary/00.
"U.S. Stays Neutral in R.P.-China Spratly Dispute." *Japan Times*, February 15, 1995.
"US Warns Against Restriction in the South China Sea." *Straits Times*, May 12, 1995.

Valencia, Mark J., Jon M. Van Dyke, and Noel A. Ludwig. *Sharing the Resources of the South China Sea*. Honolulu: University of Hawai'i Press, 1997.
"Warships Ordered to Avoid Spratlys." *South China Morning Post*, May 11, 1996.
"Who Knew What?" *Far Eastern Economic Review* 158 (April 6, 1995).
"Why China Is Creating Mischief in the Spratlys." *Straits Times*, April 7, 1995.
Wroe, David. "Making Mischief in the South China Sea." *Sydney Morning Herald*, July 15, 2016. https://www.smh.com.au/politics/federal/making-mischief-in-the-south-china-sea-20160715-gq6knp.html.
Zha, Daojiong, and Mark J. Valencia. "Mischief Reef: Geopolitics and Implications." *Journal of Contemporary Asia* 31, no. 1 (2001): 86–103.

CHAPTER 6

The Occupation in the 2000s

Abstract This chapter discusses Mischief Reef developments since the late 1990s. First, it examines China's decision to reinforce its position on the reef in 1998 and of how the shifting regional balance of power in favor of China impacted approaches to the dispute. It considers fluctuations in Manila's relationship with both the US and China. It also discusses the strategic context behind "Mischief Reef II" in 1998. The chapter looks at the factors that contributed to a relatively peaceful period of stability from the late 1990s until the late 2000s. The cautious optimism that followed an ASEAN-led "Declaration on a Code of Conduct" for maritime disputes in 2002 and progress on joint resource exploration is then examined. It shows how potentially dangerous incidents, "salami slicing" strategies and "cabbage tactics" by China in particular, and behaviour designed to emphasize and exaggerate claims continued to complicate this dispute. The chapter also examines the China's extensive construction work on the reef, creating "facts in the water", especially between 2013 and 2016. The import of a ruling against China's legal claims and activities by an international arbitral tribunal in July 2016 also receives attention, illustrating the challenges involved in finding a legal resolution.

Keywords ASEAN · Confidence-Building Measures · Declaration on the Code of Conduct of Parties in the South China Sea (DoC) · Island

S. Fox, *Mischief Reef*,
https://doi.org/10.1007/978-981-16-3884-8_6

building · Second Mischief Reef Incident (Mischief Reef II) · Sino-US relations · South China Sea Arbitration

China's Decision to Act

As mentioned in Chapter 5, some sources contend that Mischief Reef II was influenced in part by the detention of twenty-three Chinese fishermen by the Philippines in August 1998 on charges of intruding into the country's territorial waters (discussed below).[1] On August 5, 1998, US and Filipino warships and aircraft had also engaged in live-fire military exercises near the contested Scarborough Shoal. According to Lim, these followed a rejection by the PHL of an offer from China to permit Filipino fishermen to use PRC facilities on Mischief Reef.[2]

It is also important to position the second Mischief Reef incident within a wider context. For some observers, Beijing's decision to build new structures on the contested feature in late 1998 and early 1999 illustrated a Chinese penchant for capitalizing on favourable strategic opportunities, for instance when South China Sea rivals are weakened or distracted. The ten-day visit of President Clinton to the PRC in late June and early July 1998 and his public reiteration of a "Three Nos" policy in regards to Taiwan,[3] for example, were viewed by many Chinese elites as an acknowledgement of the country's new great power status in the region. The years 1997 and 1998 also witnessed a general improvement in US attitudes towards the PRC and a greater appreciation of its economic prowess. The inauguration of Joseph Estrada[4] as President of the Philippines in late June 1998 was also seen by some as perhaps heralding a worsening of bilateral ties vis-à-vis Mischief Reef.[5] This may

[1] "Spratley Dispute Flares Again," *International Herald Tribune*.

[2] Lim, "Tempest," 91.

[3] This policy declared the US did not support Taiwanese independence nor a 'one China, one Taiwan' or 'Two Chinas' solution, and would not support Taiwan's membership of international organizations which comprise of sovereign states; see *China-Embassy.org*.

[4] Estrada is sometimes referred to by his nickname "Erap" in a number of sources in this chapter.

[5] Lim, "Tempest," 89.

have strengthened the hand of those advocating a harder line on the Chinese side.

The regional economic depression, discussed below and which commenced in July 1997, had a destabilizing influence on both individual regional states and on ASEAN's ability to speak with one voice. The crisis aggravated already extant strains between member states and thus undermined group unity, temporarily incapacitated the regional body, and financially hampered the ability of states to counter China's military modernization program. This program had accelerated in the mid to late 1990s and was in part influenced by the lessons learned from the Third Taiwan Crisis in 1995–1996 when the PRC, its navy in particular, was humiliated by its own inability to keep US forces out and militarily influencing outcomes that were unfavourable to Beijing. China's "valued contribution" in dealing with the financial crisis as well as the integration of new ASEAN members Cambodia, Laos, Myanmar, and Vietnam are also cited as distractions and reasons for the muted response to the Second Mischief Reef incident. In Washington, conservative and hawkish US politicians, who might normally have been calling for a stronger line against the rising PRC, were distracted domestically by the proceedings surrounding the impeachment trial of President Clinton (late 1998–early 1999) and externally by the Kosovo crisis (February 1998–June 1999). Problems involving Iraq (late 1998) and North Korea (Autumn 1998) as well as conflict prevention following nuclear weapons testing by India and Pakistan (May 1998) were also high on the agenda. In Japan, political party instability and an economic recession kept Tokyo busy and firmly focused on problems at home.[6]

These factors in the Chinese decision to act on the reef in late 1998 are different from 1995 in that the motivation this time was largely informed by a favourable opportunity for the PRC to reinforce its position in the area and to advance foreign policy and security policy objectives. Domestic politics on this occasion were less of an influence, though not completely a non-issue for reasons explained later. This was because by October 1998, succession politics in China were not a major factor. Jiang Zemin had successfully navigated the stormy waters of the leadership transition and was accepted domestically and internationally as the country's

[6] Chung, "The Spratly Islands Dispute," 278–279; Chase et al., "China's Incomplete Military Transformation,"13–14; Tiglao et al., "Tis the Season," 18; Joyner, "The Spratly Islands Dispute," 73–74.

leader. The PLA's influence had weakened relative to the early to mid-1990s, and Jiang had consolidated his position at the top through the appointment of loyal figures to the upper echelons of the Central Military Commission (CMC).[7]

A Significantly Subdued Reaction

The reaction of the international community and particularly the US to the second incident on Mischief Reef was, in comparison to 1995, relatively tame. Some voices did express concern about the escalation in activities on the reef by the PRC. In January 1999 for example, while not expressing approval or disapproval of a proposal for a Washington-led meeting on the Spratly Islands disputes, Vietnam's foreign minister did, however, express support for a multilateral approach to the disagreements. On China's construction work on Mischief Reef, the Vietnamese declared: "We are following with deep worry the complex evolution **in the region Vhan Khan (Mischief Reef)** in the Spratlys… These developments will not help the stability and cooperation in the region."[8] During an East Asian tour in December 1998, the Pacific Commander for US forces, Admiral Joseph Prueher, also declared that his country was paying close attention to what was happening and stated that: "If nations feel like they have a strong card to play, they will try to do it, when they think they can get away with it. This is perhaps what China is trying to do in the Mischief Reef."[9] Estrada, somewhat over-confidently, would state in a message to the PHL senate on January 30, 1999 that by agreeing to the Visiting Forces Agreement (VFA) with the United States (signed in January 1998) that "the country can stop the Chinese in the Spratlys." In a radio interview on the same day, he declared: "It is good for us to have an ally, a superpower partner so our security would be safeguarded." He specifically referred to Mischief Reef, and asserted a strong alliance with the Americans would "balance power in all of Asia."[10] Lim writes that in 1999, most political leaders in the Philippines contended that the

[7] Chung, "The Spratly Islands Dispute," 275.

[8] "Vietnam Worried," *Philippine Daily Inquirer*; see also Lim, "Tempest," 94.

[9] Tiglao et al., "Tis the Season," 18.

[10] "VFA Will Stop Chinese in Spratlys- Estrada," *The Philippine Star*, February 1, 1999; see also Lim, "Tempest," 95.

occupation of Mischief Reef in 1994–1995 could have been prevented if the PHL Senate had ratified a draft for a new Military Bases Agreement with the US in the early 1990s.[11] The fallacy of Estrada's over-optimistic views were later to be displayed. Fierce debates on the pros and cons of the VFA raged on within the PHL senate until its eventual ratification in May 1999, revealing domestic fissions that arguably made approaches to recent developments on Mischief Reef less than optimal. Supporters cited China's military modernization, China's non-democratic government, and its expansionist tendencies as they saw it, as pressing reasons to ratify the VFA. The Spratlys, and Mischief Reef in particular, they argued, was more than just disputes over tiny features but emblematic of a broader stand-off between war-averse democratic states and a non-democratic state with expansionist policies.[12] This belief was also evident in President Estrada's key note address to over two hundred of the most powerful business leaders in the Pacific region in Hong Kong on May 17, 1999. During his speech, Estrada declared: "China's sweeping claim to the Spratlys is not merely about barren and uninhabitable islets. It is about Southeast Asia's bottom-line security."

He also observed that Southeast Asian states are experiencing "political anxieties currently centering on China's effort to project power" within the region's "maritime heartland."[13]

Opponents of the VFA, however, feared that the occupation of Mischief Reef was being exploited and sensationalized in order to justify the return of US military bases to Filipino territory on the pretext of defending national and regional security.[14] In May 1999 for example, Senator Raul Roco criticized Estrada for "twitching the dragon's tail" and for engaging in posturing which he claimed was aimed at provoking the PRC into responding aggressively thus providing a pretext with which to speed up the ratification of the VFA—"It seems to me we have to anger China just to approve this special treatment agreement between the US and the Philippines called the VFA."[15]

[11] Lim, "Tempest," 93.

[12] Ibid., 95.

[13] "Estrada Says China," *Philippine Daily Inquirer*.

[14] Carlito, "Diplomacy, Not VFA," *Philippine Daily Inquirer*.

[15] "Roco: Estrada Provoking China," *Philippine Daily Inquirer*.

Despite such debates and statements however, the late 1998 activities on Mischief Reef were not met with a decisive response by the US, who maintained its non-adversarial stance, or any other ASEAN member state. Aside from words of concern and warning from a select number of people in the US and elsewhere in the region, the response was very much subdued. This contrasted sharply with the collective response to the initial occupation in 1995. One explanation for ASEAN's silence may have been the greater dependence of individual states on Chinese goodwill and assistance in getting through the ongoing economic recession.[16] At the regional grouping's summit in Hanoi in December 15–16, 1998, Manila asked for a public response to the incident but ASEAN proved reluctant to get involved. It did, however, criticize China's breach of UNCLOS guidelines and regulations and the 1995 Sino-Filipino Code of Conduct in an internal report. The Philippines also invited Dana Rohrbacher, a republican US House Committee on International Relations member, to participate in a fly-over above the reef in a PAF C-130 transport place on December 10th in order to bear witness to the renewed activities. Having circled the reef three times, Rohrbacher later reported that he saw three PLAN warships and six ferry boats at the feature and accused the Chinese of "aggression" and the Clinton Administration of playing down the activities in order to deflect congressional criticism of the President's China policy.[17] He also observed: "The Chinese were frantically building these fortifications as we flew over. We saw the glitter of welding torches. What I saw was both alarming and sinister. The Chinese have sent warships hundreds of miles in order to steal territory from a neighbor." The presence of warships and other vessels in the reef's lagoon, he declared, was "an act of intimidation against the Filipino people."[18] President Estrada refused to be drawn in on commenting.[19] As noted later by Joyner, by dispatching warships to surrounding waters and engaging in substantial construction work on the reef in late 1998–early 1999, China did indeed appear to act in clear violation of the bilateral CoC of August 1995. In regards to China's apparent fast and loose approach to promises and commitments on Mischief Reef, Joyner also recalled a conversation

[16] Guan, "The South China Sea," 16.

[17] Tiglao et al., "Tis the Season," 18.

[18] Ibid.; Marfil, "*Malacañang* Mum on Rohrabacher," *Philippine Daily Inquirer*.

[19] Marfil, "*Malacañang* Mum on Rohrabacher," *Philippine Daily Inquirer*.

with the renowned scholar Victor Cha who observed that, in the end, the Chinese were able to successfully negotiate advantageous bilateral deals with the PHL and to make only token agreements on rules of conduct on and near the atoll.[20] Regarding the August 1995 CoC, Lim states that there were disagreements and misunderstandings about the obligations attached to the 1995 CoC's fourth paragraph which said: "Pending the resolution of the dispute, the two sides agreed to abide by the following principles for a code of conduct in the area." These divergences came to the fore following "Mischief Reef II" in late 1998 and early 1999 when Manila charged that Beijing had violated the earlier accord, and then the Chinese responded by denying any such commitment. It appears that the PHL saw it as a concrete code of conduct whereas the PRC viewed it as only setting out principles for a CoC minus the substantive and detailed aspects that had not yet been ironed out.[21] With both sides offering differing versions of what or had not been agreed, this arguably added confusion in terms of how the US and ASEAN for example could best respond to China's reinforced position on Mischief Reef.

With limited options open to Manila, the Filipinos could only express their displeasure and push for a more definitive and detailed region-wide multilateral code of conduct that corresponded with international law. At the aforementioned ASEAN annual summit in mid-December 1998, PHL Foreign Affairs Secretary Domingo Siazon Jr., informed journalists that his country and China would conduct further talks "when conditions are right" but emphasized on a positive note that ASEAN member states sincerely sought improved relations with the PRC.[22] Manila pressed the Chinese again at a later ASEAN meeting in early 1999 on a regional CoC to be signed by all the Spratly claimants. However, the PRC's assistant Foreign Minister Wang Yi rejected Siazon's overtures and replied that a joint statement signed by ASEAN and PRC leaders in 1997 was sufficient. He also claimed that the statement was "a confidence building measure" and "As long as both sides observe the orientation and content of the joint statement, then South China Sea will continue to maintain stability."[23]

[20] Joyner, "The Spratly Islands Dispute," 73, 76.

[21] Lim, "Tempest," 87.

[22] "ASEAN, China Pledge Anew," *Associated Press*.

[23] "China Rebuffs RP Anew," *Philippine Daily Inquirer*. See also Lim, "Tempest," 97.

At the ASEAN summit in December 1998, despite the seriousness of "Mischief Reef II", member states paid only indirect lip-service to the affair despite Filipino lobbying. China's upper hand with Mischief Reef was also reflected in their changed response to Manila's proposals to jointly develop the feature and surrounding waters in 1998–1999. The Chinese had also suggested joint development as an interim solution at various times. The offer, however, was treated with caution at the time due to concerns that it could be used as a ploy to strengthen the PRC's sovereignty claims not only on Mischief Reef but elsewhere as well. By the time of "Mischief Reef II" and the consolidation of its physical presence there, not to mention a stronger regional position, Beijing would only consent to the idea of discussing the proposal in future bilateral meetings on confidence-building measures (CBMs).[24]

Commenting on their talks with the Chinese, PHL Foreign Affairs Secretary Domingo Siazon Jr., recalled: "We told them to leave Mischief; they said no. We asked them if they'd be willing to have the disputed settled through international arbitration. We told them if they'd be willing to have a joint-development arrangement for Mischief. They said they'll think about it [sic]." Siazon also lamented the very limited resources of the Filipino navy and the way the Chinese had succeeded in keeping the Philippines away from the reef: "we just don't have access to the area."[25] Manila had also ordered Filipino naval vessels to maintain a distance from PRC personnel and ships so as to avoid a physical confrontation that could result in a diplomatic incident. PHL Secretary of National Defense, Orlando Mercado, reported that the Chinese had warned PAF reconnaissance aircraft not to fly below 1500 meters in the skies above the feature. They also warned the country's naval vessels to stay at a distance of at least five nms so as to "prevent an accidental confrontation."[26]

Despite this second "escalation" on Mischief Reef, Washington's general opinion was that the PRC did not have any expansionist tendencies with regards to the South China Sea. At a February 12 House International Relations East Asia sub-committee hearing, the Assistant Secretary of State for East Asian Affairs, Stanley Roth, reportedly told his

[24] Tiglao et al., "Tis the Season," 18.

[25] Tiglao et al., "Tis the Season," 20.

[26] Tiglao et al., "Tis the Season," 18; See also *Far Eastern Economic Review* 161 (October 1998), 20.

fellow Congressmen that the Chinese did not represent "a major security threat" in the Spratlys, and that anxiety centered on Beijing's sovereign claim to virtually all of the SCS rather than realities on the ground. The US preference was thus to address any such disputes through bodies like the ARF or the Jakarta-sponsored South China Sea Workshops.[27]

In early 1999, President Estrada met with his National Security Council, whose members declared that the ongoing maritime disputes with China were one of country's two "most urgent security concerns."[28] The other was Islamic separatist terrorist attacks on the large southern island of Mindanao. The Council concluded in agreement that the best way to deal with the PRC was through diplomacy. This would involve two approaches. The first would be through dialogue with Beijing and the second would be via international support and assistance.[29] By early 1999, the once temporary octagonal "fishing shelters" on Mischief Reef were now supplemented by an adjacent and very much permanent three-storey, fortified cement building with a helipad and two satellite dishes which had been constructed at an impressive speed and with logistical support and protection from the Chinese navy.[30]

For the Philippines, this was a clear signal of China's strategic objective to militarise the reef. Writing in early 1999, Joyner observed how the newly constructed building could easily be equipped with communication and radar systems that would help the PRC to more closely monitor aircraft and ships from other states. Anti-aircraft guns could also be readily fitted. He further noted how the Mischief Reef II move and "basing occupation" was viewed as an important element of the PRC's "forward defense and offense strategy" to eventually place and guide cruise missile systems throughout the South China Sea.[31] Diplomatically, China gave away no ground on its unchanging strategy of keeping the Americans out of any SCS negotiations. On January 10, 1999, the PRC Ambassador to the Philippines, Guang Dengming, responded to statements by US government officials that China should keep its promises and refrain

[27] "US Rejects Talk," *The Straits Times*, 1999, 28.

[28] "Trouble Brews on Mischief Reef," *BBC News—Asia Pacific*.

[29] Ibid.

[30] Baker and Wiencek, "Cooperative Monitoring," 94; Lim, "Tempest," 89.

[31] Joyner, "The Spratly Islands Dispute," 54; see also Ruth and Jimenez, "China Fortifies Hold," *Manila Times*.

from activities that escalate tensions in the Spratly Islands by saying that the Americans should not involve itself in the Mischief Reef issue. He also repeated the claim that the newly constructed structures on the atoll were not for military use,[32] and declared: “We can solve the problem among ourselves. Other countries cannot interfere. Our position is that this can be resolved by bilateral talks.”[33]

Estrada replied that while the Chinese were entitled that their opinion, Filipinos were entitled to their opinion too and that their position is that the US “has a role to play in the country’s territorial dispute with China in the South China Sea.” He reminded listeners that the PHL has a mutual defense treaty with the USA and that “we can always invoke that.”[34] He also expressed optimism on the proposal by China to jointly use facilities on Mischief Reef saying: “I think we will solve this problem. You know, China has never had a history of invading countries, so I don’t think China will ever think of invading the Philippines.”[35]

By February of the new year, the initial tensions over Mischief Reef II had begun to ease off. In the previous month, Beijing had agreed to holding talks with Manila over the new structures on the reef, and it was reported that the two sides had agreed to shelve the issue and to focus instead of joint development and exploration activities.[36] Writing at the time, Joyner commented that the appointment of Chinese and Filipino legal experts tasked with examining other such possible areas of co-operation as fisheries, environmental protection, disaster relief, search and rescue operations, and navigation all looked encouraging.[37] Weary of numerous disappointments in previous years, the Filipinos nonetheless persisted in raising the issue whenever possible. In early March, the PHL leader, put to one side China’s request to solely deal with the issue bilaterally by initiating a discussion of the PRC’s occupation of Mischief Reef

[32] During a visit to the Philippines to discuss joint co-operation in mid-July 1999 by the PRC’s Agriculture Minister Chen Yaobang, Chen reiterated the claim that the late 1998 structures on Mischief Reef were “civil structures, that is providing shelter to fishermen and to rescue distressed fishermen [sic].” See “RP, China to Undertake,” *Philippine Daily Inquirer*.

[33] Marfil and Avendano, “US has Role,” *Philippine Daily Inquirer*.

[34] Ibid.

[35] Marfil, “Next RP Map.”

[36] Marfil, “Charter Change.”

[37] Joyner, “The Spratly Islands Dispute,” 75.

with the United Nations General Secretary Kofi Annan at the UN Headquarters in New York.[38] Estrada recalled that Annan had promised to help to resolve the issue. The president continued by saying that he asked the UN leader "if he could intervene in this process so that we may have diplomatic talks for a peaceful resolution of the conflict over the Spratly Islands and Mischief Reef".... and that the General Secretary "promised that he will do everything to resolve this problem through peaceful means through diplomatic means."[39] On March 22 and 23, the PRC and PHL engaged in bilateral talks in Manila on Confidence-Building Measures and on the "Joint-Use" of China's facilities on Mischief Reef. In spite of the talks' declared objectives, in the end, joint use was not addressed over the two days. Instead, the attendees described the talks as a "fruitful discussion" and that their contrasting views had been aired in a "frank and friendly manner." Wang Yi, the PRC's Assistant Foreign Secretary, rejected claims that his side had offered the joint use of facilities on the reef. In turn, the PHL's Undersecretary of Foreign Affairs Lauro Baja Jr. called on the Chinese to dismantle the structures or to place them and their management "under a mutually agreed arrangement." The PRC delegation's reaction was to ignore these demands and to remain steadfast in their position that the feature was under Chinese sovereignty. When the Filipino delegation requested access to the structures whenever they wished, the Chinese side responded that this would not be necessary because the structures are of no military use. Critically analyzing the PHL's approach to the talks, Lim viewed the Filipinos as placing an "all or nothing" offer on the table. By this, he means that Manila demanded that Beijing engage in no new occupation of the reef and that the Chinese suspend their sovereignty claim without the Filipinos suspending their own EEZ claims. In effect, this would leave China with two unappealing options, to pack up and leave the atoll or to make their facilities available for the two sides to jointly administer. As a result, the Chinese simply repeated their position that they have "indisputable sovereignty over the Spratlys." To concede under such circumstances would have seen the PRC lose the advantages and leverage that they had gained in occupying the feature in the first place. Lim also observed that, irrespective of the outcome, the Chinese understood the importance of promising

[38] Javellana, "Estrada, UN Chief."

[39] "Erap Insists," Agence France Presse.

and proceeding with further talks because it maintained the appearance, before the region's and world's eyes, of a flexible and reasonable China, and preserved the hope of a possible solution in the future.[40]

On March 24, shortly after the conclusion of the two-day talks, an announcement on a South China Sea fishing ban by Qi Jingfa, the PRC's Agriculture Vice Minister, was reported in the China Daily. In his statement relating to the replenishment of depleted fish stocks, Qi declared: "From June 1, 1999, a two-month fishing ban will be imposed each year on the South China Sea north of 12 degrees latitude, including Beibu Gulf." President Estrada responded by saying that the PRC did not have any right to prevent or ban PHL fishermen from operating within disputed areas of the Spratlys.[41] Expressing his frustration with this ban and with China at the lack of progress on joint use following the March talks, Estrada stated:

> I think they [the Chinese] are just showing their inconsistencies before the world because, as you remember, in the ASEAN dialogue meetings in Kuala Lumpur,[42] the Chinese President Jiang Zemin made that offer and everybody remembers that.[43]

In late March 1999, Manila declared that fly-over inspections of Mischief Reef would continue.[44]

The Filipinos had little to show for their work by the end of March 1999. The talks of that month saw Beijing refusing Manila's calls to dismantle the recently built structures, to put on paper any assurance not to build any new structures, and denying that they had ever proposed the joint use of facilities on the reef. Instead they declared that the PHL should end aerial surveillance over the area. The only fruitful result from the meeting was a reluctant agreement to restrict the use of facilities to civilians only. In the same month, the Philippines asked that the case be put before the United Nations and the International Tribunal on the Law of the Sea, but China refused. In protest against Beijing's

[40] Lim, "Tempest," 96–97.

[41] Ibid., 97.

[42] Referring to the period of the Asian-Pacific Economic Co-operation summit in Kuala Lumpur from November 14–18, 1998.

[43] "China Bans Fishing," *Weathernews Philippines*.

[44] Zha and Valencia, "Mischief Reef: Geopolitics," 90–91.

seeming intransigence on the issue, Manila postponed a scheduled visit by President Estrada to the PRC in May 1999 while proceeding to honor commitments to travel to Hong Kong, South Korea, and Japan.[45] The cancellation was seen by most observers as a diplomatic reprimand against the PRC. This was because Jiang Zemin had personally invited Estrada to visit China when they first met at the Asian-Pacific Co-operation summit in Kuala Lumpur in November 1998. Upon entering office, Estrada had also declared his desire for China to be the first country he would visit. Due to a downturn in ties, however, owing to the repercussions of Mischief Reef II, the president's advisers persuaded him to visit other ASEAN member states first, as was customary. A decisive factor in the cancellation was the PRC's apparent inflexibility in talks over Mischief Reef with one senior PHL diplomat commenting "Under the present circumstances, it is inauspicious for him to go to China."[46] When Estrada visited Japan in June 1999, he used the occasion to severely criticize China's control over Mischief Reef.[47]

Following talks at the ASEAN-China forum of April 4–8, 1999, the organization could only muster an agreement from the Chinese that they would earnestly and seriously consider Manila's proposal for a more effective code of conduct for the SCS.[48]

President Estrada had also not helped himself in garnering the support of fellow ASEAN member states by previously condemning Indonesia's human rights record and Malaysian Prime Minister's Mahathir Mohamad's smear campaign against his rival Anwar Ibrahim and subsequent imprisonment on false charges. As one source argues, the reaction of ASEAN states can also often be influenced by a self-interested but understandable belief amongst members that they might fare better in a strictly bilateral deal with the PRC or that their own ties with the rising giant are more important than ASEAN solidarity.[49]

[45] Ibid., 89, 93.

[46] Lim, "Tempest," 98; see also "Erap Skips Visit to Beijing," *Philippine Daily Inquirer*.

[47] Lim, "Tempest," 99.

[48] Guan, "The South China Sea," 16.

[49] Zha and Valencia, "Mischief Reef: Geopolitics," 89–90, 96.

The Late 1990s: Another Rush for Unoccupied Features

It should be noted that China's renewed activities on Mischief Reef came in the context of renewed competition for features and an increase in the number of occupations by virtually all claimants in the area. A month prior to October 1998, for example, when the PRC upgraded its facilities on Mischief Reef, PLAN stood by and did not respond after learning that the Vietnamese had started building structures on the Beijing-claimed Nanan (*Orleana*) and Jindun (*Kingston*) shoals.[50] As explained by Emmers, many of the disputants have used military force to occupy features claimed by others. In the late 1990s, there was a noticeable rise in tensions between the Philippines and Malaysia, Vietnam and Malaysia, and the Philippines and Vietnam. In 1999, Malaysia occupied two features, Investigator Shoal and Erica Reef, claimed by the Philippines. This soured relations between the two countries and elicited protests from other claimants such as Brunei, China, and Vietnam.[51] According to Acharya, with the discovery of structures such a helipad and a two-storey building with a radar tower constructed by Malaysia on one of these PHL-claimed features, the Philippines felt betrayed by Malaysia. Singapore in particular also appeared to be reluctant to criticize China in this period while at an ARF meeting in July 1999, the Malaysians seemed receptive to Chinese proposals for bilateral approaches to the South China Sea disagreements.[52] When Manila protested the construction of new structures on Erica Reef, Kuala Lumpur said that they were for climate research and the study of marine life.[53] This atmosphere of feature-grabbing activities before and after Mischief Reef II within the Spratly area may provide another reason why the Chinese felt that they needed to reinforce their presence and facilities on Mischief Reef. They also arguably gave the Chinese a justification for their actions. Divisions among ASEAN member states over the Spratlys were also no doubt advantageous in undermining a unified response against the PRC vis-à-vis Mischief Reef.

[50] Guan, "The South China Sea," 22.

[51] Emmers, "Maritime Disputes," 53.

[52] Acharya, "Constructing a Security Community," 136; Leifer, "Dictionary of the Modern Politics," 258.

[53] Leifer, "Dictionary of the Modern Politics," 258.

By 1999, Manila's attempts to check China's late 1998 advancements on the feature appeared to be going nowhere. Filipino frustration over the diplomatic deadlock was summed up by the PHL's Foreign Affairs Undersecretary Lauro Baja Jr., when he stated that his country's determined efforts to elicit international support against the continued occupation of Mischief Reef were not bearing fruit. Baja complained that "we were left alone" and that he had effectively been told that while neighbours appreciated and sympathized with Manila, "the issue is only a Philippine–China problem."[54] By April 15, 1999, Baja lamented that the Philippines was like "an orphan in its campaign" to elicit outside and multilateral involvement, and that Mischief Reef and other PHL claimed features appeared too insignificant in the eyes of "so-called friends in the international community". He added that even amongst the ASEAN member states, some "friends" are "either mute, timid or cannot go beyond espousal of general principle of peaceful settlement of disputes and polite words of understanding given in the corridors or meeting rooms."[55]

In a move to display the extent of its sovereign claims, on June 1 Beijing unilaterally announced the previously mentioned two-month prohibition against fishing activities within the Spratly Islands area. In an attempt to check the Chinese advances in disputed areas as seen in the previous year, Vietnam and the Philippines together pushed for a more reliable code of conduct to be hammered out between the claimant states. This was aimed at preventing an escalation in clashes in the contested areas, and additionally to ensure that China and other states did not occupy any remaining uninhabited and unprotected features in the South China Sea.[56] The PHL navy stepped up its pursuance and arrest of Chinese vessels and their crews. In January 2000, PHL forces fired three warning shots in proximity to two PRC fishing vessels in the vicinity of Scarborough Shoal. In one incident in May, a Chinese fisherman was shot dead by PHL marine patrol personnel in the area.[57] Late January 2000 also saw the resumption of Filipino-US joint exercises (named "Balikatan" meaning Shoulder to Shoulder) after an hiatus of some five years.[58]

[54] Guan, "The South China Sea," 17.

[55] "Concern Over Spratly Statement," *The Straits Times*.

[56] Emmers, "Maritime Disputes," 53, 56.

[57] Zha and Valencia, "Mischief Reef: Geopolitics," 91.

[58] Romero, "RP-US 'Balikatan 2000' Launched."

Early 2001 saw the opening salvos in a diplomatic international support-centered drive led by the new PHL leader, Gloria Macapagal-Arroyo (January 2001–June 2010), and her National Security Advisor Roilo Golez, aimed at peacefully pressuring Beijing to remove its structures on the reef while not harming mutually beneficial economic ties. To this end, Golez announced: "we should use multilateral forum [*sic*] to tell the world what China is doing. Our strongest weapon against a big nation like China is noise."[59] At the same time, Arroyo knew where her country's priorities lay and described the Mischief Reef issue as an "irritant" amid the wider and much more important Sino-Filipino relationship. The PHL President's views were no doubt informed by the unprecedented growth in economic ties between the two countries in the 1990s, China's support for Manila's economic objectives, and the realities of addressing more pressing terrestrial security concerns which already required considerable military resources.[60] In October 2001, just before the PHL President Arroyo embarked on a three-day state visit to the PRC, Filipino air forces reported the presence of four Chinese vessels at Mischief Reef.[61] Despite their mutual interest in binding China to a code of conduct, tensions between the ASEAN member Spratly claimants were also apparent. In August 2002, for example, Vietnamese troops stationed on one disputed feature fired warning shots in the direction of PHL surveillance planes sent to observe them. Other states were also still utilizing non-military methods to defend or reinforce their claims.[62] By the early 2000s, it was apparent that disputes over features such as Mischief Reef remained volatile and hostage to potentially lethal incidents between military and fishing vessels in sensitive waters. These activities, which seemed to have increased dramatically since the 1990s, made the call for a new and hopefully workable code of conduct for the South China Sea all the more pressing.

[59] "New Security Adviser Wants," *Associated Press*.

[60] Chung, "The Spratly Islands Dispute," 284.

[61] *Philippine Star*, October 30, 2001.

[62] Emmers, "Maritime Disputes," 53, 56.

2002—A New "Declaration" on a Code of Conduct

Despite these challenges and occasional stand-offs over the Spratlys, in general the period from the late 1990s to the late 2000s was comparatively stable with a toning down of the frictions witnessed in the 1990s. Raditio observes how during these years a "self-restrained, accommodating, and reassuring" China concentrated its efforts on developing relationships with neighboring states by engaging in ASEAN-led multilateral talks on areas of possible co-operation rather than getting bogged down on negotiations over a lasting resolution to the disputes as well as territorial sovereignty. On the latter, China did, however, remain firm on dispute settlement through a bilateral approach. These years also witnessed no new occupations by the Chinese. The Spratly claimants appeared willing to accept the status quo, at least for the time being. This more moderate approach in the early 2000s also complemented and was influenced by the greater weight given to the PRC's "Peaceful Development Road" policy (2005)[63] and its earlier "Periphery Policy"[64] (also known the "Good Neighbor" policy).[65] These circumstances at the start of the new century certainly at least raised the possibility of a regional meeting of minds vis-à-vis disagreements in the South China Sea.

While there were lingering disagreements over the exact wording, talks between China and ASEAN aimed at finding a peaceful and manageable approach to the Spratly disagreements seemed to bear fruit in November 2002. On the margins of the ASEAN summit in Phnom Penh in Cambodia, the various foreign ministers signed a multi-lateral but non-binding "Declaration on the Code of Conduct" (DoC) aimed at addressing maritime disputes.[66] The long process leading up to the declaration was delayed in particular by the choice of language to be employed. From the PRC's perspective, this related to a quest by rival claimants for binding assurances on a ban on any future occupations or the construction of new structures on uninhabited features. The Chinese had preferred a stated commitment to refrain from the use of force.[67] The

[63] For more, see "China's Peaceful Development Road," Foreign Ministry of the People's Republic of China.

[64] See also Zhao, "China's Periphery Policy."

[65] Raditio, "Understanding China's Behaviour," 111.

[66] ASEAN, "Declaration on the Conduct."

[67] Fravel, *Strong Borders*, 271.

new DoC was characterized by a commitment by all of the signatories to adhere to UNCLOS, the UN Charter, the Five Principles of Peaceful Co-existence, and the Treaty of Amity and Cooperation[68] in Southeast Asia (TAC). The parties involved also declared a commitment to "the freedom of navigation in and over flight above the South China Sea", and resolved themselves to addressing their disputes "without resorting to the threat or use of force, through friendly consultations and negotiations by sovereign states directly concerned, in accordance with universally recognized principles of international law." On the thorny issue of future occupations and constructions, they agreed to exercise restraint and to be sensitive in their attempts to "build trust and confidence between and among them". The code also included a commitment to increase "voluntary" defense exchanges and advanced notifications, and to co-operate with rescue operations in disputed areas.[69]

While the declaration was a step in the right direction, it contained some significant shortcomings for such issues as Mischief Reef. As argued by Emmers, the declaration, though laudable, was only an interim measure until the parties could work out a more concrete code of conduct. There were obvious limitations and weaknesses, most notably its non-binding nature. This in particular frustrated Manila and Hanoi the most, because they saw the PRC's rejection of some proposals as evidence that the Chinese might again attempt to enhance their structures on occupied features. The weaknesses in the 2002 declaration are also apparent in the fact that it could not comprehensively address the politically sensitive problems of fishermen being detained by the armed forces of "foreign" states as well as the construction of new facilities on occupied but contested features. Given that it took three years of hard talk to agree on a declaration, some scholars questioned whether the disputants would ever be able to reach an effective code of conduct.[70] This question is especially relevant to conflict prevention and dispute management in the waters surrounding Mischief Reef. Developments and flawed agreements since the 1994–1995 takeover understandably gave countries like the Philippines little cause for comfort, or confidence that the Chinese

[68] China acceded to the TAC on October 8, 2003; see "Treaty of Amity and Cooperation in Southeast Asia." https://asean.org/treaty-amity-cooperation-southeast-asia-indonesia-24-february-1976/.

[69] ASEAN, "Declaration on the Conduct."

[70] Emmers, "Maritime Disputes," 58.

would not reinforce their facilities when favourable circumstances permit it. There were reasons to be concerned as well as optimistic.

Post-2002 and Cautious Optimism

Despite concerns about the weaknesses of regimes and conflict-prevention measures in the Spratlys, several scholars agreed that China, in the first decade of the new century and since the late 1990s, had mostly behaved like a status quo state generally following international norms rather than seeking to upset international order and to make new gains by force or stealth. Appreciating its far greater economic and geo-strategic interests in the region, the Chinese played a careful balancing game between moderately defending its sovereign claims from others versus the strategic necessity of not frightening or intimidating its neighbors in the South China Sea. According to one scholar, for example, the PRC's willingness to engage and cautiously compromise over these disputes was informed by its more pressing economic objectives alongside a strong desire to minimize the presence and involvement of powerful players such as the US and Japan. This fear became a more urgent concern following the September 11 terrorist attacks, a serious downturn in ties with Japan, and worries that Washington would further enhance its military presence in the region. This was in spite of ongoing attempts by virtually all of the claimants to quietly or publicly strengthen their positions in the area. For example, when Hanoi sanctioned the commencement of upgrades to a runway on the contested island of Truong Sa Lon (Big Spratly) in order to boost the number of tourist trips from Vietnam, Beijing angrily protested against the activities and denounced them as a violation of the 2002 declaration.[71] On a positive note however, the Chinese chose not to react aggressively to the move and kept its protests within the diplomatic realm.

The years immediately after the 2002 DoC also showed promise with numerous confidence-building measures in the area of joint co-operation. For instance, the Chinese proposed the joint exploration of oil reserves with the Philippines in 2003, and 2005 saw a bilateral agreement on pre-exploration surveys.[72] The two countries also signed a Memorandum of

[71] Ibid., 53.

[72] Bercovitch and Oishi, "International Conflict," 111.

Understanding in the area of defense co-operation in November 2004, and in May 2005 Manila and Beijing put pen to paper with agreements on annual defense and security dialogues, PRC technical assistance to the PHL's armed forces, the training of Filipino soldiers, and a payment of the equivalent of 6 million US dollars towards the purchase of non-lethal equipment for the Philippine military.[73] Perhaps the obvious sign of improving bilateral and regional ties since late 2002 was the signing of a Joint Marine Seismic Undertaking (JMSU) between the national oil companies of the Philippines, China, and Vietnam in March 2005. This remained effective until 2008 when regional ties again worsened. It also initially held out promise for a resolution of how Spratly disputants might be able to share competing resources in overlapping claim areas. China and the Philippines had signed bilaterally on September 1, 2004 with Vietnam joining them in the new year after initial reservations. The JMSU took effect in July 2005 and was seen as a victory for Chinese diplomacy. At the time, PHL President Arroyo described it as a "diplomatic breakthrough for peace in the region."[74] The JMSU's term ran out in June 2008 and was not extended by any of the parties. In the PHL, one cause of its demise was a result of domestic discord, with rival parties accusing the government of having weakened the country's position in the South China Sea as well as undermining the constitution by circumventing it.[75] There were also accusations that corruption and the persuasive effect of loans from the PRC had helped smooth the path to an agreement in 2005.[76] Such developments revealed a number of potential vulnerabilities in Filipino approaches to Mischief Reef.

As to the reasons for a deterioration in regional ties in the late 2000s, Batongbacal cites UNCLOS-related supplementary submissions made by Vietnam and Malaysia in May 2009 in which they claimed continental shelf areas beyond 200 nms, as a key reason for a downturn in regional relations. China immediately protested the move as a violation of jurisdictional and sovereign rights, and officially released the first publication of its nine-dashed line which encompassed virtually all of the South

[73] Storey, "China and the Philippines."

[74] Baguioro, "Three Nations Sign Pact"; Emmers, *Resource Management*, 62.

[75] See "The JMSU: A Tale of Bilateralism"; and Deogracias, "The Road to an ASEAN-China."

[76] Storey, "Trouble and Strife," 6; Emmers, *Resource Management*, 63.

China Sea. UNCLOS guidelines instructed that states that had been UNCLOS signatories before 1999 had to submit supplementary claims to economic rights before May 13, 2009 in cases where their continental shelf extended more than 200 nms beyond a state's baselines. Angry diplomatic exchanges and a return to a less stable relationship characterized by dangerous confrontations in SCS waters between the disputants followed these developments.[77]

Expressing a cautiously optimistic note, Fravel, in 2008, contended that while the PRC has benefitted from using force and occupying features in the SCS before, it may be less willing to behave similarly in the future. This, he argued, conformed with his central thesis that because its claim strength has significantly improved, its perception of the necessity to use force and its sensitivity to its position has declined. The Chinese have considerably improved their once weak relative claim strengths in areas like the Paracels and the Spratlys since the 1970s. However, by 2008, China was in a stronger negotiating position in terms of its leverage in any final resolution or possible peacekeeping measures. This was evidenced in its central role in sculpting the rules and regulations contained in the 2002 Declaration on the Code of Conduct.[78] It has, however, persisted in manipulating the rules and provisions of UNCLOS for its own ends, to the frustration of fellow claimants. In 2006, one path to a resolution was closed off by Beijing's decision not to be party to the compulsory dispute settlement mechanisms contained within the convention. This is in spite of its making occasional announcements that it would use the convention as a guideline for discussions. On August 25, 2006, the PRC submitted a written declaration to the UN regarding Article 298 of UNCLOS, whereby it stated that "The Government of the People's Republic of China does not accept any of the procedures provided for in section 2 of Part XV of the Convention."[79] Simply put, China was not willing to engage in any compulsory dispute settlement laid out in UNCLOS, including compulsory arbitration. This included maritime delimitation, as well as military and law enforcement activities. It also used the occasion to reiterate its conviction that the "most effective means" for the settlement

[77] Batongbacal, "Arbitration 101: Philippines V. China"; Raditio, "Understanding China's Behaviour," 50, 57.

[78] Fravel, *Strong Borders*, 296–299.

[79] Government of People's Republic of China. *Declaration*.

of disputes like Mischief Reef between China and its neighbouring states is through "friendly consultations and negotiations between the sovereign States directly concerned."[80]

In 2008, Fravel stated on a positive note that contrary to expectations about the rising China, in the nearly fourteen year period since the occupation of Mischief Reef, the PRC did not occupy any additional features within the Spratly Islands even though its military capabilities had increased since then. It also held back from physically removing other state's forces from PRC-claimed features even though it had steadily improved its ability to do so. This, according to Fravel, was attributable to China's stronger position and its optimism about the country's future outlook for the area. Prior to resurgent tensions in the last decade, another key explanation for a reduction of the type of tensions witnessed in the 1990s was the fact that virtually all of the features in the Spratly Islands were by 2008 physically controlled by one claimant or another, a development which has made feature-grabbing a less attractive and less feasible option.[81] This view is again a moot point open to challenge and agreement. Nonetheless, developments since Fravel's 2008 observation present a South China Sea that is vulnerable to serious and volatile fluctuations as the various claimants have not only reinforced their positions on features like Mischief Reef but have stepped up their displays of sovereignty in surrounding waters and in the skies overhead. In the last fifteen years, street protests, and domestic political pressures to defend national honor have also complicated how the Philippines in particular has approached the Mischief Reef issue.

Lingering Challenges

While the frequency of occupations such as that of Mischief Reef in 1995 has greatly decreased, potentially dangerous incidents and escalatory behavior designed to emphasize claims have remained hallmarks of the Spratly Islands disputes. Satellite imagery obtained by Jane's Information Group in November 2007, for example, showed that the PRC had

[80] Ibid.; this quote has been applied repeatedly by the PRC and can be found in a number of documents.

[81] Fravel, *Strong Borders*, 296–299.

enhanced its facilities on the feature.[82] In 2008, the Chinese formally declared the Vietnamese-claimed Sansha City to be an integral part of Hainan Province. This came in the context of the publication of details surrounding the Yulin (Sanya) submarine base on Hainan, and with it, increased concerns over the PRC's security objectives in the SCS. In March 2009, China-registered "fishing" vessels were accused of harassing a US navy surveillance vessel, the Impeccable, as it carried out duties within the Spratly group and also off the coast of Hainan Island. Problems related to selective interpretations of UNCLOS persisted when the Chinese again emphasized their SCS claims based on historical discovery by submitting their nine-dash interrupted line map encompassing most of the SCS to the UN on May 7, 2009. Malaysia, the Philippines, and Vietnam all protested against the move.[83] As noted however, this appeared to be in response to Vietnam and Malaysia's UNCLOS-related continental shelf submissions of the same month. Future military aspirations to reinforce the facilities on contested reefs were also indicated in a report on the proceedings of the sixth meeting of the eleventh National Committee of the Chinese People's Political Consultative Conference's (CPPCC) Standing Committee, "highest-level advisory body" in the PRC in June 2009. On June 18, it was reported that the former chief of the General Staff of the People's Liberation Army (PLA) and CPPCC standing committee member, General Zhang Li, recommended the Chinese build an airport and a seaport on Mischief Reef. Zhang's reasoning was, once constructed, the PRC would then be able to exercise control over the Spratly archipelago and it would give the state a platform which PLAN ships could utilize in order to bypass the region's and China's most important strategic choke point, the Straits of Malacca.[84] At the Asian Regional Forum in 2010, US Secretary of State Hillary Clinton aired US and regional concerns over the threat such activities presented to peace, international navigation, and to finding a diplomatic resolution. In response, the PRC's Foreign Minister, Yang Jiechi, accused the USA of meddling, and retorted "China is a big country and other countries are small countries and that is just a fact."[85]

[82] Fisher, "South China Sea Competition."

[83] "A Mischief Reef," *Newsbreak*.

[84] Hsiao, "PLA General; Advises Building."

[85] "ARF Makes a Contribution," *Japan Times*.

Filipino anxieties over China's intentions within its perceived EEZ persisted, regardless of reassurances from Beijing. The 2002 Declaration also proved to have had a limited influence on preventing troublesome behaviour. March 2011, for example, witnessed a Philippine oil exploration vessel, the "MV Veritas Voyager" being "harassed" and forced away by PLAN ships in the Reed Bank area. In May 2011, when PRC Defense Minister Liang Guanglie was on a "goodwill" trip to the PHL (May 21–25), the Filipino navy reported the sighting of several Chinese vessels off-loading construction materials near the Philippines-claimed but still unoccupied Amy Douglas Bank (also known as Iroquois Reef or An-t'ang Tao in Chinese). The Chinese had also positioned a buoy and numerous marker posts nearby without explaining its actions to Manila. Other media reports stated that the PRC constructed several structures on five occupied reefs within the Philippine's claimed area. Such activities in the midst of ostensibly positive ties only served to weaken confidence and to convince Filipinos that China was, as one PHL newspaper put it, talking "sweet" in its neighbour's house but acting "bitter" in its backyard. This lingering sentiment was also expressed by the Philippine's Defense Secretary Voltaire Gazmin, who remarked angrily about these apparent two sides to China's strategy, claiming publicly that "somehow I'm really affected because we have shown them our hospitality and we were talking properly. We agreed that all problems could be resolved. And yet while we're talking something was afoot elsewhere."[86] Attempts to restore confidence in ties following a recent rise in tensions suffered as a result of these activities. Such cynicism over the long term future of Mischief Reef was likewise reflected in one of the country's leading broadsheets, when it declared that PRC and PHL political leaders "can croon love songs all day long and smile at each other, but you can bet your last peso that the Chinese will not only stay on Mischief Reef but will continue to expand their holdings; and they know they can get away with it."[87] In a reflection of Filipino concerns, President Benigno Aquino III (June 2010–June 2016) announced in June 2011 that the South China Sea would henceforth be officially referred to as the "West Philippine Sea" instead. He explained that the move was due to a need to strengthen

[86] "A Mischief Reef," *Newsbreak*; "ASEAN, China Hardening Positions," *China Post*. The PHL newspaper *Business Mirror* provides details on seven such maritime incidents in the first half of 2011 alone; see *Business Mirror*, March 12, 2012.

[87] Farolan, "Mischief Reef and 'Love Me Tender'."

the country's claims and also to follow suit with other states in terms of how they referred to the area (Vietnam—*East Sea*; China—*South China Sea*).[88]

In early April 2012, Sino-Filipino tensions escalated over a sovereign rights related standoff concerning the Scarborough Shoal dispute (Philippines—*Panatag Shoal*; China—*Huangyan Dao*). The nearest PHL landmass is 124 nms (approx. 230 kms) from the feature: the municipality of Palauig in Zambales Province. The standoff followed the attempted seizure by BRP[89] Gregorio del Pillar of eight Chinese fishing vessels who were accused of illegal fishing inside the PHL's EEZ. In response, the Filipino ship was obstructed by three Chinese maritime surveillance vessels.[90] The Scarborough Shoal dispute is a decades long issue but the April 2012 incident and its on-going repercussions, which included the permanent posting of PLAN warships in proximity to the shoal and denial of access to the shoal's lagoon, represented a major escalation. The PHL's then Foreign Secretary Albert del Rosario described the PRC's activities as "dictatorial" that made the task of conflict avoidance "impossible."[91] The standoff also saw attempts from China after early April 2012 to protest the PHL's position by using "trade as a foreign policy tool" amongst other methods. Examples included a suspension or disruption of tours by Chinese tourists to the Philippines, a refusal to accept PHL banana exports in such major ports as Beijing, Shanghai, and Guangzhou as well as more strict regulations on bananas, pineapples, and other fruits, cyber attacks on important websites in the Philippines, and street protests in Beijing and Hong Kong. There were also pro- PHL demonstrations outside the PRC embassy in Manila. Given the dilemma between defending the nation's sovereign interests and its trade interests with a rising PRC, divisions between those who advocated a hard line against Chinese activities and those who feared the economic repercussions in

[88] "Manila Renames South China Sea," *Channel News Asia*.

[89] BRP is the acronym for 'Barko ng Republika ng Pilipinas' which in Tagalog means "Ship of the Republic of the Philippines."

[90] "PH, Chinese Naval Vessels," *Philippine Daily Inquirer*.

[91] Torode, "China 'Dictatorial' in Scarborough"; Bondoc, "China Invading Scarborough."

terms of trade, investment, tourism, and foreign aid were increasingly apparent.[92]

The affair no doubt reminded the Filipinos of the serious repercussions for any small state who challenged China's position in the South China Sea. July 11, 2012 saw the accidental grounding of the Jianghu V class PLAN frigate Dongguan near the disputed Half Moon Shoal (Tagalog—*Hasa Hasa Shoal*; Chinese—*Banyue Jiao*) situated just 60 nms (approx.110 kms) from Palawan in the Philippines. The frigate had been on a routine patrol in adjacent waters. In February 2011, the same frigate had fired warning shots at three Filipino fishing vessels at Jackson Atoll (Tagalog—*Quirino Atoll*; Chinese—*Wufang Jiao*), some 140 nms (approx. 260 kms) west of Palawan.[93] Commenting in July 2012, Storey noted that while all sides clearly understood that a serious conflict would hurt wider and more important national interests, such incidents as the Half Moon Shoal grounding nonetheless reflected the increased militarisation of the waters of the South China Sea and of how "resolution of the dispute is even further out of reach". In this context, there is a considerable risk of an accidental clash and subsequent escalation in which he opined "it is just a matter of time before one of these standoffs gets really ugly and people get killed."[94]

In subsequent years, the Philippines would claim that China was acting in breach of a 2012 US-brokered deal which saw the two sides withdrawing their vessels from the shoal area. According to the PHL Ambassador to the USA speaking in 2016, Jose Cuisia Jr., China had reneged on its promises and later denied the existence of an agreement. Following reports of the presence of a PRC survey vessel at the shoal, he also warned Beijing that converting the shoal into an island would aggravate SCS disputes between the PHL and the PRC. He also called upon the US to persuade China to not take such a "very provocative" step.[95] Given what had happened on Mischief Reef, the Scarborough Shoal development and the seeming failure of diplomacy compelled the militarily weak

[92] Bondoc, "Protest in Philippines"; "Hackers Bring PH-China," *Philippine Daily Inquirer*, 2012; "Protest Over Huangyan Island," *China.org.cn*, 2012; "In Philippines, Banana Growers," *Washington Post*, 2012; "HK Activists Protest Against," *Focus Taiwan*, 2012.

[93] Amurao, "A Shoal Too Far."

[94] Branigan, "Chinese Frigate Runs Aground."

[95] Gomez. "Don't Turn Shoal into Island."

Philippines to protect their interests by globally publicizing the fact that China's claims were "invalid."[96]

On January 22, 2013, the PHL's Department of Foreign Affairs presented a *note verbale* to the PRC embassy in Manila in which the Philippines' government had submitted a "Notification and Statement of Claim" before the UN's Arbitral Tribunal; this initiated compulsory arbitration proceedings under Article 287 "Choice of Procedure" and Annex VII of UNCLOS. It also related to "maritime jurisdiction" in the South China Sea and the "Settlement of Disputes Mechanism under the Convention". On the same day, in an official press statement, the PHL Secretary of Foreign Affairs Albert F. del Rosario stated "the Philippines undertook many efforts to peacefully engage China and settle these disputes" and that it "had exhausted all political and diplomatic avenues for a peaceful negotiated settlement of its maritime dispute with China." He continued by asserting: "On numerous occasions, dating back to 1995, the Philippines has been exchanging views with China to peacefully settle these disputes. To this day, a solution is still elusive. We hope that the Arbitral Proceedings shall bring this dispute to a durable solution". He also explained how the PRC's Ambassador to the PHL had been summoned to the Department of Foreign Affairs and handed a *note verbale* that outlined the Philippines' disputing "the validity of China's nine-dash line claim to almost the entire South China Sea (SCS) including the WPS [West Philippine Sea] and to desist from unlawful activities that violate the sovereign rights and jurisdiction of the Philippines under the 1982 UNCLOS."[97]

As noted by one PHL media source at the time, the legal move "was the strongest step taken by the Aquino administration against perceived Chinese aggression in the West Philippine Sea" but which also raised fears of a "backlash" from "an Asian economic giant and a major global power."[98] Nonetheless, an official Department of Foreign Affairs statement beckoned the country's citizens to display their patriotism and reflected the strength of feeling in the PHL with regards to China's

[96] "Courting Trouble—An International Tribunal Delivers," *Economist*, 2016.

[97] Embassy of the Republic of the Philippines in Japan, 2013.

[98] Del Callar, "PHL Seeks End To."

behaviour: "If someone forces himself into your house and tries to unlawfully take away what belongs to you, should you not take action against the intruder?"[99]

On the same day, an article entitled "Honor" recalled a speech in August 2012 on "Facing Up to the China Challenge" by a former National Security Adviser and Director-General of the National Security Council, Jose T. Almonte.[100] In the speech, Almonte argued that standing up to China was not only about the country's independence, dignity, and sovereignty but that the country's "national honor" was at stake. Almonte also lamented the failure of ASEAN to act collectively against China's actions in the SCS, and how Vietnam and the Philippines are "visibly alone to defend their rights in accordance with international law". The article also pointed to the failure to prevent the "trespass at will" by civilian ships, a failure that has only emboldened the Chinese to proceed with its "creeping annexation" and area denial strategy. Almonte also warned that "the quality of our response will determine how we will rise or fall as a nation" and "our bitter experience in 1995 over its occupation of Mischief Reef and gradual conversion into a command center still rankles." He continued by asserting that without a concerted and unified response then the PHL would turn into "a tributary, a vassal state or a province of a dominant power." Almonte likewise listed the features on which the PRC had constructed extensive military installations upon including Kagitingan Reef (Fiery Cross Reef), Subi Reef (also known as Zamora), Calderon Reef (Cuarteron Reef), the Gaven Reefs [sic] (also known as Burgos) and Chigua Reef (Johnson South Reef). The speech also lamented that in the five months prior to August 2012, the Chinese had roped off Scarborough Shoal, preventing Filipinos from fishing there, and had created Sansha (as part of Hainan province) as a prefecture-level city (in July 2012) with law enforcement units and a military garrison to administer the SCS. The PRC had also officially included a map of the SCS on Chinese passports (with PHL claimed areas included). He also asserted that the Chinese had also warned that after January 1, 2013, Filipino vessels within Chinese claimed areas could be intercepted and boarded.[101]

[99] Embassy of the Republic of the Philippines in Japan, 2013.

[100] Alunan, "Honor."

[101] Almonte, "Facing Up."

In response to the PHL's January 22 move, on February 19, 2013, the PRC government "solemnly declared" that it did not accept nor would not participate in the arbitration.[102] On the same day, the PRC rejected and returned the PHL's *note verbale* with the "Notification and Statement of Claim" attached. As explained in Chapter 2, the PRC government refused to participate in the arbitration proceedings and rejected its subsequent findings.[103] In March 2013, the PRC's Xinhua News Agency reported that a PLAN fleet was carrying out patrol and training exercises near Mischief Reef. According to the report, the fleet had "extended regards to other navy and fishery administration ships that have been conducting regular patrols in the waters surrounding the reef."[104] In May 2013, there was another standoff close to the nearby Second Thomas Shoal, south-east of Mischief Reef (Philippines—*Ayungin Shoal*; Vietnam—*Bãi Cỏ Mây*; PRC—*Ren'ai Jiao*), involving Chinese fishing vessels and Filipino naval vessels. The latter employed "bashing maneuvers" and "circling maneuvers" to ward off the Chinese ships whom the Filipinos accused of attempting to occupy the feature.[105] In 1999, the Filipinos had deliberately grounded a landing craft, the BRP Sierra Madre (LT-57) at the shoal as a means to prevent the feature becoming a second Mischief Reef. The ship now acts as an outpost for the PHL navy, and visually represents Filipino sovereignty over the feature.

For Philippines observers, the Scarborough Shoal and the Second Thomas Shoal incidents bore similarities to the takeover of Mischief Reef seventeen years earlier, and is where PRC vessels are currently based to display sovereignty elsewhere. Also similar is how China also breached earlier conflict prevention agreements. The accusations leveled against China of so-called "salami slicing" or more precisely, as described by journalist Robert Haddick, "the slow accumulation of actions, none of which is a *casus belli*, but which add up over time to a major strategic change" appeared to carry real weight.[106]

Both countries accused the other of violating the previously mentioned non-binding 2002 Declaration on the Conduct of Parties in the South

[102] Ministry of Foreign Affairs of the People's Republic of China, 2016.

[103] Government of People's Republic of China, Summary Position Paper, 2014.

[104] "South Sea Fleet Patrols," *People's Daily Online*, 2013.

[105] Tuyay, "Kalayaan Fortified."

[106] Haddick, "Salami Slicing."

China Sea (DoC). In September 2013, noting the seriousness of the Scarborough Shoal issue following the discovery by surveillance aircraft of concrete blocks on the feature, journalists Francisco and Mogato quoted PHL Foreign Secretary Albert del Rosario as commenting "If we looked back to what they did in Mischief Reef, this could very well be a repetition of what happened there." He also claimed that China's most recent "incursion" represented "a significant and larger challenge" for the Philippines. Del Rosario additionally noted the Chinese were aiming to take over the shoal in advance of any future binding CoC in the South China Sea, stating "We think that they have an assertion agenda that they are trying to complete before they are able to sit down and negotiate a CoC". He also observed how the activities by China on Scarborough Shoal could mark "the first case of occupation of an uninhabited feature in the South China Sea since the 2002 code was signed."[107]

The stand-off also illustrated how fishing activities around disputed features could escalate into more serious military and diplomatic confrontations as witnessed in September 2010 between Japan and China in the East China Sea.[108] From the perspective of protecting their sovereignty, Manila had also became increasingly concerned by the implications of a unilaterally imposed temporary fishing ban by China on all fishing vessels in parts of the Spratly archipelago. The seasonal fishing moratorium had been in place since 1999, ostensibly to prevent overfishing and to protect food supplies for PRC citizens. The Philippines did not recognize the ban in PHL claimed areas and in fact implemented fishing regulations of its own. However, in the four years prior to the Scarborough Shoal stand-off (ongoing since April 2012), tensions over fisheries increased as more and more PRC fishing vessels, travelling further to cleaner and more abundant waters, were spotted in the SCS, and with them more face-off incidents with the PHL coast guard for example, over who had sovereign rights in a said area.[109] All these developments, particularly in 2012, had strongly influenced the Philippines's arbitration decision of January 2013. They were determined not to have repeats of Mischief Reef. As explained below, China's response to the arbitration was to embark on an unprecedented and unparalled

[107] Francisco and Mogato, "Philippines Says China Expanding."

[108] For more, see McCurry, "Japan–China Row."

[109] Macikenaite, "The Implications."

feature reclamation and island building program on Mischief Reef and elsewhere in the Spratlys; this has transformed the security environment and seriously strained relations with rival disputants.

Creating "Facts in the Water"

Instead of being cowed by the PHL's court action and the tribunal's subsequent July 2016 finding against China, Beijing very publicly rejected Manila's legal strategy in word and in deed. If one views the photos on the Asia Maritime Transparency Initiative website (run by the Center for Strategic and International Studies), one can see in stark terms the ways in which China was creating "facts in the water", according to strategic analysts at the Pentagon.[110] On Mischief Reef, in the years from 1995 to 2013, there were at least two locations for reclamation activities. These were mostly confined to the rim of the atoll. However, from the end of 2013 until the end of 2016, the Chinese constructed an artificial island of some 1379 acres (558 hectares) that occupied the majority of the feature's perimeter.[111] In early August 2013, the Kyodo News in Japan published leaked details from a classified military document that revealed the PLAN had launched a new patrol route in waters to the west of the Philippines. The route covered Mischief Reef as well as its nearest neighbor, the Second Thomas Shoal, and Reed Bank.[112] Mischief Reef's increasingly important role as one of the PRC'S most active naval outposts and command centers, and one which helped to facilitate such patrols was also noted. The classified document also revealed that the Chinese had reinforced the feature with Cross Slot radar and satellite equipment, solar panels, dipole antennae, search lights, a windmill, a three-storey observation tower, anti-aircraft and machine gun emplacements, a helicopter landing pad and even a basketball court on a newly-constructed concrete platform. Numerous naval and civilian vessels including fishing boats were regularly observed moored at the reef in late May. In early August, it was observed that the Chinese also had strengthened their position in the waters near the Second Thomas Shoal.[113] Another source reported that

[110] Sanger and Gladstone, "Piling Sand."

[111] *Asia Maritime Transparency Initiative*, "Mischief Reef."

[112] Romero, "China Includes."

[113] Diola, "China Patrols Off Palawan."

the Philippine military had reinforced its presence on the Second Thomas Shoal and had engaged in the surveillance of surrounding features after the presence of thirty PRC "fishing vessels" from Hainan island, which included two large transport and supply ships, was confirmed within the PHL's EEZ in early 2013. A highly placed PHL source stated the vessels were often observed moored or barely moving at and around Mischief Reef. The Kyodo news story also reported that, within a matter of weeks, the Chinese had reinforced their position on at least five disputed features (not yet including Mischief Reef). As a result of the patrol route, the SCS situation had become "more volatile" and the deployment of PLAN vessels near Second Thomas Shoal in early 2013—just twenty-two nautical miles (41 kms) from Mischief Reef—represented a "significant change".[114] China was apparently concerned the Philippines might strengthen its claim over the Second Thomas Reef by building structures on the feature. In informal talks between the PRC Ambassador Ma Keqing and Defense Secretary Voltaire T. Gazmin in late May, however, Gazmin had tried to reassure Beijing that it had no intention of "violating the agreement" by building anything on the reef and that the PHL vessels were just providing Filipino soldiers on the shoal with food and water, and to rotate the personnel on the feature.[115]

Speaking in early August 2013, one observer, Rommel Banlaoi, Vice President of the Philippine Association of Chinese Studies, asserted that China's recent activities on, and emanating from, Mischief Reef were aimed at pressuring the Philippines to remove an intentionally grounded landing craft, the previously mentioned Sierra Madre, from the Second Thomas Reef. In general, most observers contended that the PRC's reinforcement and land reclamation activities in the Spratlys in the summer of 2013 were a response to Manila's arbitration case against China earlier that year. Manila's move also came in the months after an agreement between China and ASEAN at the ASEAN Ministerial Meeting in Brunei in June 2012. The members had agreed to commence formal talks on a Code of Conduct (CoC) for South China Sea dispute management during the Sixth ASEAN-China Senior Officials Meeting (SOM) in Suzhou, China in September 2013.[116] Beijing had expressed caution over hurrying

[114] Ibid.; Romero, "China Includes"; Tuyay, "Kalayaan Fortified."

[115] Romero, "China 'Concerned' Phl Will."

[116] Romero, "China Includes W. Phl Sea."

too quickly to reach a CoC. In early August 2013, PRC Foreign Minister Wang Yi warned other SCS claimant states not to rush a CoC because the SCS affects the interests of many countries, and thus requires careful coordination. He noted how some countries imagined a CoC that could be drawn up overnight. Wang also warned that the DoC of November 2002 "shall by no means be bypassed in the formulation of COC" and that "What is important now is the implementation of DoC, particularly its provisions for maritime cooperation".[117] China's ambiguity on a DoC in the months after June 2012 may also have convinced the Philippines of the need for alternative means to emphasize their superior rights and entitlements vis-à-vis features like Mischief Reef. The Chinese no doubt also felt compelled to create "new facts on the water" and to reinforce existing claims in response to as yet undeclared arbitral findings that could very publicly challenge and undermine China's interests in the archipelago.

China's land reclamation activities in mid-2013 gave rise to calls for a more decisive response within the Philippines. This was reflected in statements by PHL Defense Secretary Gazmin, who asserted in May 2013 that the Filipino military would "fight to the last soldier" for "what is ours".[118] In early June, journalist Ramon Farolan warned that the Second Thomas Shoal "must not suffer the same fate as Mischief Reef" and that via the occupied reef, the Chinese "have established a foothold in the area that serves as a forward base for the continuing "creeping" invasion of Philippine territory.[119] Rodel Rodis, a leading member of the National Federation of Filipino American Associations (NFFAA), argued that June 12, the country's Independence Day, should have been used to "rally the global Filipino community to denounce China's creeping invasion" following the loss of Mischief Reef, Scarborough Shoal, and now possibly the Second Thomas Shoal. He also lamented that "it was only a matter of time" before PRC vessels would find their way to the Second Thomas Shoal, a "gateway" to the oil and gas resource rich waters of the Recto Bank.[120] Despite such calls domestically for more decisive action, the PHL military stated that its nine naval detachments "still remained

[117] Embassy of the People's Republic of China in the Republic of Fiji, "China Warns Against Rush."

[118] "Creeping Occupation," *The Philippine Star* (editorial).

[119] Farolan, "AFP Test Missions."

[120] Rodis, "Defend Philippine Independence."

in a makeshift style" and "its defense assets are not sufficient to implement the required military actions" needed to ward off Chinese designs in the area. As such, the Philippine's defense posture was "reactive on developing situations".[121] Such realities also reflected the limited options open to the PHL in terms of defending their claim to Mischief Reef or at least pressuring China not to further consolidate its position.

In 2014, China's reclamation activities on features within the PHL's EEZ, including Mischief Reef, continued apace, and appeared to be a clear riposte to the arbitral case of January 2013. It should be noted that most other claimant states, including Vietnam, Taiwan, and Malaysia, for example, were also engaging in reclamation and fortification activities. In fact, a New York Times article observed as much in April 2015 when it stated that "in some ways, China is just catching up". It qualified this by writing that these smaller reclamations paled in comparison to the extent and scale of the PRC's island building in this period. The PRC's intensified activities on Spratly features brought the SCS to the forefront of US foreign policy concerns, with President Obama criticising the Chinese for "not necessarily abiding by international norms", for "using its sheer size and muscle to force countries into subordinate positions" and that "just because the Philippines or Vietnam are not as large as China doesn't mean that they can just be elbowed aside."[122]

Filipino newspaper articles in the first half of 2014 reported how official sources were mistaken in presuming that the Chinese could possibly refrain from reclamation activities on Mischief Reef because of its proximity to the Philippines. One article reported the views of an anonymous official who commented on how Beijing predicted that Manila would respond more stridently on the diplomatic front and would be more successful in garnering international support if the PRC engaged in any land reclamation projects on Mischief Reef.[123] However, a paper by the geopolitical analysis website Stratfor positioned China's activities in general in the Spratlys as part of a three-step strategy aimed at pushing its maritime boundaries farther without "antagonizing all of its neighbors at once" and which recognized the logistical limitations of the PLAN in

[121] "Chinese Navy Launches." *Global Post*.

[122] "Chinese Mischief at Mischief Reef," *New York Times*; "Obama Says China Bullying," *The Guardian*.

[123] Sta. Ana, "China Reclaiming Land."

terms of exercising control over such a large area that is distant from the Chinese mainland. The same paper postulated that the Chinese would reinforce their control in "tactically advantageous areas where it has an actual presence."[124] Despite these activities, in a speech to mark Filipino-Chinese Friendship Day on June 9, the PRC Ambassador to the PHL, Zhao Jianhua, asserted that the maritime disputes between the two countries were "temporary ... compared with our thousand-year friendship and extensive co-operation" and stated the neighbours "have the wisdom, the patience and the courage to settle the disputes through consultations and negotiations."[125] Developments on Mischief Reef, however, provided irrefutable evidence of China's intention to remain permanently on the feature, and to fully exploit it to project Chinese maritime and aerial power.

In October 2014, Lee Hsiang-Chou, the director-general of Taiwan's National Security Bureau, informed his country's parliament that Admiral Wu Shengli, the PLAN commander, had in September personally inspected each one of the reefs where reclamation projects had taken place in (in an "unprecedented survey" over the course of one week), including Mischief Reef. Wu also had observed a joint aerial and naval drill at Fiery Cross Reef, the site of the largest and most important Chinese base in the archipelago.[126] Describing the end objective of these activities, Lee stated that "the goal is to turn islets into ramparts and islands into battlefields." Keck also observed that by transforming underwater features into islands, the Chinese aim to physically assert and strengthen their EEZ claims in the eyes of international law, despite the weaknesses in their claims.[127] According to Lin Chong-pin, a former deputy defence minister of Taiwan, the reclamation projects are also part of a "long-term diplomatic and legal strategy to win legitimacy for the proclamation of sovereignty in the international community".[128]

[124] "China Uses Deep-Sea Exploration," *Stratfor Worldview*.

[125] Sta. Ana, "China Reclaiming Land."

[126] For more on Fiery Cross Reef, see Keck, "China May Build 'Artificial Island' in South China Sea," *The Diplomat*, June 7, 2014, https://thediplomat.com/2014/06/china-may-build-artificial-island-in-south-china-sea/.

[127] Keck, "China Naval Chief Conducts."

[128] Chan, "PLA Navy Chief."

The state-of-the-art air power-related facilities on features like Mischief Reef also bolstered the PRC's ability to monitor and exercise control over the skies. In November 2013, China had provoked the ire of neighbours such as Japan and South Korea (as well as the United States) by unilaterally declaring an Air Defence Identification Zone (ADIZ) over the East China Sea. Many regional observers today believe that it is only a matter of time before the Chinese make a similar declaration over the SCS.[129] For example, as recently as May 2020, an anonymous PLA source revealed that China has been planning to declare an ADIZ over the South China Sea since 2010. Other expert sources have pointed to the PRC's increasing ability to patrol a SCS ADIZ due to state-of-the-art radar facilities and runways on now reclaimed features like Mischief Reef. Indeed, the sources claim that a central reason for the island building activities has been to achieve this aim. At the same time, the Chinese are hesitant to declare an ADIZ in the area "due to a number of technical, political, and diplomatic considerations", notably the adverse impact that an ADIZ declaration would have on China's relationship with other SCS claimant states as well as the US and Japan (Chan, *South China Morning Post*, May 31, 2020).[130]

In a reflection of their significance to the PRC, Lee also claimed that PRC President Xi Jinping had personally authorized the militarization and fortification of the five Spratly features in question (projects at two other features had already commenced before his reign began in late 2012). Lee Hsiang-Chou noted how rare it was for such a high-ranking official like Wu to embark on an extended visit to the Spratlys and that this reflected the PRC's determination to strengthen their position there.[131]

The PRC published its "Position Paper of the Government of the People's Republic of China on the Matter of Jurisdiction in the South China Sea Arbitration Initiated by the Republic of the Philippines" on December 7, 2014. Described in greater detail in Chapter 2, China stated in the document that the Philippines had breached a bilateral agreement, that the arbitration violated UNCLOS, that it was contrary to

[129] Keck, "China Naval Chief Conducts."

[130] Chan, "Beijing's Plans for South."

[131] Keck, "China Naval Chief Conducts."

accepted international legal procedures, and that the arbitral tribunal had no jurisdiction.[132]

By early 2015, satellite imagery brought the public's attention to the extent of China's unprecedented reclamation activities on Mischief Reef. From March 16, 2014 onward, ships were observed inside the lagoon. Island building and dredging commenced on and after January 30, 2015 with the reef reaching its maximum land area of 20.94 square kilometres on May 30, 2015. It was assumed that once the dredging operations had ceased then the objective switched to heightening the feature. The activities included landfill operations involving cutter suction dredgers, which contributed to significant environmental damage to the reef and its surrounding waters. This damage was cited by the PHL in its January 2013 arbitration case. Such was the extent of this dredging ("1,379 acres of land reclamation, and the construction of a 2,644 m by 55 m runway") that one journal article selected Mischief Reef as a worthy case study in terms of the "possible biological impact" of these activities in the Spratlys.[133] The article noted the reef was mostly underwater in 2014, but was mostly above water in 2015 due to the extensive dredging activities of that year, and that by 2016, when the arbitration findings were released, it had an airstrip and living quarters.[134] The last satellite image of the dredging activities was from November 30, 2015.[135] The research found that no new further dredging was detected beyond April 30, 2016, and that no new land areas were detectable up to November 2017.[136] It also found that the biological impact caused by plumes from dredging, backscatter, excess sediment, and the absorption of sediment on the coral reef was dramatic. Negative consequences included the smothering of reef complexes and reduced light to these complexes.[137] On some dates, backscatter was detectable as much as 30 kms from the reef, and the impacted area stretched some 20 kms from the center of the feature while the total impacted area consisted of approximately 1200 square kms. The inner reef area was also "likely heavily impacted". In its

[132] Foreign Ministry of the People's Republic of China.

[133] Smith et al., 3.

[134] Ibid., 2.

[135] Ibid., 6–7.

[136] Ibid., 3.

[137] Ibid., 9.

conclusion, the paper emphasized the geo-political significance of these environmental impacts because "pollution by one country into another country's waters aggravates territorial disputes".[138] It also referenced expert testimonies from the Philippines–China arbitration hearings who claimed that the feature reclamation projects by the PRC in the Spratlys represented the quickest deterioration of coral reefs in human history. According to the journal authors, this view was "consistent with the decrease in chlorophyll-a seen from 2016 from 2018 in the lagoon and surrounding waters." It also noted how such destruction concerned not only the reef itself or others like it, but also "reduces commercially vital fish stocks, and the ability of the Pacific Ocean to detoxify waste that can impact climate." The construction of man-made airfields and the reclaimed islands, which is often irreversible, also destroy reef habitats, and could cause leaching, and contribute to the "extinction of local fish, invertebrates, and other critical components of the local ecosystem."[139]

By April 2015, globally recognized newspapers such as the New York Times were reporting on satellite photos by Airbus Defence and Space, and published by IHS Jane's Weekly that showed how Mischief Reef was, through massive dredging operations, being transformed within a matter of weeks since January 2015, from a submerged coral reef into an island with an amphibious warship guarding its artificially widened southern entrance. The operations, the article claimed, showed "the remarkable speed, scale and ambition of China's effort to literally gain ground in the dispute" by creating, as Pentagon military analysts described it, "facts on the waters" that were happening so quickly that they could not be undone or prevented. The pace of these activities was a cause for concern for all the claimant states as well as major allies like the United States.[140]

In March 2015, the commander of the US Pacific Fleet, Admiral Harry Harris, warned that "China is creating a great wall of sand with dredges and bulldozers" and that its reclamation activities, lack of clarity, pattern-like provocative behavior, and the "deep asymmetry between China's capabilities and those of its smaller neighbors...raise serious questions about China's intentions." Harris also emphasized that all the parties in the SCS disputes should honor the 2002 ASEAN-China Declaration on

[138] Ibid., 10.

[139] Ibid.

[140] Sanger and Gladstone, "Piling Sand."

the Conduct of Parties in the South China Sea.[141] in which the signatories agreed to "exercise self-restraint in the conduct of activities that would complicate or escalate disputes and affect peace and stability" and cautioned China's next steps "will be a key indicator of whether the region is heading towards confrontation or cooperation."[142]

A month earlier, the Asia–Pacific editor of IHS Jane's Weekly, James Hardy, contended that the satellite photos were proof of a "methodical, well-planned campaign to create a chain of air and sea-capable fortresses."[143] In April 2015, the New York Times quoted Mira Rapp-Hooper, then director of the Center for Strategic and International Studies' (CSIS) Asia Maritime Transparency Initiative, which was monitoring activities in the Spratlys. Rapp-Hooper stated that Mischief Reef is one of seven outposts employed by China to exert control over the SCS and that its metamorphosis will, together with other PRC-occupied features, allow Beijing to conduct regular, sustained patrols of the airspace and water, and to attempt to press its far-flung maritime claims as many as 1000 miles from its shores". She acknowledged that while outposts like Mischief Reef would be too difficult for China to defend in a war, they nonetheless "could certainly allow it to exert significant pressure on other South China Sea claimants, such as the Philippines and Vietnam."[144] In a mark of how seriously Washington was taking Mischief Reef and other Spratly disputes, early April 2015 witnessed US Defense Secretary Ashton B. Carter warn "we take a strong stance against the militarization of these disputes" and urged "China to limit its activities and exercise restraint to improve regional trust." In the same month, the US and Filipino militaries also jointly participated in the largest drills between the two allies since 2000.[145] The Obama administration also committed to a strategy of keeping US vessels sailing unhindered in the Spratlys so as to emphasize their commitment to freedom of navigation in those waters and to publicly reject the PRC's claim to exclusive maritime and aerial rights

[141] Also see "2002 Declaration on Conduct of Parties in the South China Sea", https://cil.nus.edu.sg/wp-content/uploads/2017/07/2002-Declaration-on-the-Conduct-of-Parties-in-the-South-China-Sea.pdf.

[142] Harris, untitled speech at the Australian Strategic Policy Institute.

[143] Alexander Smith, "China Builds Islands."

[144] Sanger and Gladstone, "Piling Sand."

[145] Brunnstrom and Takenaka, "U.S. Defense Chief Warns."

in the area.[146] The encounters between US and Chinese vessels and aircraft became markedly more tense in this period. A November 2015 US Congressional Report observed the evolution in US responses to the PRC's island building activities particularly from mid-2015 onwards. The Wall Street Journal wrote on May 12 that US Secretary of Defense Ashton Carter cited "growing momentum with the Pentagon and the White House for taking concrete steps in order to send Beijing a signal that the recent buildup in the Spratlys went too far and needed to stop." As such, Carter was considering dispatching US Navy surveillance aircraft and vessels within twelve nms of the PRC's island building projects[147] (Map 6.1).

Words were soon converted into more determined and more frequent actions. One such example was the case of a US Navy P-8A Poseidon surveillance airplane that departed on May 20, 2015 from the Philippines' Clark Air Base on a reconnaissance trip. The aircraft flew over the "Big Three" PRC outpost features of Subi Reef, Mischief Reef, and Fiery Cross Reef and surveilled the island building projects taking place below them. As recalled by a CNN reporter, Jim Sciutto, who was permitted to join and observe the mission, the PLAN radioed the US plane and demanded that they leave the airspace on at least eight occasions. These demands included the following messages: "You are approaching our military alert zone. Leave immediately" and the yelling of "You go" as the Chinese radio operator became more irritated. The November 2015 US Congressional Report also complained that the term "military alert zone" is not an internationally recognized term so it is difficult to comprehend how exactly the PLAN defines the area in question. The same report cited the surveillance flights over such features as Mischief Reef as possible proof that the US sought to "impose reputational costs on China as its land reclamation and construction activities continue."[148] CNN also reported that while P-8 crew members had been engaging in such surveillance operations for months and had received warnings from the PRC, they noted that the warnings had become more aggressive after the island building projects had commenced. In May 2015, an unnamed US defense

[146] Sanger and Gladstone, *New York Times*.

[147] Poling, "Carter on the South China Sea"; Entous and Barnes, "U.S. Military Proposes Challenge"; *Report to Congress* (November 2015), 472.

[148] Scuitto, "Behind the Scenes"; *Report to Congress* (November 2015), 472.

Map 6.1 Image (June 2018) showing the changes to Mischief Reef after major construction projects in the period from 2014 to 2016. A runway is visible at the bottom center of the image while dozens of vessels can be seen moored inside the reef's lagoon. Public Domain/Creative Commons Image (*Source* Tony Peters (photographer), June 7, 2018: https://www.flickr.com/people/7538452@N03; https://en.wikipedia.org/wiki/Mischief_Reef; https://commons.wikimedia.org/wiki/File:Mischief_Reef_(40836669690).jpg)

official revealed that these flights were taking place on an almost-daily basis.[149] One such flight included.

[149] Cooper and Perlez, "U.S. Flies Over"; "High Stakes Surveillance," CNN; *Report to Congress* (November 2015), 472.

Admiral Scott Swift, commander of the U.S. Pacific Fleet, as an observer.[150] Reflecting American weariness with China's activities, in late May 2015 Carter called for "a lasting halt" to the land reclamation projects and severely criticized Beijing for its behaviour declaring: "Turning an underwater rock into an airfield simply does not afford the rights of sovereignty or permit restrictions on international air or maritime transit."

Carter also reiterated his country's right and intention to "fly, sail, and operate wherever international law allows."[151] Reflecting a stronger but sometimes still indecisive line by Washington,[152] on October 27, President Obama ordered a US navy guided missile destroyer to conduct a FONOP within 12 nms of Subi Reef, aimed at showing the Chinese that they do not recognize any territorial sea around the feature. China responded by dispatching at least one of its ships to observe the destroyer. A PRCFM spokesperson also warned: "If the relevant party keeps stirring things up, it will be necessary for China to speed up its construction activities."[153] The risk of confrontation thus became more pronounced than previously. As one observer noted, it was apparent that China was reclaiming these submerged features and then declaring them military no-go zones in complete contravention of international laws and norms. Such behaviour again begged serious questions about China's intentions and about whether or not the Chinese would use features like Mischief Reef to keep other military forces out of the waters in and the airspace above the South China Sea.[154]

When the PRC's Foreign Ministry spokesperson, Lu Kang, stated on June 16 that "the land reclamation project of China's construction on some stationed islands and reefs of the Nansha (Spratly) Islands will be completed in the upcoming days", the other SCS claimants remained

[150] Pearson and Blanchard, "U.S. Admiral Says"; *Report to Congress* (November 2015), 473.

[151] U.S. Department of Defense, *IISS Shangri-La Dialogue*; *Report to Congress* (November 2015), 473.

[152] Wright, Ewing, and Bender, "Obama Team, Military"; De Luce and Mcleary, "In South China"; *Report to Congress* (November 2015) 473.

[153] Perlez, "Beijing Calls U.S."; Savastopulo and Clover, "China Accuses US Navy"; PRCFM, "Remarks on USS Lassen's Entry"; *Report to Congress* (November 2015), 473.

[154] Wingfield-Hayes, "Why China Warned the US."

unconvinced (Lee, *The Diplomat*, June 19, 2015). The government statement was apparently a damage-limitation exercise aimed at reassuring China's neighbours that the reclamation activities would be limited in terms of time and scope. According to Ruan Zongze from the China Institute of International Studies, a think tank affiliated with the PRC's Foreign Ministry, the statement was "a sign of transparency showing that China is proceeding according to its pre-established schedule." In addition to securing the PRC's defense objectives, the statement emphasized that the activities were civilian in nature, and not focused on any third party. It added that the activities were within China's sovereign rights, were "lawful, reasonable and justified", and were not harmful to the marine environment. The reclamation projects also "do not affect the freedom of navigation and overflight enjoyed by all countries in accordance with international law in the South China Sea", however, despite the initial reassurances, the Foreign Ministry's website stated that the Chinese would continue with construction projects aimed at permitting maritime search and rescue, environmental conversation, and scientific research among other objectives.[155]

Apparently land reclamation was only a stage in a process of militarizing and installing state-of-the-art facilities on features like Mischief Reef. On June 23, the China Daily, a mouthpiece for the PRC government, cited a maritime expert who claimed that China's intensive land reclamation projects on Mischief Reef were a "response to the arbitration case filed by the Philippines." The same China Daily article included an English language translation of an "On Military and War" column report in the news.ifeng.com Chinese media website. The title of the original Chinese language article translated as "Turning Mischief Reef into the Pearl Harbor of the South China Sea is of vital importance." It set out the benefits of island building on the reef because it could serve as "China's forefront outpost in the South China Sea with an integrated air, sea, and land garrison." It also noted how land reclamation activities had been completed on Fiery Cross Reef on June 15, but were still on-going on Mischief Reef with only 5.6 of the planned 8 kilometers of land having been reclaimed since January. Comparisons were made with the large US-UK operated Diego Garcia naval base in the Indian Ocean. The article lauded the more favourable depths at Mischief Reef, with a large area lagoon (of some 36 square kilometers) with depths of between 20 to 30 meter, and surrounding waters of more than 1000 meter depths that provided "an ideal berth for submarines." These characteristics made the atoll favourable to protecting vessels and warships of

[155] "China Says South China," *Taipei Times*.

all sizes from high waves and inclement weather. Due to all these advantages, the report contended that an outpost on Mischief Reef was more important than one on Fiery Cross Reef. In fact, its strategic value to the PRC, it claims, was evident from the presence of the large "Jinggangshan" amphibious warship at the reef during the reclamation period.[156] The tribunal held a hearing on "jurisdiction and admissibility" in July 2015, declared an award on the same on October 29 of that year, and then convened another hearing on the merits of the said award in late November 2015 (November 24–30).

In response to an award by the Arbitral Tribunal on jurisdiction and admissibility that was favourable to the PHL on October 29, Beijing rejected the decision on October 30 as null, void, and non-binding.[157] The arbitration procedures continued nonetheless with numerous hearings, requests, and statements made, particularly in November and December of 2015. The "Hearing on the Merits" took place from November 24–30 during which time "outstanding issues of the Tribunal's jurisdiction and admissibility and the merits of the Philippines' submissions", including Submission 12, were heard.[158] Similarly, as explained in the same, July 2016 marked a watershed for the Mischief Reef dispute. On July 12, the Arbitral Tribunal granted a "final and binding" award in favour of the Philippines and unanimously found that China's claims and activities on and around the feature and its surrounding waters had no basis under UNCLOS and thus were unlawful. While not changing one jot to the "facts on the water", the findings were a publicity victory for the Philippines. The July 2016 findings and the subsequent news coverage once again brought the irretrievable loss of Mischief Reef, and China's slow but comprehensive takeover of the atoll to the world's attention. As illustrated in the next and final chapter, the years since the 2016 award have not provided any evidence of China relenting in any way vis-à-vis the once submerged feature.

[156] "China to Turn Mischief Reef," *China Daily*.

[157] For the formal documents, see https://docs.pca-cpa.org/2016/07/PH-CN-20160712-Award.pdf and https://www.fmprc.gov.cn/nanhai/eng/snhwtlcwj_1/t1379492.htm.

[158] For more, see Chapter 2 herein.

References

"A Mischief Reef in the Making?" *Newsbreak*, June 2, 2011. http://archives.newsbreak-knowledge.ph/2011/06/02/a-mischief-reef-in-the-making/.

Almonte, Jose T. "Facing Up to the China Challenge." Speech, August 22, 2012, Makati Business Club General Membership Meeting, *Perspectives on Dealing with China*, MBC Forum No. 12 Series 2012. www.mbc.com.ph and https://www.yumpu.com/en/document/read/11886814/mbc-forum-2012-almonte-sta-maria-4dpmd-makati-business-club.

Alunan, Rafael M. III. "Honor." *Business World*, January 22, 2013. http://www.bworldonline.com/content.php?section=Opinion&title=Honor&id=64610

Acharya, Amitav. *Constructing a Security Community in Southeast Asia—ASEAN and the Problem of Regional Order*. Oxford, UK: Routledge, 3rd edition, 2014.

Amurao, George. "A Shoal Too Far in South China Sea." *Asia Times Online*, 2012. https://namvietnews.wordpress.com/2012/07/20/a-shoal-too-far-in-south-china-sea/.

"ARF Makes a Contribution." *Japan Times*, July 30, 2011. https://www.japantimes.co.jp/opinion/2011/07/30/editorials/arf-makes-a-contribution/.

ASEAN. "China Hardening Positions on Overlapping Claims in South China Sea." *China Post*, May 31, 2011. http://www.chinapost.com.tw/commentary/the-china-post/special-to-the-china-post/2011/05/31/304386/ASEAN-China.htm.

"ASEAN, China Pledge Anew to Settle Dispute Peacefully." *Associated Press*, December 17, 1998.

ASEAN. "Declaration on the Conduct of Parties in the South China Sea." Phnom Penh, Cambodia, November 4, 2002. https://asean.org/?static_post=declaration-on-the-conduct-of-parties-in-the-south-china-sea-2

Asia Maritime Transparency Initiative. "Mischief Reef." Center for Strategic and International Studies (CSIS), 2020. https://amti.csis.org/mischief-reef.

Baguioro, Luz. "Three Nations Sign Pact for Joint Spratlys Survey." *The Straits Times*, March 15, 2005.

Batongbacal, Jay. "Arbitration 101: Philippines V. China." *Asia Maritime Transparency Initiative*, January 21, 2015. https://amti.csis.org/arbitration-101-philippines-v-china/.

Baker, John C., and David G. Wiencek (eds.). *Cooperative Monitoring in the South China Sea: Satellite Imagery, Confidence-Building Measures and the Spratly Islands Disputes*. Westport, CT: Praeger, 2002.

Bercovitch, Jacob, and Mikio Oishi. *International Conflict in the Asia-Pacific: Patterns, Consequences, and Management*. Routledge, Oxford (UK), 2010.

Bondoc, Jarius. "China Invading Scarborough, but Phl Thinks It Will Pass." *The Philippine Star*, December 14, 2012. https://www.philstar.com/opinion/2012/12/14/885753/china-invading-scarborough-phl-thinks-it-will-pass.

Bondoc, Jarius. "Protest in Philippines Over South China Sea Stand-Off." *BBC News*, May 11, 2012. https://www.bbc.com/news/world-asia-18030805.

Branigan, Tania. "Chinese Frigate Runs Aground in Disputed Part of South China Sea." *The Guardian*, July 13, 2012. https://www.theguardian.com/world/2012/jul/13/chinese-frigate-runs-aground-sea.

Brunnstrom, David, and Kiyoshi Takenaka. "U.S. Defense Chief Warns Against Militarization of Territorial Rows in Asia." *Reuters*, April 8, 2015. https://jp.reuters.com/article/us-usa-japan-carter-militarisation-idUSKBN0MZ05W20150408.

Carlito, Pablo. "Diplomacy, Not VFA, Urged on Spratly Row." *Philippine Daily Inquirer*, November 9, 1998.

Chan, Minnie. "Beijing's Plans for South China Sea Air Defence Identification Zone Cover Pratas, Paracel and Spratly Islands, PLA Source Says." *South China Morning Post*, May 31, 2020. https://www.scmp.com/news/china/military/article/3086679/beijings-plans-south-china-sea-air-defence-identification-zone.

Chan, Minnie. "PLA Navy Chief Visited Paracels, Taiwan's Intelligence Boss Says." *South China Morning Post*, October 17, 2014. https://www.scmp.com/news/china/article/1617943/pla-navy-chief-visited-paracels-taiwans-intelligence-boss-says.

Chase, Michael S., Jeffrey Engstrom, Tai Ming Cheung, Kristen A. Guinness, Scott Warren Harold, Susan Puska, and Samuel K. Berkowitz. "China's Incomplete Military Transformation: Assessing the Weaknesses of the People's Liberation Army (PLA)." Rand Corporation, Santa Monica, CA, USA, 2015. https://www.uscc.gov/sites/default/files/Research/China's%20Incomplete%20Military%20Transformation_2.11.15.pdf.

"China Bans Fishing." *Weathernews Philippines*, March 25, 1999.

"China Rebuffs RP Anew." *Philippine Daily Inquirer*, April 6, 1999.

"China Rejects Philippines' Tribunal Challenge: Paracels Dispute and the Impacts Towards Southeast Asian Human Life." *Agence France Presse*, April 1, 1999. https://paracels74.tripod.com/index.htm.

"China Says South China Sea Work to Finish Soon." *Taipei Times*, June 17, 2015. http://www.taipeitimes.com/News/front/archives/2015/06/17/2003620885.

"China to Turn Mischief Reef into 'Pearl Harbor of the South China Sea'." *China Daily*, June 23, 2015. http://chinadailymail.com/2015/06/23/china-to-turn-mischief-reef-into-pearl-harbor-of-the-south-china-sea/.

"China Uses Deep-Sea Exploration to Push Its Maritime Claims." *Stratfor Worldview*, May 8, 2014. https://worldview.stratfor.com/article/china-uses-deep-sea-oil-exploration-push-its-maritime-claims.

"Chinese Mischief at Mischief Reef." *New York Times*, April 11, 2015. http://www.nytimes.com/2015/04/12/opinion/sunday/chinese-mischief-at-mischief-reef.html.

"Chinese Navy Launches New Patrol Route in the S. China Sea." *Global Post*, August 5, 2013. https://www.imoa.ph/chinese-navy-launches-new-patrol-route-in-the-s-china-sea/.

Chung, Christopher. *The Spratly Islands Dispute: Decision units and Domestic Politics*. Canberra: Australian Defence Force Academy: School of Humanities and Social Science, 2004. https://www.unsworks.unsw.edu.au/primo-explore/fulldisplay/unsworks_3198/UNSWORKS.

Cooper, Helene, and Jane Perlez. "U.S. Flies Over a Chinese Project at Sea, and Beijing Objects." *New York Times*, May 22, 2015.

"Concern Over Spratly Statement." *The Straits Times*, April 27, 1999.

"Courting Trouble—An International Tribunal Delivers a Blow to China's Claims in the South China Sea." *Economist*, July 16, 2016. https://www.economist.com/china/2016/07/16/courting-trouble.

"Creeping Occupation." *The Philippine Star*, May 24, 2013. https://www.philstar.com/opinion/2013/05/24/945627/editorial-creeping-occupation.

Dacanay, Barbara Mae. "China Builds on Five More Reefs Near Philippine-Claimed Island." *Gulf News*, May 24, 2011. http://gulfnews.com/news/world/philippines/china-builds-on-five-more-reefs-near-philippine-claimed-island-1.812272.

De Luce, Dan, and Paul Mcleary. "In South China, a Tougher U.S. Stance." *Foreign Policy* (blog), October 2, 2015.

Del Callar, Michaela. "PHL Seeks End to Chinese Occupation of 8 Reefs and Shoal in UN Complaint." *GMA News*, January 23, 2013. https://www.gmanetwork.com/news/news/nation/291632/phl-seeks-end-to-chinese-occupation-of-8-reefs-and-shoal-in-un-complaint/story/.

Denyer, Simon, Craig Whitlock, and Steven Mufson. "U.S. Warship Sails Within 12 Miles of Chinese-Built Island in South China Sea." *Washington Post*, October 26, 2015.

Deogracias, Charmaine C. "The Road to an ASEAN-China Code of Conduct in the South China Sea." *ABS-CBN News*, August 10, 2017. https://news.abs-cbn.com/focus/08/10/17/the-road-to-an-asean-china-code-of-conduct-in-the-south-china-sea.

Diola, Camile. "China Patrols Off Palawan, Builds a Basketball Court in Reef—Report." *The Philippine Star*, August 6, 2013. https://www.philstar.com/headlines/2013/08/06/1058591/china-patrols-palawan-builds-basketball-court-reef-report.

Embassy of the People's Republic of China in the Republic of Fiji. "China Warns Against Rush to Set Code of Conduct in South China Sea." Press Release, August 6, 2013. http://fj.china-embassy.org/eng/gdxw/t1064432.htm.

Embassy of the Republic of the Philippines in Japan. "Notification and Statement of Claim." No. 13-2011, January 22, 2013. https://tokyo.philembassy.net/02events/statement-by-secretary-of-foreign-affairs-albert-del-rosario-on-the-unclos-arbitral-proceedings-against-china-to-achieve-a-peaceful-and-durable-solution-to-the-dispute-in-the-wps/.

Emmers, Ralf. "Maritime Disputes in the South China Sea—Strategic and Diplomatic Status Quo." In *Maritime Security in Southeast Asia*, edited by Kwa Chong Guan and John K. Skogan. Oxford: Routledge, 2007.

Emmers, Ralf. *Resource Management and Contested Territories in East Asia.* London, UK: Palgrave Macmillan, 2013.

Entous, Adam, and Julian A. Barnes. "U.S. Military Proposes Challenge to China Sea Claims." *Wall Street Journal*, May 12, 2015.

"Erap Insists on UN Intervention." *Agence France Presse*, March 23, 1999.

"Erap Skips Visit to Beijing." *Philippine Daily Inquirer*, April 1, 1999.

"Estrada says China 'Biggest Threat'." *Philippine Daily Inquirer*, May 18, 1999.

Far Eastern Economic Review 161 (October 1998).

Farolan, Ramon. "Mischief Reef and Love Me Tender." *Philippine Daily Inquirer*, July 18, 2011. https://opinion.inquirer.net/7987/mischief-reef-and-%E2%80%98love-me-tender%E2%80%99.

Farolan, Ramon. "AFP Test Missions." *Philippine Daily Inquirer*, June 2, 2013. https://opinion.inquirer.net/53841/afp-test-missions.

Fisher, Richard, Jr. "South China Sea Competition: China Contemplates More Mischief." *International Assessment and Strategy Center*, June 28, 2009. http://strategycenter.net/research/pubID.209/pub_detail.asp.

Foreign Ministry of the People's Republic of China. "China's Peaceful Development Road." December 12, 2005. https://www.fmprc.gov.cn/ce/cegv/eng/zywjyjh/t227733.htm.

Foreign Ministry of the People's Republic of China. *Statement on the Award of the Arbitral Tribunal in the South China Sea Arbitration.* July 12, 2016. https://www.fmprc.gov.cn/nanhai/eng/snhwtlcwj_1/t1379492.htm.

Francisco, Rosemarie, and Manuel Mogato. "Philippines Says China Expanding Territory Before Code Takes Effect." *Reuters*, September 4, 2013. https://fr.reuters.com/article/uk-philippines-china-idUKBRE9830M420130904.

Fravel, M. Taylor. *Strong Borders, Secure Nation—Co-operation and Conflict in China's Territorial Disputes.* Princeton: Princeton University Press, 2008.

"General Chi to Sign Defense Loan Accord in Manila." *South China Morning Post*, February 5, 1997.

Gomez, Jim. "Philippine Diplomat to China: Don't Turn Shoal into Island." *The Philippine Star*, December 4, 2016. https://www.philstar.com/headlines/2016/04/12/1572446/philippine-diplomat-china-dont-turn-shoal-island.

Government of People's Republic of China. "Summary of Position Paper on the Matter of Jurisdiction in the South China Sea Arbitration." December 7, 2014. http://english.www.gov.cn/archive/press_briefing/2014/12/07/content_281475020440060.htm.

Government of People's Republic of China. *Declaration*, August 25, 2006. https://www.wipo.int/treaties/en/remarks.jsp?cnty_id=6638C.

Guan, Ang Cheng. "The South China Sea Dispute Re-visited." Working Paper No. 4, Institute of Defence and Strategic Studies, Singapore, Working Paper Series, August 1999. https://www.rsis.edu.sg/wp-content/uploads/rsis-pubs/WP04.pdf.

"Hackers Bring PH-China Dispute to Cyberspace." *Philippine Daily Inquirer*, April 23, 2012. https://globalnation.inquirer.net/34379/hackers-bring-ph-china-dispute-to-cyberspace.

Haddick, Robert. "Salami Slicing in the South China Sea." August 3, 2012. https://foreignpolicy.com/2012/08/03/salami-slicing-in-the-south-china-sea/.

Harris, Admiral Harry B., Jr. Speech at the Australian Strategic Policy Institute, Canberra, Australia, March 31, 2015. http://www.cpf.navy.mil/leaders/harry-harris/speeches/2015/03/ASPI-Australia.pdf.

"High Stakes Surveillance Over the South China Sea." CNN, May 20, 2015.

Himmelman, Jeff. "A Game of Shark and Minnow." *New York Times Magazine*, October 27, 2013. https://www.nytimes.com/newsgraphics/2013/10/27/south-china-sea/index.html.

"HK Activists Protest Against Standoff Near Scarborough Shoal." *Focus Taiwan*, October 5, 2012. https://focustaiwan.tw/politics/201205100037.

Hsiao, Russell. "PLA General Advises Building Bases in the South China Sea." *China Brief* 9, no. 13 (June 24, 2009), Jamestown Foundation. http://www.jamestown.org/single/?no_cache=1&tx_ttnews[tt_news]=35169.

"In Philippines, Banana Growers Feel Effect of South China Sea Dispute." *Washington Post*, June 10, 2012. https://www.washingtonpost.com/world/asia_pacific/in-philippines-banana-growers-feel-effect-of-south-china-sea-dispute/2012/06/10/gJQA47WVTV_story.html.

Javellana, Juliet. "Estrada, UN Chief to Discuss Row Over Spratlys." *Philippine Daily Inquirer*, March 18, 1999.

"The JMSU: A Tale of Bilateralism and Secrecy in the South China Sea." Newsletter, *Center for Strategic and International Studies*, July 27, 2010. https://www.csis.org/analysis/jmsu-tale-bilateralism-and-secrecy-south-china-sea.

Joyner, Christopher C. "The Spratly Islands Dispute in the South China Sea: Problems, Policies, and Prospects for Diplomatic Accommodation." In *Investigating Confidence-Building Measures in the Asia-Pacific Region*, edited by Ranjeet K. Singh, 53–108. Report No.28, Henry L. Stimson Center, Washington, DC, USA. May 1999. https://www.stimson.org/wp-content/files/file-attachments/Investigating%20Confidence-Building%20Measures%20in%20the%20Asia-Pacific%20Region.pdf.

Keck, Zachary. "China Naval Chief Conducts 'Unprecedented' Survey of Disputed Reefs." *The Diplomat*, October 17, 2014. https://thediplomat.com/2014/10/china-naval-chief-conducts-unprecedented-survey-of-disputed-reefs/.

Klare, Michael T. *Resource Wars—The New Landscape of Global Conflict*. New York: Owl Books, 2001.
Leifer, Michael. *Dictionary of the Modern Politics of Southeast Asia*. Oxford, UK: Routledge, 2013.
Lim, Benito. "Tempest Over the South China Sea: The Chinese Perspective on the Spratlys." *Asian Studies* 36, no. 2 (2000): 69–132. http://www.asj.upd.edu.ph/mediabox/archive/ASJ-36-2-2000/lim.pdf.
Lum, Thomas, and Larry A. Niksch. "The Republic of the Philippines: Background and US Relations." Congressional Research Service, 2009. https://apps.dtic.mil/dtic/tr/fulltext/u2/a494140.pdf.
Macikenaite, Vida. "The Implications of China's Fisheries Industry Regulation and Development for the South China Sea Dispute." *Keio University*, 2014. http://citeseerx.ist.psu.edu/viewdoc/download?doi=10.1.1.1003.1586&rep=rep1&type=pdf.
Manila Business World. 13 April 1999 in *FBIS-EAS*-1999-0413.
"Manila Renames South China Sea." *Channel News Asia*, June 14, 2011.
Marfil, Martin P. "Charter Change: Next RP Map to Include Spratly Islands–Estrada." *Philippine Daily Inquirer Interactive, NEWS*, January 27, 1999.
Marfil, Martin. "*Malacañang* Mum on Rohrabacher." *Philippine Daily Inquirer*, December 12, 1998.
Marfil, Martin. "Next RP Map to Include Spratly Islands—Erap." *Philippine Daily Inquirer*, January 27, 1999.
Marfil, Martin, and Christine Avendano. "US Has Role in Spratlys—Erap." *Philippine Daily Inquirer*, January 12, 1999.
McCurry, Justin. "Japan-China Row Escalates Over Fishing Boat Collision." *The Guardian*, September 9, 2010. https://www.theguardian.com/world/2010/sep/09/japan-china-fishing-boat-collision.
"New Security Adviser Wants Aggressive Stance Against China Over Spratlys." *Associated Press*, February 22, 2001.
"Obama Says China Bullying Smaller Nations in South China Sea Row." *The Guardian*, April 10, 2015. https://www.theguardian.com/world/2015/apr/10/obama-says-china-bullying-smaller-nations-in-south-china-sea-row.
Pearson, James, and Ben Blanchard. "U.S. Admiral Says His South China Sea Surveillance Flight 'Routine'." *Reuters*, July 20, 2015. https://www.reuters.com/article/us-southchinasea-usa-idUSKCN0PU08720150720.
Perlez, Jane. "Beijing Calls U.S. Warship's Route in South China Sea a 'Provocation'." *New York Times*, October 27, 2015.
"PH, Chinese Naval Vessels in Scarborough Shoal Standoff." *Philippine Daily Inquirer*, May 9, 2012. https://globalnation.inquirer.net/32341/ph-chinese-naval-vessels-in-scarborough-shoal-standoff.
Philippine Star, October 30, 2001. http://www.philstar.com/Article.aspx?articleId=138432.

"Philippines: Shots in the Spratlys." *Jane's Intelligence Review*, March 1, 1996.

Poling, Gregory. "Carter on the South China Sea: Committed and (Mostly) Clear." *Center for Strategic and International Studies Asia, Maritime Transparency Initiative*, June 3, 2015.

PRCFM. "Foreign Ministry Remarks on USS Lassen's Entry into Waters Near Relevant Islands and Reefs of China's Nansha Islands." October 27, 2015.

"Protest Over Huangyan Island Dispute Held in Beijing." *China.org.cn*, May 12, 2012. http://www.china.org.cn/china/2012-05/12/content_25367605.htm.

Raditio, Klaus Henrich. *Understanding China's Behaviour in the South China Sea—A Defensive Realist Perspective*. London: Palgrave Macmillan, 2019.

Report to Congress (2015) of the US-China Economic and Security Review Commission: Executive Summary and Recommendations. 114th Congress. First Session, Chapter 3, Section 2: "China and Southeast Asia", 428–490. https://www.uscc.gov/files/000977.

"Roco: Estrada Provoking China." *Philippine Daily Inquirer*, May 21, 1999.

Rodis, Rodel. "Defend Philippine Independence Against China Invasion Threat." *Global Nation*, June 18, 2013. http://globalnation.inquirer.net/77919/defend-philippine-independence-against-china-invasion-threat.

Romero, Alexis. "China 'Concerned' Phl Will Build Structures in Ayungin Shoal." *The Philippine Star*, May 29, 2013. http://www.philstar.com/nation/2013/05/29/947745/china-concerned-phl-will-build-structures-ayungin-shoal.

Romero, Alexis. "China Includes W. Phl Sea in Patrol Route—Report." *The Philippine Star*, August 7, 2013. https://www.philstar.com/headlines/2013/08/07/1060871/china-includes-w-phl-sea-patrol-route-report.

Romero, Paolo. "RP-US 'Balikatan 2000' Launched." *The Philippine Star*, January 29, 2000. https://www.philstar.com/headlines/2000/01/29/94581/rp-us-balikatan-2000-launched.

"RP, China to Undertake Joint Research in the Spratlys." *Philippine Daily Inquirer*, July 13, 1999.

Ruth, Annie, and Raffy Jimenez. "China Fortifies Hold on Spratlys." *Manila Times*, January 21, 1999.

Sanger, David E., and Rick Gladstone. "Piling Sand in a Disputed Sea, China Literally Gains Ground." *New York Times*, April 8, 2015. http://www.nytimes.com/2015/04/09/world/asia/new-images-show-china-literally-gaining-ground-in-south-china-sea.html?_r=0.

Savastopulo, Demetri, and Charles Clover. "China Accuses US Navy of Illegal Incursion in South China Sea." *Financial Times*, October 27, 2015.

"Scarborough Shoal Stand-off: A Timeline." *Philippine Daily Inquirer*, May 9, 2012. https://globalnation.inquirer.net/36003/scarborough-shoal-standoff-a-historicaltimeline.

Scuitto, Jim. "Behind the Scenes: A Secret Navy Flight over China's Military Buildup." *CNN*, May 26, 2015.

Smith, Alexander. "China Builds Islands in Disupted [sic] South China Sea." *IHS Jane's Defense Weekly/ NBC News*, February 19, 2015. https://www.nbcnews.com/news/china/china-builds-islands-disupted-south-china-sea-ihs-janes-defense-n308856.

Smith, Leland, Peter Cornillon, Don Rudnickas, and Colleen B. Mouw. "Evidence of Environmental Changes Caused by Chinese Island-Building." *Scientific Reports* 9, no. 5295 (2019). https://doi.org/10.1038/s41598-019-41659-3.

"South Sea Fleet Patrols Meiji Reef." *People's Daily Online*, March 29, 2013. http://en.people.cn/102774/8187210.html.

"Spratley Dispute Flares Again." *International Herald Tribune*, December 1, 1998.

Sta. Ana, David Jude. "China Reclaiming Land in 5 Reefs?" *Philippine Star*, June 13, 2014. http://news.abs-cbn.com/nation/06/13/14/china-reclaiming-land-5-reefs.

Storey, Ian. "China and the Philippines: Moving Beyond the South China Sea Dispute." *China Brief*, October 25, 2006, The Jamestown Foundation.

Storey, Ian. "Trouble and Strife in the South China Sea Part II: The Philippines and China." *China Brief* 8, no. 9 (April 28, 2008), The Jamestown Foundation.

Storey, Ian James. "Creeping Assertiveness: China, the Philippines." *Contemporary Southeast Asia: A Journal of International and Strategic Affairs* 21, no. 1 (April 1999): 95–119.

Summary of World Broadcasts, Asia, Pacific, Issues 3373–3384, 14.

Tiglao, Rigoberto, Andrew Sherry, Nate Thayer, and Michael Vatikiotis. "Tis the Season." *Far Eastern Economic Review* 161 (December 24, 1998).

Tordesillas. Ellen. "Bring China's 9-Dash Line to UN: Justice Carpio." *GMA News Online*, November 8, 2011. https://www.gmanetwork.com/news/opinion/content/237813/bring-china-s-9-dash-line-to-un-justice-carpio/story/.

Torode, Greg. "China 'Dictatorial' in Scarborough Shoal Dispute, Says Albert del Rosario." *South China Morning Post*, November 30, 2012. https://www.scmp.com/news/asia/article/1094200/china-dictatorial-scarborough-shoal-dispute-says-del-rosario.

"Trouble Brews on Mischief Reef." *BBC News*, January 22, 1999. http://news.bbc.co.uk/2/hi/asia-pacific/260762.stm.

Tuyay, Francisco. "Kalayaan Fortified Amid China Threats." *Manila Standard Today*, May 13, 2013. http://manilastandardtoday.com/2013/05/13/kalayaan-fortified-amid-china-threats/.

U.S. Department of Defense, *IISS Shangri-La Dialogue: "A Regional Security Architecture Where Everyone Rises."* May 30, 2015.
"VFA Will Stop Chinese in Spratlys- Estrada." *The Philippine Star*, February 1, 1999.
"Vietnam Worried by China Buildup." *Philippine Daily Inquirer*, January 14, 1999.
Wingfield-Hayes, Rupert. "Why China Warned the US to Stay Away." *BBC News*, June 24, 2015. http://www.bbc.com/news/magazine-33205815.
Wright, Austin, Philip Ewing, and Bryan Bender. "Obama Team, Military at Odds Over South China Sea." *Politico*, July 31, 2015.
Zha, Daojiong, and Mark J. Valencia. "Mischief Reef: Geopolitics and Implications." *Journal of Contemporary Asia* 31, no. 1: 86–103.
Zhao, Suisheng. "China's Periphery Policy and Its Asian Neighbors." *Security Dialogue* 30, no. 3 (September 1999): 335–346.

CHAPTER 7

Post-Arbitration and Looking to the Future

Abstract This concluding chapter begins by discussing Mischief Reef developments since the July 2016 South China Sea Arbitration. Particular attention is given to Freedom of Navigation Operations (FONOPS) as the United States defended this red line issue while China attempted to consolidate its position. The implications of the PRC's continued militarization of Mischief Reef are also addressed. The chapter also shows how despite extensive constructions, there are still significant vulnerabilities involved in defending the feature. It then moves on to addressing technological advances in resource exploration and extraction. The chapter also discusses very recent developments including the influence of President Rodrigo Duterte, as well as a seeming hardening of Washington's position over the Spratlys issue. The chapter then considers the future outlook, factoring in such variables as domestic politics, economic incentives, and the policy goals and strategic objectives of the two protagonists as well as the US. China's desire to discourage an enhanced US naval presence, and how this may contribute to a more stable quid-pro-quo relationship of engagement with Manila are also examined, as are the compelling incentives to address the dispute peacefully. Lessons learnt as well as proposals for resolving or at least managing the dispute are also featured.

Keywords ASEAN · Code of Conduct (CoC) · Confidence-Building Measures · Freedom of Navigation Operations (FONOPS) · Natural resources · Rodrigo Duterte · South China Sea Arbitration

S. Fox, *Mischief Reef*,
https://doi.org/10.1007/978-981-16-3884-8_7

Post-July 2016 Developments

The years since the watershed tribunal findings in July 2016 arguably point more to reasons to be concerned than reasons to be optimistic. Potentially dangerous incidents, the militarization of features, so-called "hybrid warfare"[1] or "grey zone"[2] tactics such as "salami slicing"[3] and "cabbage tactics"[4] by China in particular, and behaviour designed to stake and emphasize claims continue to complicate this dispute. As noted, the tribunal findings have not cowed the Chinese. Indeed, in addition to their 2013–2016 island building projects, the PRC's position on Mischief Reef has been reinforced and will, in all likelihood, continue to be so.

Aside from the defensive strategic benefits of occupying the feature, technological advancements and access to once inaccessible resources in the Spratly Islands have also made the outpost reef and its surrounding waters more valuable than ever. From installations once described by China as mere "fishermen's shelters", Mischief Reef is now one of the so-called "Big Three" (in addition to Fiery Cross Reef and Subi Reef) and as such a key command center for the projection of Chinese power and the protection of Chinese interests in the South China Sea. The significance of Mischief Reef to the PRC's long-term goals in the area is clearly exemplified by the extensive construction work on the reef, especially between 2013 and 2016. From fishermen's shelters in 1994–1995, the outpost now includes a 3 kilometre runway, a port, high-tech radar and communications systems (include military jamming equipment), underground storage facilities, surface to air missile (SAM shelters), anti-ship cruise missiles, gun batteries, and a research station[5] (Map 7.1).

[1] Dowse and Bachmann explain: "Hybrid warfare is an emerging, but ill-defined notion in conflict studies. It refers to the use of unconventional methods as part of a multi-domain warfighting approach. These methods aim to disrupt and disable an opponent's actions without engaging in open hostilities." Dowse and Bachmann, "Explainer: What Is 'Hybrid Warfare'."

[2] These are "operations [that] may not clearly cross the threshold of war. That might be due to the ambiguity of international law, ambiguity of actions and attribution, or because the impact of the activities does not justify a response." Ibid.

[3] Discussed in Chapter 6.

[4] Himmelman describes how this term was coined; Himmelman, "A Game of Shark and Minnow."

[5] "China's Activities," Ministry of Defense Japan; Long, "Deep Plowing the South."

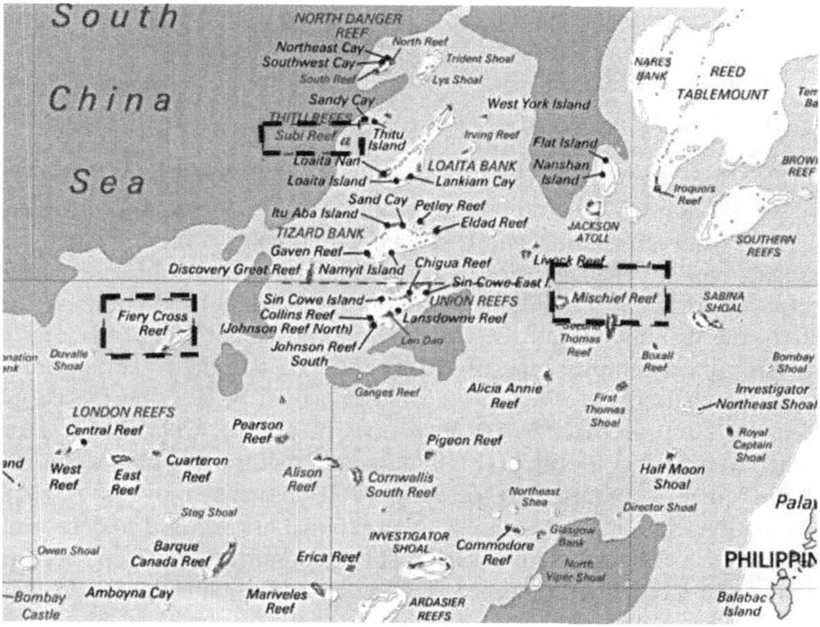

Map 7.1 Image (1995) showing the PRC's "Big Three" outposts (Fiery Cross Reef, Mischief Reef, and Subi Reef) in the Spratly Islands. Public Domain Image (*Source* Central Intelligence Agency [CIA], United States, 1995. https://www.loc.gov/resource/g9237s.ct002223/?r=-0.998,-0.072,2.996,1.443,0; https://en.wikipedia.org/wiki/Spratly_Islands#/media/File:Mapspratly.jpg)

These developments enhance China's ability to attain key strategic objectives vis-à-vis features like Mischief Reef—keeping US forces and their allies out via an anti-access/area denial (A2/AD) strategy[6] and ultimately exercising greater control over the Spratly archipelago. The pattern of events since 1994–1995 suggest that the Filipinos have justifiable cause for their concerns that they not only will never retrieve Mischief Reef, but that their position in the "West Philippine Sea" will continue to be eroded by Chinese activities on and around the feature in the near future. The question of whether or not Manila and Beijing can stabilize this dispute to the satisfaction of both states amid a larger and more complex maritime

[6] Ngo, "China's A2/AD Challenge."

dispute remains as pressing today as it did in the mid-1990s. Some of the key recent issues in relation to Mischief Reef are discussed below.

Freedom of Navigation Operations (FONOPS)

Incidents in recent years close to Mischief Reef illustrate how FONOPS by the US and China's response to them carry the potential for a violent skirmish between Chinese and US or Filipino military forces. As discussed earlier, freedom of navigation is a red line issue for Washington. Even before major island building projects on the reef had been completed in 2016, the Commander of the US Pacific Fleet, Admiral Harry B. Harris Jr. was publicly emphasizing (in 2015) the US' "steadfast" commitment to ensure that 60% of US naval capabilities would be based in the Pacific Fleet by 2020 so that "if any crisis does break out, we're better positioned to quickly respond." He also reiterated that the US and its regional allies "remain committed to fostering a rules-based system that respects international law and adherence to international norms" and to "ensuring unfettered access to shared spaces."[7] These assurances, however, have not altered the Chinese commitment to further consolidate their hold over the reef, in the air and in surrounding waters. Nor has an increase in US FONOPS in close proximity to Mischief Reef since October 2015 and particularly during the Trump presidency (January 2017 to January 2021) distracted the Chinese from their objectives.[8]

Freedom of navigation activities and responses to them in proximity to Mischief Reef since 2015 reflect a hardening of positions by all sides. Widespread concerns over the PRC's 2013–2016 island building projects and its apparent rejection of international law following the tribunal findings in July 2016, as well as a tougher foreign policy approach under the presidency of Donald J. Trump (January 2017 to January 2021), have all contributed to heightened tensions in the area. Trump had accused the Obama administration (2009–2017) of being too soft on China in the South China Sea by not going beyond "innocent passage" FONOPS.[9]

In May 2017, in an intentional rejection of the PRC's territorial sea claims around the feature, an American warship, the USS Dewey, sailed

[7] Harris, Untitled speech.

[8] Panda, "China Condemns US FONOP."

[9] "South China Sea: USS Dewey Warship," ABC.

within 12 nms of Mischief Reef and conducted a “manoeuvring drill” in adjacent waters. It was the Trump presidency’s first challenge to China’s attempts to restrict the movement of vessels from other states in the area. In response, the PRC lodged “stern representations” with Washington, protested that the Dewey had entered the area “without permission”, and that they had warned it, with the aid of two PLAN guided missile warships, to leave the area. A spokesperson for the PRC’s Foreign Ministry, Lu Kang, protested “the act damaged China’s sovereignty and security interests, and could have easily led to an air or sea accident”. Lu continued by asserting that the SCS-related tensions had eased due to joint discussions between the PRC and ASEAN states but US activities such as FONOPS had “seriously disrupted the process of dialogue and consultation.”[10] Such expressions of anger reflected prevailing opinions in the PRC that it is in fact the US who is militarizing the South China Sea disputes by intensifying their freedom of navigation patrols. Mischief Reef and other features, they asserted, were built up for self-defense as well as civilian purposes. Indeed, Chinese experts argue that how the disputes play out in the coming years will rest on how the PRC perceives regional security trends with their eyes focused particularly on such issues as FONOPS.[11]

The May 2017 FONOP stood out from earlier operations. US officials, speaking anonymously, informed media sources that the Dewey’s undeclared mission was to send a message of defiance against China’s claims, particularly to show that “Mischief Reef is not entitled to its own territorial sea regardless of whether an artificial island has built on top of it”. Experts also observed how, previously, FONOPS were characterized by a so-called “innocent passage” exercise whereby US naval vessels would pass through waters without prior notification as demanded by China but without stopping. These “innocent passage” FONOPS struck a balance between ignoring China’s claims while not risking a serious escalation. The USS Dewey, however, carried out a “man overboard” normal operation exercise inside the 12 nms area to show that it was not an “innocent passage” exercise, thus unambiguously rejecting China’s territorial sea claim.[12] The following March saw a US Navy Arleigh Burke-class guided

[10] “South China Sea: US Warship,” BBC.

[11] Torode and Scarr, “Subi Reef, Built Up by Chinese.”

[12] “South China Sea: USS Dewey Warship,” ABC.

missile destroyer, the USS Mustin, also conducting a normal maneuvering (not an "innocent passage") operation within 12 nms of Mischief Reef, and displaying an exercise of rights on the "high seas". The exercise was anonymously acknowledged by US officials, who were cited in a Reuters report. This was after Ren Guoqiang, a spokesperson for the Chinese Ministry of National Defense publicized the freedom of navigation exercise on March 23, calling it a "serious military provocation" and declaring that China "resolutely opposes any illegal provocation in the name of "freedom of navigation."[13] November 2019 also saw the US Navy conduct another FONOP, when the USS Gabrielle Gifford, a littoral combat ship (LCS), sailed within 12 nms of the feature. Afterwards, the Chinese said that they had "tracked, monitored, identified, warned and expelled" the ship, and demanded that the US "stop flexing muscles". By this stage, the PRC's Mischief Reef claims had been directly challenged by the Americans on no less than six occasions (out of twenty-one FONOPS) in the past few years.[14] A Beijing-based think tank, the South China Sea Strategic Situation Probing Incentive, observed that 2020 had seen the highest number of US naval vessels (nine) for five years sailing within 12 nms of PRC-claimed features.[15] This escalation in FONOPS-related tensions in recent years illustrates how the Americans are running out of patience with China's activities, and how US approaches to the SCS are vulnerable to shifts according leadership and policy orientations. Even if one sides with the US, this adds more uncertainty to how the PRC interprets Washington's objectives. As China pushes on regardless to keep others out of the Mischief Reef area, these realities do not bode well for a long-term de-escalation.

Continued Militarization

Another troublesome characteristic of recent years has been the militarization of the Mischief Reef issue on land, sea, and air. In early April 2018, surveillance photographs by the Digital Globe satellite company showed that the Chinese had placed radar-jamming equipment on Mischief Reef as well as Fiery Cross Reef sometime within the previous ninety days.

[13] Panda, "China Condemns US FONOP."

[14] Liu, "China Deploys Airship"; Johnson, "U.S. Sends Warships."

[15] Huang, "South China Sea."

This came to light amidst the largest ever military exercises in the SCS by the Chinese army, navy, and air force and which included the PRC's first aircraft carrier, the Liaoning.[16] That same month, Batongbacal commented on these as then yet unconfirmed reports that a signal jamming device had been installed on Mischief Reef by noting it would be a "serious development from a military perspective" because it could "literally blind the entire AFP [Armed Forces of the Philippines]."[17]

By mid-2018, Mischief Reef (to the east), together with the two other "Big Three" Spratly outpost features, Subi Reef (to the north) and Fiery Cross Reef (to the west), each located at the corner of a defensive triangle, were all characterized by 3-km runways, missile launching emplacements, massive storage facilities, and state of the art surveillance equipment capable of monitoring the communications, satellite, and military activity of foreign states in the area. Observers speculated that the first Chinese soldiers could soon be stationed on Subi Reef. Mischief Reef could possibly follow later. Previously unpublished data analysis by Earthrise Media revealed that Mischief Reef contained up to 190 different buildings and structures, including a basketball court. Security analyst Collin Koh postulated that Mischief Reef had the ability to host an entire regiment ranging from 1,500 to 2,400 soldiers.[18] In May 2018, intelligence officials in Washington confirmed the veracity of a report by CNBC detailing the PRC's clandestine installation of surface-to-air missile systems and YJ-12B anti-ship cruise missiles on all of the "Big Three" Spratly features. The cruise missiles will permit Chinese forces to hit any ship within 295 nms of the three reefs. The HQ-9B long-range surface-to-air missiles are capable of hitting any foreign aircraft, drone, or cruise missile within a distance of 160 nms. Shortly before this, the installation of military jamming equipment was confirmed. In response, one Pentagon official declared, "the further militarization of outposts will only serve to raise tensions and create greater distrust among claimants."[19] In May 2018, the PRC announced that PLA bomber aircraft had conducted

[16] Gordon and Page, "China Installed Military Jamming"; Morgan, "US State Dept. Calls."

[17] Bondoc, "No Confirmation on Signal Jammers."

[18] Torode and Scarr, "Subi Reef, Built Up by Chinese."

[19] Macias, "China Quietly Installed"; Gordon and Page, "China Installed Military Jamming."

take-off and landing exercises on islands and other features in preparation for what the Chinese termed "the battle for the South China Sea". The Japan Times also reported an increasingly worrying trend of naval vessels and aircraft from an array of countries including not only the Philippines, Vietnam, and Malaysia but also the US, Australia, France, India, Japan, and New Zealand being warned to stay out of certain areas of the SCS. It also noted how the PLAN was using features like Mischief Reef to patrol what Chinese naval officers refer to as a "military alert zone" aimed at keeping other naval forces at bay, and that such activities "are far more frequent than is widely known". Commenting on the likely outcome of these militarization activities before becoming the commander of US Indo-Pacific Command in late May 2018, US Navy Admiral Philip Davidson expressed concern because the Chinese had completed their bases in the SCS and only lacked deployed forces. "In short", he argued, "China is now capable of controlling the South China Sea in scenarios short of war with the United States".[20] Chinese experts like Zhang Bouhai, however, contended that the completion of the island building project would see Beijing acting cautiously before making a major move such as stationing combat aircraft and soldiers in the Spratlys because this "would really cross a threshold for China's neighbors."[21] Early August [2018] saw a US reconnaissance aircraft, a US Navy P-8A Poseidon, flying at 16,500 feet above the Spratlys, being warned to "leave immediately," an all too common occurrence in the area in recent years. On board the plane were reporters from CNN and the BBC invited to witness for themselves Chinese activities on Mischief Reef as well as Subi Reef, Fiery Cross Reef, and Johnson Reef. Six separate warnings were issued across the airwaves, each one demanding that the plane vacate the area and reminding them that they were inside PRC territory. "Leave immediately and keep out to avoid any misunderstanding" they were warned. The crew responded, however, that they were engaged in "lawful military activities beyond the national airspace of any coastal state." A PHL aircraft flying nearby was also apparently warned to leave but the onboard journalists noted the much harsher tone and words employed by the Chinese when issuing their warnings to the Filipinos: "Philippine military aircraft, I'm warning you again. Leave immediately

[20] Torode and Scarr, "Subi Reef, Built Up by Chinese."

[21] Ibid.

or you will bear responsibility for all the consequences!" Considering the fact that bilateral political relations had improved following the departure of PHL President Benigno Aquino III (June 2010 to June 2016), a leader who helped initiate the 2013 tribunal proceedings, this had not softened China's line. Under the influence of the mercurial Rodrigo Duterte (President from June 2016 to the present day), the PHL has adopted a much softer approach to the Spratlys disputes in spite of the ongoing militarization, with Duterte announcing in late October 2016 on a visit to Beijing of his "separation" from the United States and alignment with the PRC. "Both in military, not maybe social, but economics also. America has lost,"[22] he declared. As the above aerial incidents reveal, it remains to be seen if that will be the most fruitful course of action. Today, many observers are questioning what exactly Duterte has to show for his softer line with the Chinese.

Regarding the August 2018 aerial incident, US frustration over China's unabashed assertiveness was apparent when all three of the US military's verified and official Twitter accounts responded with unusually strong words to condemn the PRC's behavior. The US Navy's account retorted "We will sail, fly and operate wherever international law allows" while the US Indo-Pacific Command's account asserted "the United States will not be "warned off" from lawful operations in international waters and airspace." The US reconnaissance plane in question had emanated from Japan so US Forces Japan's account also weighed in by tweeting "Japan-based US Navy P-8As contribute to regional peace and security every day by flying wherever international law allows."[23] In late 2018, a research station, under the authority of the Chinese Academy of Sciences' Integrated Research Center for Reefs and Islands, was constructed on Mischief Reef.[24] This represented a stronger push by China to conduct research exploration and exploitation in the area, a development discussed below. In June 2019, a steel-hulled Chinese fishing vessel allegedly rammed and sank a wood-hulled Filipino vessel that had been anchored at the disputed and resource-rich Reed Bank tablemount area to the northeast of Mischief Reef. Afterwards, the Chinese crew sailed away and did not offer assistance to the twenty-two Filipinos in the water who

[22] Blanchard, "Duterte Aligns Philippines."

[23] Johnson, "U.S. Military Has Strong Words."

[24] Long, "Deep Plowing the South."

had to be rescued by a Vietnamese fishing vessel nearby. The incident was later described by Batongbacal, as "unprecedented" and one which could prove to be a "tipping point" in Sino-Filipino relations in the SCS because it could "herald a new phase in Philippine-China interaction in the West Philippine Sea: one where we (the Philippines) will be forced out of the West Philippine Sea". Batongbacal also saw parallels with how China forced Vietnamese vessels out of parts of the SCS in May 2014 and warned that "it is enough reason for this administration [under Rodrigo Duterte] to seriously reconsider its friendship policy towards China."[25] In July 2019, the PRC published a defense white paper, the first in many years, and one which emphasized China's conflict capabilities, and "combat readiness" in the South China Sea and the western Pacific. The paper reiterated that "the South China Sea islands ... are inalienable parts of Chinese territory" and that "China exercises its national sovereignty to build infrastructure and deploy necessary defensive capabilities on the islands and reefs in the South China Sea". Related activities include defending "important waters, islands and reefs ... in the South China Sea", acquiring "full situation awareness of adjacent waters", and "resolutely respond[ing] to security threats, infringements, and provocations on the sea."[26]

Such incidents and statements reflected China's objective of not only strengthening their control over the waters around Mischief Reef, but the sky above it via a more comprehensive and complementary system of terrestrial, maritime, and aerial surveillance. In November 2019, ImageSat International (ISI) published satellite images revealing that an operational reconnaissance airship (known as an aerostat) had been deployed above the feature to more closely monitor activities by foreign states in the sea and in the air. All-weather, efficient and comparatively low-cost, aerostats can remain in the air for long periods and assist the Chinese to receive early warnings of low-flying aircraft and to survey a wide area (up to 300 nms). They also help fill the role of surveillance aircraft that might not always be available at short notice. The move was the first time that the Chinese had placed such aircraft in that area.[27] All these developments,

[25] Esmaquel II, "Sinking of Filipino Vessel."

[26] People's Republic of China State Council Information Office, "China's National Defense," 7, 12.

[27] Liu, "China Deploys Airship"; Johnson, "U.S. Sends Warships."

including China's ADIZ discussed in Chapter 6, point to real challenges for how China, the US, and other claimant states find a modus vivendi in the sea and in the air over features like Mischief Reef.

Present Day Vulnerabilities

Despite China's extensive militarization and island-building activities, Mischief Reef and others like it are nonetheless very vulnerable in terms of defense. This begs questions about the PRC's expectations regarding the long-term utility of the outpost. In December 2019, CNN published details of a report by "Naval and Merchant Ships", a Chinese language magazine overseen by the Chinese State Shipbuilding Corporation, a supplier to the PLA. The report pointed to the difficulties faced by China in the SCS because such isolated "lonely in the distant sea" outposts, which are far from both mainland China and other significant PRC-controlled islands, can be easily attacked and are all but impossible to defend in a full-scale conflict. The report asserted, "Islands and reefs in South China Sea have unique advantages in safeguarding national sovereignty and maintaining a military presence in the open sea, but they have natural weaknesses with regard to their own military defense". Citing the example of Fiery Cross Reef, the report warned, "even if the support fleet rushes at the fastest speed, it will take more than a day to reach it." The report also lamented the fact that even with runways, the PLAAF control of the skies is limited and it would take crucial time and most of their fuel supplies for jet fighters to respond effectively. Features under attack would also need to be fortunate enough for one of two of China's combat-ready aircraft carriers, the Liaoning and the Shandong, to be within proper range. Mischief Reef and other similar outposts are also within range of US and Japanese long-range missile systems, not to mention the naval forces of other claimant states. Short of war, such features could also easily be placed under siege and blockaded, denying the occupants the possibility of resupply. The constructed shelters and other facilities on Mischief Reef are devoid of vegetation, and natural rock or soil formations, and thus stick out like a sore thumb on the horizon. The groundwater level is also high, and facilities do not allow personnel and materials to be kept underground for long periods. Such shelters therefore have "very limited" anti-strike defenses. CNN additionally cites Malcolm Davis, a Senior Analyst in Defence Strategy and Capability at the Australian Strategic Policy Institute, who observed "The harsh environmental conditions in the South China Sea – salt water corrosion, poor weather – make it almost impossible to deploy anything on the islands in a manner that could allow them to defend these bases." This would make any high tech and exorbitant expensive aircraft on a feature like Mischief Reef unserviceable within a matter of a week or so. He also asserted that some features would become primary targets in the event of a SCS conflict and that it is "just physically impossible to build an island that is essentially defensible" due to the characteristics of the reefs and sandbars in the area.[28]

Not all observers agree with the view that certain aircraft would be unserviceable. In August 2020, Storey pointed to China's aerial weaknesses in an article analyzing the reasons why the PRC has not yet deployed jet fighters to its occupied features in the Spratly Islands, including Mischief Reef. These include: (a) Beijing's preference to avoid escalating tensions with its SCS neighbours; (b) the difficulty of maintaining aircraft due to exposure to sea salt and humidity resulting in metal corrosion; and (c) the possibility that weaknesses within the structural integrity of the features (including runways) may be causing the Chinese to hesitate in sending their state-of-the-art aircraft to the area. To explain further, Storey discounts the first explanation due to China's already provocative actions in the SCS since the start of 2020, and he discounts the second explanation by pointing to the US and its aircraft carriers, which continually manage this problem. In fact, large, most likely air-conditioned, hangars on PRC-occupied features also would permit them to deal with this problem. Moreover, a short deployment from any of the "Big Three" Chinese outposts would thus not inflict an unmanageable amount of wear and tear on PLAAF jet fighters, which could be easily rinsed with fresh water. The third explanation is that of structural integrity caused by substandard construction that resulted in rushed work (which has not allowed the reclaimed land to settle), although this usually takes months if not years prior to the start of construction activities. Related to this is the possibility of subsidence. Storey questions if "short cuts and shoddy construction" within an endemically corrupt building construction industry in China resulted in an artificial island that might be sinking or cracking in places, particularly the all-important runways. Unlike other

[28] Griffith, "Beijing May Have Built Bases."

slower turboprop engine aircraft, the landing of jet fighters requires that the surface integrity of a runway be of a very high standard. Satellite imagery cannot easily discern this problem but "the image-conscious and risk-averse PLA would be keen to avoid the public relations debacle that would accompany a mishap involving one of its fighters" when landing or taking off on one of the "Big Three" reefs. If this possible structural integrity explanation is true, Storey asserts, it begs questions about the "strategic utility" of Mischief Reef for the PLAAF, particularly their future aspiration to enforce an ADIZ in the SCS.[29] Nonetheless, despite these apparent weaknesses, Davis comments on the reasoning behind occupying and fortifying a number of seemingly indefensible South China Sea atolls and reefs. In this regard, he says: "What the Chinese are trying to do is annex an international maritime space, to control and own international waters, and to do that they need to have a permanent presence there."[30] As to the gamble being taken by China, he surmises that the Chinese may be banking that no power would dare engage in an attack that could result in an all-out war against a military heavyweight with nuclear weapons for the sake of undoing China's gains on tiny features like Mischief Reef. At the very least, any devastating attack on PRC outposts would almost certainly result in a commensurate response targeting American bases in Okinawa and Guam, an objective that the PRC is perfectly capable of, and of which it has warned in years past.[31]

Advances in Resource Exploration and Extraction

Yet another factor that emphasizes the economic strategic value of the Mischief Reef outpost for China in recent years has been the considerable technological strides made in terms of accessing the once inaccessible deep-sea resources of the South China Sea, most of which China claims as its own. These include rare earth elements (REEs), oil and gas, and vast quantities of natural methane gas hydrates (also known as flammable or combustible ice). Polymetallic nodules such as nickel, copper, manganese and cobalt are also sometimes found clustered on the seabed. These are essential materials in key advanced technologies such as smartphone

[29] Storey, "Why Doesn't China Deploy."

[30] Griffith, "Beijing May Have Built Bases."

[31] Ibid.

components and electric car batteries. They also meet the goal of diversifying supply.[32] As explained by one source, "The stakes for deep sea research have raised over the past decade, as everything from genetic material derived from biological organisms to critical components for advanced technology have been found in deep sea environments".[33] It also noted how the rich biodiversity of the South China Sea made it an especially appealing location for research-related exploration and extraction. In one case, microbes extracted from the seabed played a role in the development of coronavirus test kits.[34]

The economic potential of these resources for China was acknowledged as recently as 2017 when the China Daily wrote that scientists see natural gas hydrates as the most attractive future substitute for oil and natural gas and noted that "one cubic meter of flammable ice, a natural gas hydrate, is equal to 164 cubic meters of regular natural gas". This followed the announcement on May 18 of a "great technological" and "historic" mining mission in the SCS that may result in a "global energy revolution". It followed nearly two decades of research and endeavors by the Chinese, after which Li Jinfa, deputy director of the China Geological Survey, stated that the PRC would intensify related activities.[35] In October 2019, the Secretary-General of the UN's International Seabed Authority, Michael W. Lodge, predicted that the PRC would be the first state to commercially exploit deep-sea minerals. He also noted that there is an "enormous" demand for minerals.[36] On March 26, 2020, the Chinese officially declared, via their Ministry of Natural Resources, the setting of world records by operating at a depth of 1,225 meters and extracting 861,400 cubic meters of gas at an average of 28,700 cubic meters per day. This was in the Shenhu area of the Pearl River Mouth Basin in the waters of the northern South China Sea. It followed the launching of China's second trial exploration of maritime "flammable ice" in October 2019 and the commencement of mining activities on February 17, an endeavor that involved over seventy entities such as the China

[32] Long, "Deep Plowing the South"; Adomaitis, "China Leads the Race."

[33] Long, "Deep Plowing the South."

[34] Ibid.

[35] "China's Combustible Ice Estimated," *Xinhua*.

[36] Adomaitis, "China Leads the Race."

National Petroleum Corporation (CNPC) and Peking University. Additionally, it was an achievement which saw the PRC produce 2.8 times the gas output compared to the sixty-day exercise in 2017. Acknowledging the record's significance, an article by the government-sponsored Xinhua news outlet proudly stated "China has mastered key technologies of horizontal drilling and independently developed a set of core equipment for industrial prospecting and exploring of flammable ice, laying a solid technical foundation for commercial mining." The same article controversially stated the operation proved that "flammable ice" could be extracted in an environmentally safe manner without any geological hazards or pollution, and that the outbreak of the COVID-19 epidemic had not slowed the Chinese in their endeavors.[37] In this regard, China continues to be strongly criticized for the impact on the environment of its island-building and resource exploration and extraction activities in the SCS.

An April 2020 report focused on China's accelerating research exploration and exploitation initiatives evidenced by the construction of two new and operational research stations on the two other "Big Three" reefs, Fiery Cross Reef and Subi Reef. This move, in addition to the landing of military aircraft on Fiery Cross Reef, during the peak of the COVID-19 pandemic, elicited a very strongly worded response from Washington. As noted, a research station had been built on Mischief Reef in late 2018. Other claimants, particularly Vietnam, are wary of the repercussions of the ramping up of such activities. Under the umbrella of the South China Sea Innovation Institute for Ecological and Environmental Engineering, the research stations and their related activities have a stated mission of "keeping a foothold in those islands and reefs" and "deep plowing the South China Sea's islands and reefs."[38] Such developments show why Chinese interests in maintaining a strong footing and in strengthening power projection capabilities in the South China Sea via major outposts like Mischief Reef are destined to grow.

The Very Recent Past

A worrying characteristic of US-China relations vis-à-vis the South China Sea disputes in 2019 and 2020 has been the particularly fervent language employed by both sides to emphasize their positions. For instance,

[37] "China Sets New World Records," *Global Times*.

[38] Long, "Deep Plowing the South"; US Dept. of State, "PRC's Reported Sinking."

when the PRC allegedly sank a Vietnamese fishing vessel in the Paracel Islands in early April 2020 at the peak of the COVID-19 crisis, the US Department of State's Morgan Ortagus said that the US was "seriously concerned". As mentioned, the Chinese had also constructed research stations and landed military aircraft on a disputed feature in the Spratlys in the same period. The Americans thus called "on the PRC to remain focused on supporting international efforts to combat the global pandemic, and to stop exploiting the distraction or vulnerability of other states to expand its unlawful claims in the South China Sea."[39] Such strong statements from the US were repeated throughout 2020. Undaunted, on April 18, the PRC's State Council, in a further sign of China's tightening grip, declared the establishment of the Xisha (the Paracel Islands) and Nansha (the Spratly Islands) administrative districts as subdivisions of Sansha city on Hainan Island. Fiery Cross Reef will be the administrative center for the Spratlys.[40] A day later, in a move aimed at emphasizing administrative control, the PRC's Ministry of Civil Affairs and the Ministry of Natural Resources published an updated map showing the standardized names of 25 above water and 55 submerged features in the SCS. The last such update had been in 1983.[41]

A few days later on April 23, US Secretary of State Michael R. Pompeo complained to ASEAN state foreign ministers during an online meeting to discuss the COVID-19 outbreak that recent developments proved that the PRC "has moved to take advantage" of the chaos and disruption caused by the pandemic. He went on to also complain that the Chinese were using militarized ships to prevent rival claimant states from exploring for and extracting offshore oil and gas resources.[42] It would appear the accusations that China was making the most of the coronavirus distraction were not entirely without foundation. On April 15, for example, the PRC government-sponsored Global Times published an article in which a Chinese military expert observed the difficulties faced by the US Navy with four aircraft carriers "unsuitable for deployment" and with no carrier in the Asia–Pacific region because of on-board COVID-19 infections. China, on the other hand, had "done a good job in controlling the

[39] US Dept. of State, "PRC's Reported Sinking."

[40] Hadano and Onishi, "Vietnam Protests China's New."

[41] Long, "China Ups Ante"; Leng, "Names of Islands, Reefs."

[42] "US Blasts China," *Voice of America*.

epidemic" with no comparable operational problems.[43] As earlier chapters have shown, China has often been accused of exploiting windows of opportunity to reinforce its position over features and areas of the SCS.

As with before, the Filipinos have often been helpless in the face of China's growing assertiveness. When PLAN sailors pointed their target acquisition laser radar at a PHL navy vessel on April 22, Manila, while downplaying the seriousness of the incident, issued a protest and told the press that perhaps the Chinese were testing how the Filipinos might respond. The Chinese had also pointed a laser beam at an American surveillance aircraft in the Philippine Sea (west of Guam) in February. As the region was dealing with the peak of the COVID-19 pandemic, maritime specialists such as Batongbacal stated that the PRC was using its leverage in terms of medical assistance and expertise to simultaneously stifle any attempts to regionally co-ordinate protests against an apparent escalation in Chinese activities in the "West Philippine Sea". When a retired PHL Supreme Court Judge, Antonio Carpio, called for the Philippines, Vietnam, and Malaysia to conduct joint patrols as a counter to China, his suggestion was rejected by Presidential spokesperson Harry Roque, reflecting a softer line by the Duterte regime vis-à-vis China in PHL-claimed areas.[44]

On July 13, 2020, Mike Pompeo released a very strongly worded press statement in which he emphasized a "strengthening US policy" in the SCS. The world, he warned, "will not allow Beijing to treat the South China Sea as its maritime empire." Pompeo asserted that his country "champions a free and open Indo-Pacific", was committed to upholding freedom of navigation "in a manner consistent with international law," and along with its allies, "have long-endorsed a rules-based international order." China's claims, he stated, were "completely unlawful" and the PRC was engaged in a "might makes right" strategy as well as a "campaign of bullying" aimed at achieving "unilateral dominion." China's "predatory world view", he protested, "has no place in the 21st century." Pompeo also used the occasion to align Washington's position on the SCS with the 2016 Tribunal's "final and legally binding" conclusions. In his comments, Pompeo directly referred to Mischief Reef and

[43] Liu, "Epidemic Hinders US Military."

[44] "Manila Downplays Chinese Laser," *Radio Free Asia*.

the "harassment" of PHL fishermen and personnel involved in offshore energy development when he said:

> In line with the Tribunal's legally binding decision, the PRC has no lawful territorial or maritime claim to Mischief Reef or Second Thomas Shoal, both of which fall fully under the Philippines's sovereign rights and jurisdiction, nor does Beijing have any territorial or maritime claims generated from these features.[45]

The PHL's Foreign Affairs and National Defense departments apparently supported Pompeo's assertions, revealing splits over how best to address the threat posed by China to Filipino maritime rights. However, Manila's weak hand, just four years after the July 12, 2016 Tribunal findings, was again evident in late July when Duterte, during his country's annual State of the Nation Address, informed the Filipino Congress that he was powerless and penniless to defend the Philippines' maritime claims vis-à-vis China. The speech reflected both realistic assessments and Duterte's own desire for "an independent foreign policy" illustrated when he said "we worked without fail to protect our rights in the South China Sea, neither beholden nor a pawn to anyone." Arguing that he had no gripe with either the Chinese or the Americans, he saw real dangers in drawing closer to the US, warning that if American naval forces and their "atomic arsenals" returned to Subic Bay and a war broke out, the result would be the "extinction of the Filipino race." Addressing criticisms of his China-leaning and friendlier, non-confrontational approach to the PRC's occupation and control of PHL features and waters, Duterte argued that "unless we [Filipinos] are prepared to go to war", then maritime disputes with China should be treated as "diplomatic endeavours." On the numerous contests for features, resources, and waters between China and the Philippines, the PHL President stated,

> China is claiming it. We are claiming it. China has the arms, we do not have it [sic]. So, it is simple as that. They are in possession of the property.... So what can we do? We have to go to war and I cannot afford it. Maybe some other president can, but I cannot.[46]

[45] Pompeo, "U.S. Position on Maritime Claims."

[46] Duterte, "State of the Nation Address."

Duterte also said that he had made a recent plea with Xi Jinping for his country to be one of the first to receive vaccine shipments from China for free or on credit. In late December 2020, after learning about procurement delays, he also threatened to repeal the Visiting Forces Agreement (VFA) with Washington if it does not provide millions of vaccines.[47] This is despite the 2016 Tribunal findings and strong assertions of support from its ostensible mutual defense treaty ally, the US, the only power capable of challenging the Chinese quest for control of the South China Sea; Duterte has not attempted to do more to assert the PHL's internationally-recognized maritime rights.[48] This can be understood to reflect how approaches to disputes like Mischief Reef are often hostage to domestic politics at any given time, and to the influence of China's rising power upon the Philippines. At the time of writing, Duterte's China-friendly policies since 2016 have not shown any tangible sovereignty-related dividends in reversing the loss of Mischief Reef. Notwithstanding Duterte's foreign policy strategy, geo-political and military realities have left the Philippines with limited options. Noting the realities on the water, Gregory Poling, a South-east Asia specialist, stated "There is no putting these artificial islands back in the ocean. They are a fact of life. Now the US and its partners need to focus on dissuading Beijing from using the bases to coerce its neighbours."[49] China's activities on Mischief Reef have continued apace. In early August 2020, the deployment of two PLAN warships, a Type 054A frigate and a Type 056 corvette, were confirmed via satellite images showing the vessels inside the atoll's lagoon. The images also showed numerous other vessels transporting materials and supplies to and from the reef.[50] Later that month, the US again showed a tougher line regarding the PRC's South China Sea activities when the Department of State announced that Washington had imposed export restrictions against twenty-four Chinese state-owned enterprises, companies, and their divisions. These entities were known to be involved in island building projects and the militarization of features like Mischief Reef. These include the massive China Communications

[47] Ibid.; Sarmiento, "COVID-19: Duterte seeks China's Help"; Venzon, "Duterte Threatens to End US Military Pact."

[48] "Duterte Says Philippines Powerless," 2020.

[49] Brennan, "Beijing's South China Sea Military Bases."

[50] Long, "China Warships, Fighter Jets Deployed," 2020.

Construction Company (CCCC). Washington also imposed visa restrictions on numerous executives attached to these companies. According to the contents of a US Department of State special teleconference briefing "on U.S. visa restrictions and [the Department of] Commerce's entity listing for PRC companies and individuals tied to malign activities by the PRC in South China Sea" [sic] on August 26, the restrictions were designed to "impose costs on bad actors" and "to encourage all sorts of parties and institutions and governments around the world to assess risk and reconsider business deals with predatory Chinese state-owned enterprises."[51]

The restrictions are largely symbolic and without real teeth in a direct sense because the companies involved imported the relatively small figure of five million US dollars in the five years prior to the move. The real impact of the restrictions lies in the fact that a lot of companies will probably shy away from any named parties on the list because of the potential reputational damage caused by such an affiliation. There would also be a fear among business partners of closer than usual scrutiny being placed on whether or not Export Administration Regulations are being followed. The State Department's special briefing also specifically mentioned Mischief Reef, claiming:

In the case of Mischief Reef and the Spratly Islands, which was determined by the 2016 arbitral tribunal ruling to be within the Philippines' exclusive economic zone and on its continental shelf, Beijing's development there—its building and militarization—is a violation of the Philippines' sovereign rights and jurisdiction under the Law of the Sea Convention.[52]

Whatever the eventual business impact, the exports and visa restrictions' move, at the very least, reflected a hardening of the US' approach to Chinese activities on Mischief Reef and served also to damage China's image in the eyes of the international community where such restrictions and sanctions are normally reserved for renegade states.

On the same day as the special briefing, in what was perhaps an omen of things to come, should the US continue to challenge Chinese power over features like Mischief Reef, the South China Morning Post reported

[51] US Dept. of State, "Briefing on Visa Restrictions for the People's Republic of China and Commerce Department Restrictions on Chinese Corporate Entities."

[52] Ibid.

that the Chinese had launched two "aircraft carrier killer" class missiles from the mainland into the South China Sea. Both missile types (an intermediate range DF-26B launched from 1,200 miles inland and a medium-range DF-21D launched from Zhejiang province) are capable of hitting aircraft carriers from a position beyond the range of fighter jets. The missile launches were interpreted by observers as a warning to the US, a day after an American U-2 spy plane had been spotted observing a PLAN naval drill from inside a PRC-imposed no-fly zone over the Bohai Sea in northern China. The spy plane incident elicited a strongly worded protest from the PRC against what a Ministry of Defense spokesperson called "provocative actions" that could lead to misjudgments and which "seriously violated the code of safe behavior for air and sea between China and the US and international norms."[53]

One month later, the US State Department released another very strongly worded press statement entitled "China's Empty Promises in the South China Sea" in which a department spokesperson Morgan Ortagus called out the PRC over the apparent contradictions between its words and deeds in the South China Sea in the past five years. For instance, the statement reserved considerable criticism for PRC General Secretary Xi Jingping for declaring in the White House Rose Garden in September 2015 that "China does not intend to pursue militarization" and that outposts like Mischief Reef would not "target or impact any country." It contrasted this assurance with China's "reckless and provocative" extensive island-building activities and its militarization of disputed features and areas in recent years. Ortagus also complained that "the CCP does not honor its words or commitments" and that recent months had witnessed "an unprecedented number of states express their formal opposition at the United Nations to China's unlawful maritime claims in the South China Sea". Protesting the PRC's "unacceptable and dangerous behavior", Ortagus called on the international community to "raise its opposition", promised that the US will hold the CCP to account, and that it would "continue to stand with our Southeast Asian allies and partners in resisting China's coercive efforts to establish dominion over the South China Sea."[54] Both Department of State statements in August and September also emphasized the irreparable environmental damage

[53] Huang, "Chinese Military Fires."

[54] US Dept. of State, "China's Empty Promises."

and destruction caused to coral reefs features like Mischief Reef by the PRC's land reclamation and militarization projects. Ortagus also noted how these "disputed outposts" were being used as "platforms of coercion against their neighbors." These "platforms" she declared, "serve as staging grounds for the hundreds of maritime militia vessels and China Coast Guard ships that regularly harass civilian craft and impede legitimate law enforcement activities, offshore fishing, and hydrocarbon development by neighboring states."[55] Despite such harsh criticisms, the Chinese persist in strengthening their position and displaying their resolve to defend their territory as they see it. This was again evident as recently as Christmas Day 2020 when, in another first, China flew the Y-20 transport aircraft, its largest aircraft and capable of transporting troops and heavy equipment like missile launchers, to Fiery Cross Reef. This took place just three days after the US destroyer, the USS John S. McCain, sailed within 12 nms of Mischief Reef.[56] On February 4 this year, Simularity, a company that analyses changes to geospatial imagery and data, published photographic evidence of new construction and other related preparatory activities at seven different locations on the reclaimed parts of the atoll. The first construction activity had begun in October 2020 and all appear to relate to the port, radar, and antennae facilities.[57] The Philippine Star also reported Batongbacal as saying that these developments are evidence that the areas being cleared are probably for "more planned buildings."[58] Writing in March 2021, such activities continue to beg questions of how and if tensions over Mischief Reef and other such features can be eased and reflect the fact that the occupation remains as pertinent as ever.

Reflections

When examining the significance of the occupation of Mischief Reef in 1994–1995, it is apparent that the initial take-over was both remarkable and unremarkable. In the latter case, the occupation was just one

[55] Ibid.

[56] Huang, "South China Sea: Why Did the PLA."

[57] Simularity and AllSource Analysis, "New Construction on Mischief Reef."

[58] Viray, "Photos Show More Chinese."

of many carried out by all the other claimants, the forty-fourth occupation since the 1950s,[59] and which reached a crescendo in the 1990s. Despite this, the reef's occupation stands out for a number of important reasons. Most notably, the furtive and seemingly unprovoked seizure of a feature situated within the EEZ of an ASEAN member-state sent alarm bells ringing amongst all the other disputants and throughout the region. The incident led many to fear that it might be a harbinger of events to come. The PRC is not the only claimant in these complex disputes but regional states are almost unanimous in their view that it is the principal cause for concern in the South China Sea. Their reasons are understandable. China is the largest and most powerful regional player in the Spratlys disagreements. Prior to the incident, the country's military capabilities had been expanding dramatically since the late 1980s, and there seemed to be a disconnect between Beijing's assurances and its behaviour in the South China Sea. It also claims not merely a portion of the contested area as other claimants do, but virtually all of it, and contends that its sovereignty over the area is "indisputable" and not open to compromise. These assertions are not based on, or consistent with, UNCLOS or customary international law. The reef's take-over thus fed fears that Beijing was choosing "might" over "right" by sanctioning PLAN to quietly occupy the feature and then later defend the act with force. Speaking in 2021, given the major developments in and around Mischief Reef since the mid-1990s, all of these initial fears appear to have been warranted. China's reassurances did and continue to do little to assuage its neighbour's concerns.

Prior to late 1994 and early 1995, when Filipino patrol and fishing vessels spotted PRC structures on and PLAN ships in the vicinity of the reef, the Philippines, as well as neighbouring states and numerous scholars, held the view that the military element of the SCS disputes was an exclusively China-Vietnam affair. The taking of the feature in 1994–1995, the first such case of the post-Cold War era, however, ended the myth that the Chinese would not target an ASEAN member-state, would not invite regional opprobrium upon themselves, or risk the return of US forces to the Philippines, all for the sake of an uninhabited and submerged reef. For proponents of the China Threat argument, the incident indicated that the Chinese were going as far as their new military

[59] See Dzurek, "China Occupies."

capabilities would allow them to in defending "their" maritime claims, and served as a reminder that the new China was willing and able to defend its interests in the Spratly Islands. Subsequent developments have also proven the strategic and economic value to China of holding and projecting its power from this once uninhabited and submerged reef. The PRC's patient "salami slicing" strategy and "cabbage tactics" in relation to Mischief Reef in tandem with its exponential rise in terms of economic and political influence since the mid-1990s have also helped China to continue on a dual track of defending both territorial and wider regional interests. Indeed, the PRC's sheer economic clout and skilful diplomatic manoeuvres, have, to a large extent, helped to shelter it from more severe sanctions for its SCS activities by ASEAN, the UN, and major regional players like the US and Japan. The future may see the Chinese consolidating its established gains on and around Mischief Reef and elsewhere via strategies aimed at keeping the United States, the only power capable of seriously challenging China's growing presence in the area, away. The PRC has its work cut out in this regard but the years since 1994–1995 have shown that the Chinese are capable of weathering the occasional diplomatic storm and avoiding a direct confrontation with the Americans. The events and developments of 2020, most notably the economic downturn caused by COVID-19 as well as an upsurge of incidents by China in the "West Philippines Sea", however, appear to finally have influenced a drifting away by an unpredictable Duterte from his friendly approach to China. At an address to the UN in September 2020, the Filipino leader, for the first time, resolutely demanded that the 2016 Tribunal decision be respected and "firmly reject[ed] attempts to undermine it." Other developments since mid-2020, including a move by Manila to suspend an earlier decision in February of last year to terminate the 1998 Visiting Forces Agreement (VFA) also pointed to closer ties with the US, a development that runs counter to the PRC's strategic goals with the Philippines. Indeed, when Duterte originally announced the termination of the VFA, the CCP-aligned Global Times noted the benefits of this for the PRC's position in the SCS because "without the VFA, US interference in the South China Sea will be constrained" and this "will upset US meddling." The same article observed possible divisions over approaches to the US in the PHL between the Office of the President and the Department of National Defense.[60] Fluctuations and uncertainties like these present observers with some real challenges in terms of how to foretell the likely future of Sino-US-Filipino relations and their approaches to disputed maritime areas.

The Future Outlook for Mischief Reef

A quarter century after the discovery of PRC structures on Mischief Reef, the central elements of this dispute still remain. The Philippines persists in publicly contesting China's control of the reef but China's position on the feature is now unassailable and unofficially accepted as permanent. While possession is nine-tenths of the law as the saying goes, the Filipinos may be able to extract concessions in other fields from Beijing in exchange for Manila's time and silence regarding Chinese boots on Mischief Reef. Up to 2020, President Duterte's China-leaning strategy has mostly proved to be a false dawn with lessons for future PHL administrations. If, as certain developments in 2020 point to, Duterte deviates from his "independent" policy of the last four years and draws closer to a post-Trump White House, then it may see a stronger and more assertive line by the Filipinos on such issues as freedom of navigation and over-flight as well as resource extraction in the Mischief Reef area. A lot will depend on the SCS stance of the new Biden administration. Various observers see the new US President, while certainly more of a multilateral leader and more calculating than Trump, continuing the practice of asserting its perceived maritime and aerial rights, for example by sending American warships into waters that China aspires to control. Biden's designated National Security Advisor, Jake Sullivan, has gone as far as calling for a ramming up of FONOPS, a scenario certain to aggravate the South China Sea disputes.[61] The Obama years (2009–2017) were also years in which the PRC consolidated its position in the Spratlys without any serious repercussions. This may also point to a Biden leadership that may very well seek to emphasize a stronger policy shift that marks his presidency out from his vice-presidency, and more resolutely counters Chinese designs.

[60] Li, "Manila's Termination of Military Pact."

[61] Ding, "On South China Sea, Expect More"; Donnelly, "South China Sea"; Heydarian, "Biden to Follow Trump's Lead."

The Philippines' relative weakness leaves it with limited options save the garnering of regional and international support, and any possible gains from a risky stepping up of brinkmanship by its ally, the United States, scenarios that Duterte himself has recognized. Recent trends point to continued and potentially violent confrontations in the Mischief Reef area over those aforementioned free movement issues that cannot be easily ignored. At the same time, as painfully evidenced by the "opportunism" of the Mischief Reef incident, the absence of a countervailing military power to check Chinese forces in the area or at least compel them to carefully consider their actions, showed how states such as the Philippines cannot depend on bodies such as ASEAN alone. Despite claims of a united front, the reality is that the reliability of ASEAN to come to the rescue of a member-state is often conditional and often depends on the context, as the contrasting responses to the early years of the occupation in 1995 and 1998–1999 showed. It is apparent also that each member sees China differently based on their respective historical ties, economic relations, domestic politics, and international circumstances. As such, responses and the atmosphere surrounding incidents are often informed and characterized by these differences between the member-states (Emmers, 2007, 54). The PHL, for one, has arguably learned that they cannot depend on regional bodies alone when responding to countering China's military capabilities, necessitating a discussion of more assertive US involvement. The 2016 tribunal findings and international law, while serving to bolster Manila's position publicly, have not changed a jot the realities on the ground. These realities beg the question in 2021 (and post-Duterte[62] in 2022) will the PHL fully back a harder and more physical line in alliance with the USA with its attendant risks or stick to alternative long-term approaches that have yet to produce tangible dividends.

Regional attempts to honour the spirit of the non-binding 2002 Declaration of Conduct (DoC) or on finalizing a workable code of conduct (CoC) aimed at preventing conflict and building confidence have often proved disappointing and have been painstakingly slow. This delay is mostly due to failures or refusals to address the thorny issue of sovereignty, questions about who would enforce the rules, near-incidents in the air and water, and so forth. The wording and particulars remain

[62] Under the PHL's constitution, a President can only sit for a maximum of one term consisting of six years.

a serious stumbling block to finally agreeing on a binding code that ostensibly might ease tensions in the SCS. It took well over a decade after regional CoC guidelines were first drawn up (in 2005) before a negotiating draft was announced by China and ASEAN at the ASEAN Ministerial Meeting in Singapore in 2018, and completed in 2019. It is expected that CoC negotiations can be completed in 2021. Experts have expressed confidence that an agreement can be found in the near future with ramifications for the Mischief Reef area. Central to this outlook has been the Chinese aim of keeping the US out diplomatically as well as militarily by putting itself at the center of any future CoC. At the very least, the Chinese cannot be seen to not engage seriously with its neighbours on the South China Sea. In terms of diplomatic strategy, Beijing needs to be able to say to the international community that they are on track to an eventual CoC and thus US involvement is unwarranted. For the PRC to do otherwise would very well see the US being drawn deeper into the SCS disagreements at the request of numerous claimant states. The serious tensions of 2020 have also convinced the Chinese of the pressing need to offset a serious showdown with the US that could reverse some of the cost-free gains already made by the PRC. During the 37th ASEAN summit in early November, PRC Premier Li Keqiang, via video-link, called upon ASEAN states to speed up CoC consultations. According to the China Daily, Li said that such a move would "demonstrate to the international community that they have the wisdom and capability to properly manage the situation in the South China Sea and safeguard its peace and stability." He also stated that once the COVID-19 situation has stabilised, China would positively consider holding face-to-face talks with the aim of bringing forward a second reading of the CoC's draft, and that his country was determined and firmly committed to finalizing consultations in the near future.[63] These developments suggest that China is indeed eager to at least work or be seen to seriously work towards a CoC, if for no other reason than to pre-empt further American entanglement in the SCS disputes.

Since the 1994–1995 occupation, South China Sea claimant relations have been characterized by non-binding commitments, which have gone hand in hand with the physical strengthening of claims and displays of

[63] Chang, "Uncertain Prospects"; Jennings, "Why China, Once Coy"; "Asean Eyes Code of Conduct," *Philippine News Agency*; Zhang, "Li Urges Speedy Consultations."

sovereignty, which belittle promises and pacts made to date as mere lip-service. The advice of one source, writing in 2001, still appears true today. This is that the "do nothing" status quo position is untenable and a recipe for conflict because it has seen states such as China engage in a risky game of advancing their position on features such as Mischief Reef through incremental activities. These were calculated to appear so insignificant that the costs of calling their bluff were deemed too large by other claimants and external actors such as the United States.[64] Despite the 2016 tribunal findings, China still persists in trying to reassure the PHL and the USA that its activities are on Mischief Reef do not pose a threat to anyone. The outcome of the "do nothing" approach will sooner or later either see the PRC consolidate its position over most of the SCS, a rival reacting with lethal force rather than diplomacy, or an outside player, most notably the US, being drawn into a violent confrontation. The pattern so far suggests that the Chinese will continue to roll the dice, and proceed to construct facilities and enhance their position on and around contested features such as Mischief Reef with potentially dangerous consequences for the peace and stability of the area. Whether or not any near future CoC can put a check on greater Chinese assertiveness in the Spratlys and elsewhere is one of key questions regarding the South China Sea disputes for the coming years.

There is also the dilemma of how to reconcile the workable CoC agreed by China with UNCLOS and the landmark 2016 Tribunal findings, if this is even possible, and in ways that do not appear to diminish either side's position vis-à-vis the feature. Another cause for concern around the waters of Mischief Reef is how to manage the growing thirst for resources in a rapidly developing economic region of the world. Technological and seabed mining advances by China in recent years point to the atoll been increasingly utilised to protect the resources of adjacent waters and also to prevent others from exploring and extracting. The discovery of any further viable and accessible reserves could further raise tensions as rival claimants rush to stake their claims, as happened in the years leading up to the initial Mischief Reef take-over in the mid-1990s.

Closing Thoughts and Looking Ahead

At the time of writing, while the signs may point to a worsening of relations over Mischief Reef and the South China Sea disputes in general,

[64] Zha and Valencia, "Mischief Reef: Geopolitics."

the current situation does not necessarily mean that the Philippines, China, and the US are irrevocably headed towards a physical confrontation. There are numerous political, geo-political, economic, strategic, and diplomatic variables that will influence how the coming years pan out. For one thing, China's desire to discourage an enhanced US naval presence may compel the Chinese to address Mischief Reef less aggressively and to deflect criticism via non-military means such as via diplomatic manoeuvres and economic incentives. Fear of an escalation with currently superior US forces may also influence a more stable quid-pro-quo relationship of engagement with Manila with tangible benefits to offset PHL losses in the "West Philippine Sea." Duterte's 2016–2020 China-leaning approach has done little to soothe public anger in the Philippines over the PRC's apparent assault on their country's dignity. This is not to say that a rapprochement is not possible if Beijing treads more carefully and shows the Filipinos in word and deed the rewards of positive ties with the rising dragon versus destabilising brinkmanship if their American allies test Chinese resolve on issues like Mischief Reef.

The PRC's multi-faceted strategy of consolidating its control of the reef area and wider afield, keeping the US out, and placing itself at the center of regional diplomacy will likely see it playing a careful but resolute balancing act between the three objectives. In waters around features such as Mischief Reef, it is almost a certainty that Chinese military forces will enhance their presence and activities in the area. Unless a binding and comprehensive resolution is found in terms of managing such disputes, the frequency of near-misses, stand-offs, brinkmanship over markers, aircraft, and fishing vessels, and so forth is sure to increase. Given the PRC's record since the reef was first taken over in the mid-1990s, there are sufficient grounds to be sceptical about the fruits of a code of conduct if it materialises. At a minimum, it certainly serves China's interest to be seen to be serious about a binding agreement. At the very least, code of conduct talks in their advanced stages should lessen the possibility of conflict and create a more conducive atmosphere prior to a longer term resolution of disputes between China and the Philippines. Only time and events in the Mischief Reef area will tell. The reef itself is irretrievable but the air above it and the waters and seabed around it remain potential testing grounds for the future trajectory of the South China Sea disputes.

References

Adomaitis, Nerijus, and Barbara Lewis. "China Leads the Race to Exploit Deep Sea Minerals: UN Body." *Reuters*, October 23, 2019. https://www.reuters.com/article/us-mining-deepsea/china-leads-the-race-to-exploit-deep-sea-minerals-un-body-idUSKBN1X213T.

"Asean Eyes Code of Conduct for Disputed South China Sea." *Philippine News Agency*, November 12, 2020. https://www.pna.gov.ph/articles/1121661.

Blanchard, Ben. "Duterte Aligns Philippines with China, Says U.S. Has Lost." *Reuters*, October 20, 2016. https://www.reuters.com/article/us-china-philippines-idUSKCN12K0AS.

Bondoc. "No Confirmation on Signal Jammers." *GMA News*, April 13, 2018. https://www.gmanetwork.com/news/news/nation/649912/no-confirmation-of-signal-jammers-in-mischief-reef-says-lorenzana/story/.

Brennan, David. "Beijing's South China Sea Military Bases Now Have Jammers That Can Block American Radar and Communications, U.S. Claims." *Newsweek*, April 9, 2018. https://www.newsweek.com/beijings-south-china-sea-military-bases-now-have-jammers-can-block-american-877604.

Chang, Felix K. "Uncertain Prospects: South China Sea Code of Conduct Negotiations." *Foreign Policy Research Institute*, October 6, 2020. https://www.fpri.org/article/2020/10/uncertain-prospects-south-china-sea-code-of-conduct-negotiations/.

"China Sets New World Records in Flammable Ice Exploration." *Global Times*, February 27, 2020. https://www.globaltimes.cn/content/1183963.shtml.

"China's Combustible Ice Estimated at 80b Tonnes." *Xinhua*, June 2, 2017. https://www.chinadaily.com.cn/china/2017-06/02/content_29595522.htm.

Ding, Duo. "On South China Sea, Expect More of the Same from US President Joe Biden." *South China Morning Post*, December 8, 2020. https://www.scmp.com/week-asia/opinion/article/3112866/south-china-sea-expect-more-same-us-president-joe-biden.

Donnelly, Dylan. "South China Sea: Biden 'Unlikely' to Stop Trump Anti-Beijing Policy in 'Larger' Trade War." *Daily Express*, December 26, 2020. https://www.express.co.uk/news/world/1376310/South-China-Sea-news-Joe-biden-Donald-trump-Beijing-trade-war-POTUS-ont.

Dowse, Andrew, and Sascha-Dominik Bachmann. "Explainer: What Is 'Hybrid Warfare' and What Is Meant by the 'Grey Zone'?" *The Conversation*, June 17, 2019. https://theconversation.com/explainer-what-is-hybrid-warfare-and-what-is-meant-by-the-grey-zone-118841.

"Duterte Says Philippines Powerless Over South China Sea Rights." *Radio Free Asia*, July 27, 2020. https://www.rfa.org/english/news/china/philippines-southchinasea-07272020185402.html.

Duterte, Rodrigo Roa. "State of the Nation Address of Rodrigo Roa Duterte, President of the Philippines, to the Congress of the Philippines." July 27, 2020. https://www.officialgazette.gov.ph/2020/07/27/rodrigo-roa-duterte-fifth-state-of-the-nation-address-july-27-2020/.

Dzurek, Daniel J. "China Occupies Mischief Reef in Latest Spratly Gambit." *International Boundaries Research Unit Boundary and Security Bulletin*, April 1995, 65–71.

Emmers, Ralf. "Maritime Disputes in the South China Sea—Strategic and Diplomatic Status Quo." In *Maritime Security in Southeast Asia*, edited by Kwa Chong Guan and John K. Skogan. Oxford: Routledge, 2007.

Esmaquel II, Paterno R. "Sinking of Filipino Vessel 'a First' in Philippines-China Row." *Rappler.com*, June 12, 2019. https://www.rappler.com/nation/sinking-filipino-vessel-first-philippines-china-dispute.

Gordon, Michael R., and Jeremy Page. "China Installed Military Jamming Equipment on Spratly Islands, US Says." *Wall Street Journal*, April 9, 2018. https://www.wsj.com/articles/china-installed-military-jamming-equipment-on-spratly-islands-u-s-says-1523266320.

Griffith, James. "Beijing May Have Built Bases in the South China Sea, but That Doesn't Mean It Can Defend Them, Report Claims." *CNN*, December 7, 2020. https://edition.cnn.com/2020/12/07/china/south-china-sea-bases-military-intl-hnk/index.html.

Hadano, Tsukasa, and Tomoya Onishi. "Vietnam Protests China's New South China Sea Districts." *Nikkei Asia*, April 20, 2020. https://asia.nikkei.com/Politics/International-relations/Vietnam-protests-China-s-new-South-China-Sea-districts.

Harris, Admiral Harry B., Jr. Untitled Speech at Australian Strategic Policy Institute (ASPI), Canberra, Australia, March 31, 2015. http://www.cpf.navy.mil/leaders/harry-harris/speeches/2015/03/ASPI-Australia.pdf.

Heydarian, Richard Javad. "Biden to Follow Trump's Lead in South China Sea." *Asia Times*, December 18, 2020. https://asiatimes.com/2020/12/biden-to-follow-trumps-lead-in-south-china-sea/.

Himmelman, Jeff. "A Game of Shark and Minnow." *New York Times*, October 27, 2013. https://www.nytimes.com/newsgraphics/2013/10/27/south-china-sea/index.html.

Huang, Kristin, "South China Sea: Why Did the PLA Land Its Massive Y-20 Warplane on Fiery Cross Reef." *South China Morning Post*, January 1, 2021. https://www.scmp.com/news/china/military/article/3116028/south-china-sea-why-did-pla-land-its-massive-y-20-warplane.

Jennings, Ralph. "Why China, Once Coy, Suddenly Wants to Discuss a Code of Conduct for a Disputed Sea." *Voice of America News*, September 23, 2020. https://www.voanews.com/east-asia-pacific/voa-news-china/why-china-once-coy-suddenly-wants-discuss-code-conduct-disputed.

Johnson, Jesse. "U.S. Military Has Strong Words for Beijing After Warnings During Flight Over South China Sea." *Japan Times*, August 11, 2018. https://www.japantimes.co.jp/news/2018/08/11/asia-pacific/u-s-military-strong-words-beijing-warnings-flight-south-china-sea/.

Johnson, Jesse. "U.S. Sends Warships Near South China Sea Isles After Beijing Demands It 'Stop Flexing Muscles'." *Japan Times*, November 22, 2019. https://www.japantimes.co.jp/news/2019/11/22/asia-pacific/us-warships-south-china-sea/.

Leng, Shumei. "Names of Islands, Reefs in South China Sea Named." *Global Times*, April 19, 2020. https://www.globaltimes.cn/content/1186084.shtml.

Li, Kaisheng. "Manila's Termination of Military Pact Will Upset US Meddling in South China Sea." *Global Times*, February 13, 2020. https://www.globaltimes.cn/content/1179439.shtml.

Liu, Xuanzun. "Epidemic Hinders US Military Presence Near China." *Global Times*, April 15, 2020. https://www.globaltimes.cn/content/1185735.shtml.

Liu, Zhen. "China Deploys Airship on Outpost in Disputed South China Sea, Satellite Firm Says." *South China Morning Post*, November 29, 2019. https://www.scmp.com/news/china/military/article/3040019/china-deploys-airship-outpost-disputed-south-china-sea.

Long, Drake. "China Warships, Fighter Jets Deployed." *Radio Free Asia*, March 8, 2020. https://www.rfa.org/english/news/china/spratlys-jets-08032020192013.html.

Long, Drake, "'Deep Plowing the South China Sea': China Eyes Resources, Steps Up Research." *Radio Free Asia*, April 7, 2020. https://www.rfa.org/english/news/china/southchinasea-research-04072020184044.html.

Long, Drake. "China Ups Ante in South China Sea With New Place Names, Administrative Districts." *Radio Free Asia*, April 20, 2020. https://www.rfa.org/english/news/china/southchinasea-names-04202020180723.html.

Macias, Amanda. "China Quietly Installed Missile Systems on Strategic Spratly Islands in Hotly Contested South China Sea." *CNBC.com*, May 2, 2018. https://www.cnbc.com/2018/05/02/china-added-missile-systems-on-spratly-islands-in-south-china-sea.html.

"Manila Downplays Chinese Laser Gun Incident in South China Sea." *Radio Free Asia*, April 28, 2020. https://www.rfa.org/english/news/china/philippines-southchinasea-04282020185403.html.

Ministry of Defense, Japan. "China's Activities in the South China Sea (China's Development Activities on the Features and Trends in Related Countries)." October 2020. https://www.mod.go.jp/e/d_act/sec_env/pdf/ch_d-act_b_e.pdf.

Morgan, Ryan. "US State Dept. Calls Out China for 'Empty Promises' Not to Militarize South China Sea." *American Military News*, September 29, 2020. https://americanmilitarynews.com/2020/09/us-state-dept-calls-out-china-for-empty-promises-not-to-militarize-south-china-sea/.

"New Construction on Mischief Reef." Simularity and AllSource Analysis, February 4, 2021. https://simularity.com/feb-2021-new-construction-on-mischief-reef/.

Ngo, Minh Tri. "China's A2/AD Challenge in the South China Sea: Securing the Air from the Ground." *The Diplomat*, May 19, 2017. https://thediplomat.com/2017/05/chinas-a2ad-challenge-in-the-south-china-sea-securing-the-air-from-the-ground/.

Panda, Ankit. "China Condemns US FONOP Near Mischief Reef in the South China Sea." *The Diplomat*, March 25, 2018. https://thediplomat.com/2018/03/china-condemns-us-fonop-near-mischief-reef-in-the-south-china-sea/.

People's Republic of China, State Council Information Office. "China's National Defense in the New Era." *White Paper*, July 24, 2019. http://english.www.gov.cn/archive/whitepaper/201907/24/content_WS5d3941ddc6d08408f502283d.html.

Pompeo, Michael R. "U.S. Position on Maritime Claims in the South China Sea." *US Department of State*, July 13, 2020. https://www.state.gov/u-s-position-on-maritime-claims-in-the-south-china-sea/.

Sarmiento, Prime. "COVID-19: Duterte Seeks China's Help with Vaccine." *China Daily*, July 28, 2020. https://www.chinadailyhk.com/article/138255.

"South China Sea: US Warship Sails Close to Disputed Mischief Reef." *BBC News*, May 25, 2017. https://www.bbc.com/news/world-asia-40040231.

"South China Sea: USS Dewey Warship Meant to defy Beijing's Territorial Claims, US Officials Say." *ABC News*, May 26, 2017. https://www.abc.net.au/news/2017-05-26/us-warship-meant-to-defy-chinas-claim-over-artificial-island/8561040?nw=0.

Storey, Ian J. "Why Doesn't China Deploy Fighter Jets to the Spratly Island?" *The Diplomat*, August 14, 2020. https://thediplomat.com/2020/08/why-doesnt-china-deploy-fighter-jets-to-the-spratly-islands/.

Torode, Greg, and Simon Scarr. "Subi Reef, Built Up by Chinese, Appears Nearly Ready to Host First Troops Based in Heart of South China Sea." *Japan Times*, May 25, 2018. https://www.japantimes.co.jp/news/2018/05/25/asia-pacific/subi-reef-built-chinese-appears-nearly-ready-host-first-troops-based-heart-south-china-sea/.

"US Blasts China at Southeast Asian Meeting on Coronavirus." *Voice of America News*, April 23, 2020. https://www.voanews.com/usa/us-blasts-china-southeast-asian-meeting-coronavirus.

US Department of State. Special Briefing on Visa and Commerce Restrictions. August 26, 2020. https://www.state.gov/briefing-with-senior-state-department-and-commerce-officials-on-state-department-visa-restrictions-placed-on-individuals-from-the-peoples-republic-of-china-and-commerce-department-restri/.

US Department of State. Press Statement, "PRC's Reported Sinking of a Vietnamese Fishing Vessel in the South China Sea." April 6, 2020. https://www.state.gov/prcs-reported-sinking-of-a-vietnamese-fishing-vessel-in-the-south-china-sea/.

US Department of State. Press Statement, "China's Empty Promises in the South China Sea." September 27, 2020. https://www.state.gov/chinas-empty-promises-in-the-south-china-sea/.

Venzon, Cliff. "Duterte Threatens to End US Military Pact If No Vaccines." *Nikkei Asia*, December 27, 2020. https://asia.nikkei.com/Politics/International-relations/Duterte-threatens-to-end-US-military-pact-if-no-vaccines.

Viray, Patricia Lourdes. "Photos Show More Chinese Construction, New Radars on Mischief Reef." *The Philippine Star*, February 18, 2021. https://www.philstar.com/headlines/2021/02/18/2078658/photos-show-more-chinese-construction-new-radars-mischief-reef.

Zha, Daojiong, and Mark Valencia. "Mischief Reef: Geopolitics and Implications." *Journal of Contemporary Asia* 31, no. 1 (2001): 86–103.

Zhang, Yunbi. "Li Urges Speedy Consultations on S. China Sea Conduct Code." *China Daily*, November 13, 2020. https://www.chinadaily.com.cn/a/202011/13/WS5fadde7ea31024ad0ba93d5f.html.

Index

S. Fox, *Mischief Reef*,
https://doi.org/10.1007/978-981-16-3884-8

R

S

The manufacturer's authorised representative in the EU is Springer Nature Customer Service Centre GmbH, Europaplatz 3, 69115 Heidelberg, Germany. If you have any concerns regarding our products, please contact ProductSafety@springernature.com

Printed and bound by CPI Group (UK) Ltd, Croydon, CR0 4YY
30/09/2026
02225326-0005